we
Nehrus

We Nehrus

BY KRISHNA
NEHRU
HUTHEESING

WITH
ALDEN
HATCH

HOLT, RINEHART
AND WINSTON
NEW YORK CHICAGO
SAN FRANCISCO

Library of Congress Catalog Card Number: 67–19635
Published simultaneously in Canada by Holt, Rinehart
and Winston of Canada, Limited.
First Edition

Grateful acknowledgment made to John
Day Company Inc. Publishers for
permission to quote excerpts from
Toward Freedom by Jawaharlal Nehru.

Designer: Ernst Reichl
8654808
Printed in the United States of America

contents

Sixteen pages of black and white photographs appear following page 152.

we
Nehrus

1
a walk
around
the fire

One of the most exciting moments of my childhood was the day I met my brother, Jawaharlal Nehru. It is a strange thing to meet one's brother; usually he is just there when we are growing up, and is accepted as part of the family scene. But then we Nehrus have led strange lives, infinitely remote from our expectations on that June day in 1912 when Jawahar came home to us from England. He was eighteen years older than I and had been away for seven years studying at Harrow and Cambridge and reading law at the Temple in London. I was five years old.

A tremendous hustle and bustle of preparations had been going on for a week. My tiny mother with her long auburn hair and delicate fair skin was constantly on the move, her hazel eyes sparkling with excitement, seeing to it that everything was perfect. Though my father, Motilal Nehru, was outwardly calm, following the emotion-hiding form of the British whom he so greatly admired, inside he was boiling with excitement. For Jawahar, his only son, was all the world to him, with the moon and the stars thrown in for good measure.

Because it was summertime, when our home town of Allahabad down in the plains gets unbearably hot, Father had rented a big house at Mussoorie, a hill station or resort, where the snow-cooled winds from the Himalayas temper the climate. In his usual lavish fashion he had moved our whole family up there, my mother, sister and I as well as various aunts, uncles and cousins who lived with us in the Indian joint-family fashion, together with perhaps fifty servants to take care of us, and half a stableful of his beautiful horses. Of course, some of his favorite dogs came, too.

I think that all the fuss about Jawahar made me a little jealous; for though I was excited I was not looking forward with much pleasure to the arrival of competition for the favored place I had occupied as the baby of the family. That morning my father and some of the other men and boys, with a mounted groom leading one of the finest horses, had ridden off to meet Jawahar at the railroad station in Dehra Dun. I moped around the grounds and then went in to read a book. Long before they were due back my English governess had made me take off my everyday clothes and put on a fine silk dress sent out from Liberty's in London, warning me on pain of dire punishment not to get it dirty. Mama was wearing one of her prettiest saris, and so were the other ladies. The servants were in clean, long white shirts and baggy trousers, and some of them even wore the fitted white coats and turbans they used for formal dinners.

Almost exactly on time there was a great clatter of hooves and everybody poured out of the house to welcome Jawahar home. Feeling very shy and out of it, I hung back beside a pillar of the verandah staring at the horsemen cantering up the drive. Looking backward down half a century I can still see them: Father in his superbly cut white breeches and polished boots on a big bay horse, roaring with happy laughter, and beside him a slim, handsome young man with rather delicate features, except for the strong Nehru nose. He slipped out of the saddle throwing the reins to a groom, and ran lightly to hug my mother, lifting her right off the ground. Then he was engulfed in a multicolored wave of female relatives, embracing him in Kashmiri fashion.

Presently, looking over their heads, he spotted me and broke away. I was almost frightened as he came toward me and swung me up in his arms. When my face was level with his laughing eyes, he said, "You must be Choti Beti [little daughter]," and kissed me.

In spite of this warm and loving greeting I did not like my brother much at first. I always called him Bhai ("brother") just as

I called my older sister Didda, because in India, in those days at least, it was disrespectful for a younger person to call an older one, even a brother, by his first name. He called me Betty, which came from Choti Beti, which my ineradicably English governess had promptly made into Betty, just as she changed my sister Swarup's* nickname from Nanhi ("little one") to Nan, which we all still call her. In a sense I returned the compliment. Because I could not say Miss Hooper, which was my governess' name, I called her Toopie and soon she was Toopie to the whole family.

Bhai brought me beautiful presents from England and almost every time he went out he brought back a new toy for me, but still our relations were strained. The truth is I was a little afraid of him. He always seemed to be in tearing high spirits and he was the most awful tease. I lived in dread of what new prank he would play on me next. When I mounted my pony he might sneak up behind and tickle its flanks with a whip, which made it rear or bolt. If I fell off, being taken unaware, he made me mount again immediately so that I would not lose my nerve, which is quite proper training according to horsemen, though his exciting the pony definitely was not. When the pony ran away with me clinging to his back, even my father protested, but Bhai only laughed and said it was good for me.

Father had taught me to ride at the age of three. He, too, was a rugged teacher of horsemanship, and almost my first memory of him is when I fell off my pony and began to cry. The groom picked me up and carried me to him. I expected him to comfort me. Instead he gave me two hard whacks and said, "No daughter of mine must show weakness of this sort. No matter how much you are hurt you are not supposed to cry." Another time when I was much older I had a really bad fall. I picked myself up and rushed to him screaming with blood streaming from my head—it took nine stitches to close the cut. Father shook me and said, "Haven't I told you again and again you must not behave like this no matter how badly you are hurt? You must keep a stiff upper lip like the British!"

Perhaps the meanest thing Bhai ever did to me was after we went home to my father's big house in Allahabad, which was called Anand Bhawan ("House of Happiness"). It had an indoor swimming

* Now Mrs. Vijaya Lakshmi Pandit.

3

pool in a great, cavernous, damp-smelling room. At one end of the pool there was a large carved-stone cow's head from whose mouth fresh water poured to fill it. There were small dressing rooms around the pool, for men on one side and women on the other. I was just learning to swim and was much more timid in the water than I was about riding, which I always loved.

One day as I was cautiously climbing down the steps of the pool, Bhai came thrashing across it, and before I knew what was happening he grabbed my leg and threw me into deep dark water. I forgot everything I knew about swimming and went down like a rock. Of course Bhai dove to the rescue and soon had me up on land dumping the water out of me. But it was several years before I got over my fear of water.

If I tell these stories about my dearly beloved brother it is to show a frivolous, thoughtless side of him that was soon lost in the long, tragic struggle for Indian independence and is now forgotten. The world remembers him as a dedicated leader of that movement and later as the Prime Minister of India, carrying on his slight shoulders the enormous weight of welding five hundred million people—speaking nearly a hundred languages and dialects—into a modern nation. They remember his face chiseled and refined by suffering, his gentle eyes that could yet flash lightning when the famous Nehru temper was loosed; and they remember the single red rose on his immaculate *sherwani* that was the final expression of his youthful dandyism and became a symbol of the Nehru clan.

What they mostly do not know is that he never lost his sense of fun. In the dreary prisons where, off and on, he spent nineteen years of his life, and even in the luxurious and perhaps more arduous prison of the Prime Minister's House, it would suddenly bubble up and his laughter would ring out, astounding the inmates of those very different dwellings.

Anything I say about his career in the early days is hearsay, for we were strangers living under our father's roof. I was so much younger and I was under the rigid, British-style nursery rule, packed off to bed at seven or eight after a dismal supper of milk and a boiled egg. He was twenty-three, a man among men, starting his career as a lawyer, my father's junior. Incidentally, my father had

4

another famous junior, Mohammed Ali Jinnah, a Mohammedan, though this difference of religion did not impair their relationship in those days.

It has been said that Jawaharlal Nehru gave the lie to Kipling's famous line that "Never the twain shall meet," by being, in his own person, the meeting place of East and West. When he came back to us from England he was more West than East, with his superbly tailored clothes from Savile Row and his head full of radical ideas that the young intellectuals at Cambridge were tossing around. They had made him a convinced Socialist following the thought of the Fabians of Chelsea: the Webbs and Edward R. Pease, Bernard Shaw and H. G. Wells; and even delving back into the deeper waters of Karl Marx and Friedrich Engels. In some ways he was a utopian Marxist until he died.

Bhai was not the only member of the family in whom East met West. All of us except my mother, who was an orthodox Hindu, were Westernized. Our conversation was a mixture of English and Hindustani—three sentences in one, two in the other with a French word or two thrown in. My father liked and admired the British enormously. In Anand Bhawan we had a Western wing and an Indian wing complete with two dining rooms and two kitchens. The Western wing was staffed by Muslim and Christian servants. Chief among them were my father's valet, Bhola, a grand old Muslim whom we all adored, and Ashgar Ali, the butler, who at dinner stood behind Father's chair, magnificent in dark red livery and a gold turban. The chef was usually a Christian from Goa.

On the Indian side the cook and the servants were all Hindus, and there was also a Muslim chef to prepare meals for us and our Mohammedan guests. Head of the household was Munshi Mubarak Ali, white-bearded, dignified and very kind. He had belonged to a wealthy Muslim family that lost all their money in the revolt of 1857—the "Indian Mutiny" as the British called it. Munshiji,* as we all called him, lived in a little cottage in the spacious grounds of Anand Bhawan with his orthodox Mohammedan wife who never let any other man see her unveiled.

* Adding *ji* to a name is a mark of respect. For example, we always referred to Mahatma Gandhi as Gandhiji, or more intimately as Bapu ("Father").

5

Munshiji was almost like one of the family. He had Father's and Mother's fullest confidence, and he looked after our entire staff, paid their salaries, and saw to it that they carried out their work properly. We children loved him dearly. I liked to sit on his knee while he told me true stories from Indian history and legends from our mythology as well as tales from the Arabian Nights. My brother and sister were equally fond of him, for he was a grand character who, though long dead, is vividly alive in our memories.

Six days a week we ate in Western style, wearing our English clothes and sitting in Victorian chairs at the big dining table that would seat twenty-four people. On the seventh day, and on Hindu festivals, we ate in the Indian manner. Colorful little mats on which we sat cross-legged were placed on the inlaid marble floor of the Indian dining room. Small tables, twelve inches high, were put in front of us, on which the servants set large silver platters called *thalis,* holding six or more little silver cups containing meat flavored with freshly ground spices (whose pale imitation is known as "curry" in the West), two kinds of vegetables, dal (lentils prepared with spices), and raw cucumber and radishes seasoned with salt and cayenne pepper. Bread and *chapattis* were passed separately, and we ate them with the first course. Long-grained Indian rice flavored with saffron and cooked with almonds or pistachios was the second round and that was the end; you never ate bread after eating rice— it just was not done; I don't know why.

We ate very daintily, with the tips of our fingers—Father would allow no sloppiness. After the main course, if only the family were there, we got up and washed our hands in a row of basins just outside the dining room; but if guests were present the servants brought each of us a carved silver basin and a pitcher with hot water and soap. We washed our hands sitting down and dried them on fine linen towels before eating dessert—with a spoon. Tea and coffee were not served though we drank lots of them between meals.

Our Western meals were thoroughly British. The Nehrus were originally Brahmans from Kashmir and the people of that cold country have always been meat-eaters, unlike the Hindus of southern India who are vegetarians. Though she was also from a Kashmiri family my mother never ate meat. Out of respect for her feelings Father never did have beef at home, nor did he have pork because it would offend the Muslim servants. But we made out very well with lamb and chicken, fish and game. Occasionally we sneaked in some of the sausages which we all loved. In addition, Father had one of the finest wine cellars in the United Provinces (Uttar Pradesh) and, of course, scotch, gin, brandy and every other sort of liquor anyone wanted.

He was not a religious man, though he was a highly ethical one. He regarded religion with benevolent tolerance as women's foolishness. So also did Bhai until later in life when the terrible communal riots* and massacres between Hindus and Mohammedans tore India apart. Marx had called religion "the opiate of the people," but in India it appeared to be their firewater. For this reason my brother became antireligious in later life.

My own religious feelings are inevitably mixed. My first indoctrination as a child was going to the nearby Anglican Church of the Holy Trinity with Miss Hooper on Sundays. I enjoyed helping her arrange the flowers for Christmas and Easter.

Sometimes my mother took me to the Hindu temples. These I disliked. There were fat priests who came and forced you to eat food they had placed before the idol of whatever god it was—Rama or Vishnu or some other—and you were supposed to give them money in return. The temples were full of greasy smoke from the oil lamps; bells were always clanging and different groups of people were chanting different verses from the scriptures. It was very rowdy. But I do love to visit the very ancient temples with their beautiful lacy stonework and superbly wrought idols hundreds, even thousands, of years old.

The best definition of our religion I have heard came from our old Sanskrit teacher who told us that Hinduism was a way of life; that life was truth and, if you lived a truthful and honest life, that sufficed. You did not have to go to a temple and pray, though if you wanted to that was all right, too. I think my father and brother would have subscribed to that.

In spite of my family skepticism I believe in reincarnation.

* Disagreements between the religious communities in India—hence "communal."

Brahmans are twice born—having reached that plane we have only two incarnations more. I hope I am due for another one, But Bhai, who went so far beyond us spiritually, has surely earned his rest in *Svarga* or wherever he may be.

In those short gay years before Mahatma Gandhi came to change all our lives Bhai did not worry much about either religion or socialism. He was practicing law and leading the life of a rich young man with sporting proclivities and a fond father. He was an excellent athlete, good at riding, shooting, tennis and swimming. Occasionally he played polo with the British and the Maharajas. Even in his frivolous stage Bhai made a great point of excellence. "Whatever you do you must do well" he told me again and again. And in his later years, in jail or out, he kept fit. At the age of seventy his intimates might find the Prime Minister of India standing on his head with his elbows braced against the floor and his hands supporting the back of his neck in one of his favorite Yoga exercises. Until his illness of 1962, he always ran up and down stairs.

One of my father's most important preoccupations was to find a wife for his son. In this serious business he forswore Western ways and returned to the ancient customs of our people. When Father talked the matter over with him, Bhai, in spite of his British education, was perfectly willing to accept his decision. He had no prior attachments, for he knew very few Indian girls at that time.

Even before Bhai came home Father had begun lining up possible brides; looking them over and having them and their parents to tea to decide whether the family and the girl were the right ones. None of them met his exacting standards until, about three years after Bhai's return from England, Father saw Kamala.

She was sixteen and very lovely; slim and rather tall for an Indian girl, with the typically fair skin of Brahmans of Kashmiri descent. Her hair was dark brown and she had large brown eyes and a very gentle disposition. It is surprising that so little has been written about Kamala, for she was one of the most beautiful women I knew or ever have known.

She came from an orthodox Hindu family who lived in Old Delhi. Her father's name was Arjun Lal Kaul. Kaul had been our own surname two hundred years ago before we left Kashmir, but I think we were not related. What made Father like her, apart from her sweetness and beauty, was that she looked very healthy. My mother had been a semi-invalid most of her life and, though Father treated her and taught us to treat her as a very precious delicate piece of china, he wanted a strong wife for his son.

Because Jawahar had lived so long in England and probably could not entirely submerge his Western ideas, no matter how willing he may have been to try, Father decided to let them meet— a very unusual practice in those days. It was arranged that Kamala should come to stay with an uncle in Allahabad. She came to our house off and on, and of course saw quite a bit of Bhai. He still had not fallen in love with anyone else and was attracted to her, so he consented to marry her, though it was more his father's choice than his.

As soon as that was settled Father insisted that Kamala come to Anand Bhawan as often as possible, since, being from such an orthodox family, she knew nothing of Western ways. He arranged for Toopie to give her lessons in English manners and customs so that she could learn to be mistress of a house run in the Western fashion and be at ease at the parties he often gave for foreigners.

At first poor Kamala was completely confused and uncomfortable in a place so different from her home. The big dinners with crystal and china on the long table and rows of wine glasses at everyone's place, the strange food, and, most of all perhaps, the quick, loud voices of our many British guests, made her feel lost and lonely. But all the family liked her and did their best to help. Being very intelligent she soon learned how to handle herself. When eventually she came to live at Anand Bhawan as a daughter-in-law, she won all our hearts. My father doted on her, and my mother was very fond of her. They had their disagreements, though, because Mother was quite a queen in her own domain and Kamala, for all her sweetness, was a spirited girl—as she was to show when the going got rough in our long fight for independence.

My sister Nan, who was almost exactly her age, felt the usual complicated sister-in-law feeling toward her. Though I was so much younger I grew tremendously fond of her and she treated me more like a much loved daughter than a sister-in-law. Bhai absolutely adored her.

The man who was to lead India into the modern world was married with pomp and panoply in the ancient Vedic rites that have changed little in three thousand years. The year was 1916 and the date was set for the first day of spring, the festival called *Basanta Panchami*, a most auspicious day. Father brought several hundred guests and members of the family from Allahabad to Delhi in the "Nehru Wedding Train," decorated from the engine to the guard's van at the back with ribbons and bunting and flowers. At nine years of age, or any age, it was tremendously exciting to me. Because no place in Delhi could accommodate us all, Father set up an encampment just outside the old city. There were colorful bedroom tents, and living and dining room tents, all handsomely furnished, with oriental rugs laid on their wooden floors and hung from the walls. Naturally, there were also kitchen tents and so forth, a large staff, and an orchestra to add to the gaiety. The entrance was a high archway on which was written in flowers:

NEHRU WEDDING CAMP

The priestly astrologers, after studying the horoscopes of the bride and groom, selected the hour just after midnight as the most auspicious for the ceremony. In the early evening we all went to the Kaul family's house in the heart of Old Delhi. Bhai, according to our ancient custom, rode there on a white horse. He was wearing tight white trousers and a knee-length fitted coat, called a *sherwani*, made of beige brocade; on his head was a pink turban. Father's closest friend, Mr. Haksar, had wound the turban, and at each turn of the silk he kissed my brother's forehead and blessed him.

The Kauls lived in a very large house built around four sides of a central court in the eighteenth-century Indian fashion. In the center of the court was a platform on which the sacred fire burned in a brick fireplace. Over it a brocaded canopy was supported by four tall poles, and on each side seven jars were piled. The guests were massed around the platform and servants peered down from a hundred windows. There were seats for the bride and groom on the platform, as well as for their parents.

My brother, his brocade shimmering in the firelight, looked very handsome and completely at ease. Kamala was at the height of her beauty, in a pink sari (Indian brides never wear white, which is the color of mourning). She wore bangles and necklaces and ornaments all made of flowers of the shape and color of the jewels Father would give her next day. Her only real jewelry was a gold chain around her neck and two bangles, which are considered essential. The custom of wearing flowers arose because the priests always demanded whatever jewels the bride wore as part of their fee—heavy enough in any case.

The ceremony began with the priests asking Kamala's father if he was willing to give his daughter in marriage to Jawaharlal Nehru. He solemnly replied, "Yes." Then the bride and groom exchanged vows. The ceremony continued for over three hours. There was interminable chanting of prayers by the priests and, every so often, they ladled ghee onto the fire, causing it to blaze up, emitting clouds of black smoke.

The most sacred moment of the rite is the *sapta pad*—the seven steps which the bride and groom take around the fire. Bhai and Kamala, moving with youthful dignity and grace in the flamelight were so beautiful they stopped your heart.

After the long ceremony we all remained at the Kauls' house until dawn. Then the young couple left. The priests usually chant a Sanskrit song of blessing, but Father insisted that this should be done by the couple's young relatives—we had practiced for months. As Bhai and Kamala came out of the house we stood in rows, the girls dressed in the colors of springtime, pale yellow saris with green or white blouses, the boys in yellow turbans. As we sang each of the ancient verses of blessings and good wishes, the guests showered petals on Kamala and Bhai.

Father and Mother and the rest of our family dashed ahead to be ready to receive them ceremoniously at their house, which was, of course, the Nehru Wedding Camp. They stood waiting with silver trays on which were sweets and flowers, the red powder to make the *tika*, the lucky sign on the forehead which Indian women wear.

When they arrived, Mother made the *tika* on Kamala's forehead and then on Bhai's. Then she gave them each a sweet to nibble on, to sweeten their future lives.

After spending the day at the groom's house, it is the Kashmiri custom for the young couple to return to the bride's home for dinner with her family so they can get to know her husband, since they usually have had little opportunity to do so. So, in the evening, Bhai and Kamala prepared to leave our camp. This is the time when the bride wears all the finery she has been given by her husband's family. To my child's eyes, and to older eyes as well, Kamala looked absolutely dazzling in a cream-colored sari embroidered with pink flowers that were studded with real pearls. Father had sat over the weavers and sewing women who made it at Anand Bhawan. Her jewelry, which he had designed, had been made by jewelers and goldsmiths brought from Delhi and Bombay. They worked on the verandahs of Anand Bhawan while he watched them critically. He would buy nothing in a shop. Everything had to be specially made for the son he loved so dearly and the daughter-in-law he grew to love as much as, and perhaps more than, his own daughters.

So that evening Kamala was ablaze with diamonds and pearls and emeralds and rubies wrought into bracelets, necklaces, brooches and rings; far too much to wear at any one time, other than this, when the bride is supposed to show her parents how highly her husband's family regard her. Somehow Kamala's beauty triumphed over this ostentatious display, not overwhelmed but enhanced by the glittering jewels.

In a chorus of compliments she and Bhai drove away. In the Western world this would have brought the exciting but tiring business to an end. But not in India. For ten days more the festivities kept on, with parties at different houses and many at the Nehru Wedding Camp. That we all survived to ride wearily homeward on the Nehru Wedding Train was a tribute to our sturdy constitutions, soon to be put to more rigorous tests.

I have described my brother's wedding at some length because it showed a little-known side of his character—the Eastern side. Even in those days, and to a far greater degree as he grew older, he was the epitome of modern man. His aim was always to industrialize India and fit her to take her place, not in the world of today, but in the world of tomorrow: a rather frightening world of machines and computers; of science triumphant over the harsh circumstances of natural environment, over illness, hunger and war. He envisioned a world of equal opportunity, education, and living standards for all mankind, made safe and just by enlightened government operating on socialistic principles. He was not frightened by the prospect of mechanization. He had little patience with those who were, and who sought to turn India back to cottage industry and "the good old days." This became his principal point of disagreement with Mahatma Gandhi.

Despite these ideas, which had already become convictions, Jawahar was capable of taking part in an ancient ritual which had been handed down from a world even further removed from present reality than that scientifically managed future on which he had set his sights. Not only did he take part in it, he did so with grace and aplomb and serious dignity, completely unself-conscious in his glittering clothes, under hundreds of watching eyes. It was not that he believed in the chanted prayers and the sacred fire and all the other mumbo-jumbo of the rite; but he did believe in the sanctity of marriage and of family, and in the value of traditional Indian culture and customs. He was proud to share in them, so long as they did not hold back his great dream for the future of India.

2

we come from Kashmir

The origins and early history of the Nehru family have become worn with twenty tellings. Yet to make this book complete they must be told again if only for the record. The usual beginning is that the Nehrus were Brahmans of Kashmiri descent. However, I should like to explain just what a Brahman is.

There were four basic castes in the caste system, one Indian tradition my father took delight in upsetting. These were, first, the Brahmans, who were supposed to be scholars, priests and sages, the reason all Brahman men were entitled to be called *Pandit*. Next came the Kshatriyas, the warrior caste, to which the kings and maharajas belonged, as well as their fighting men. The third caste was the Vaisyas; they were the merchants, bankers, jewelers, professional men, farmers who owned their land, and most other people of ordinary occupations. Finally came the Sudras, landless peasants, some of whom later on, but not in the beginning, were known as the Untouchables because they did all the dirty work, scavenging, cleaning toilets, everything that would, in the minds of the higher castes, defile them.

Brahmans were thus the highest order of Indian society. Because learning was more honored than war, they were above the kings, who always belonged to the warrior caste. Throughout our history a Brahman has been prime minister to the greatest of kings; but the kings themselves bow to the Brahman. He stands bolt upright and blesses them, but he will not bow. The Kashmiri Brahmans go beyond that. Though in other parts of India it is customary for younger people to bow and touch the feet of their elders as a sign of respect, we Kashmiris bow only to God.

The Kauls (then our family name) left Kashmir over two hundred years ago, but we are always drawn back to that high green land of lakes and mountain-cold rivers and lush meadows under the towering escarpment of the Himalayas. About 1719, the Mogul Emperor Farukhsiyar, on a visit to Kashmir, received my ancestor, Raj Kaul, who was a very learned man. Raj Kaul must also have been endowed with great charm, for the Emperor invited him to come to Delhi to add the luster of his learning to the court. Not only that, but he presented him with a house in Delhi and several villages to give him an income. The house stood on the banks of a *nahar* ("canal") and our family became known in Delhi as Kaul-Nahar, which was corrupted to Kaul-Nehru. Eventually the Kaul got lost and our name became Nehru.

Though the Mogul emperors were, of course, Muslims, there was no difficulty about a Brahman being in their service. The emperors treated their own people and the Hindus alike. There was virtually no tension between the religious communities and, indeed, the last Mogul Emperor, Bahadur Shah, celebrated the major Hindu festivals as well as the Mohammedan ones. In the early nineteenth century my great-grandfather, Kakshmi Narayan Nehru was the first *vakil* ("legal representative") of the British East India Company at the Mogul Court, and my grandfather, Ganga Dhar Nehru, became the Kotwal of Delhi, the last Emperor's chief of police. We have a portrait of Ganga Dhar in the Mogul court dress, looking like a Muslim nobleman, with his full curling black beard and long-sleeved white tunic, with a cloak thrown over one shoulder and a long curved sword cradled in his arms.

The revolt or mutiny of 1857 ended all that. It started in Meerut in northern India where the sepoys, the East India Company's private army, mutinied and killed their English officers. They headed for Delhi, which they entered on May 11, 1857. There, feeble old Emperor Bahadar Shah and his shadow court in the old Red Fort were swept into the revolt. Meanwhile, British troops entrenched themselves on a ridge beyond the walls. For nearly four months Delhi was in chaos, which ended in terrible slaughter as the reinforced British shelled the city and then burst through the

15

Indian lines, shooting every able-bodied Indian man they saw.

As the British broke through on one side, half the population of the city fled from the other—among them my grandfather and grandmother and their two teen-aged sons and two young daughters. As they made their way along the Jumna River toward Agra, some British soldiers stopped them and accused them of kidnapping one of the little girls, who with her fair skin and chestnut hair resembled an English child. It looked like the end of the Nehrus; for the British, in their furious mood of the moment, were ready to hang them all from the nearest trees. Luckily my Uncle Nandlal could speak English, and while he argued with the soldiers someone came by who could identify the children as his sisters.

The family reached Agra safely and started life again, having lost almost everything they owned in the fall of Delhi. A few years later Ganga Dhar died, at the age of thirty-four. Three months after his death, on May 6, 1861, my father, Motilal Nehru, was born.

My father's upbringing was peculiar by any standard of East or West. My grandmother, Indrani Nehru, whom I do not remember, was a short, almost circular woman, very severe and very proud. She was a perfect dragon. Once at a wedding she overheard some women make disparaging remarks about one of her children. She walked up to them and said, "Do you know what happens if you try to spit at the sun or the moon? The spit falls back in your face."

Everyone was afraid of her except my father. She doted on him and spoiled him outrageously. Even as a little boy he was ungovernable and had a violent temper, a Nehru characteristic we all share. When a friend of the family protested that unless Motilal were curbed and disciplined he would come to a bad end, Grandmother delivered an oration: "Curb Motilal? Discipline him? As well control the winds and storms, thunder and lightning. My son has all these elements in one. He cannot be curbed but when he grows up you'll see that people will bow to his wisdom and respect his character." Unlikely as it seemed at the time, my grandmother was right.

The only person who had any influence over young Motilal was his brother Nandlal, whom he adored. At my grandfather's death, the support of the whole family fell upon his two older sons, then barely in their twenties. Bansi Dar got a position in the judicial department of the British Government of India, eventually becoming a subordinate judge. Nandlal, who also had acquired some legal training, got a job as teacher to Raja Fateh Singh of the small independent state of Khetri in Rajasthan. The raja took such a liking to Nandlal that he soon made him *diwan* ("prime minister.")

My father spent part of his early life at home, cosseted by an adoring mother and two much older sisters, and part of it with his brother at the court of Khetri, where he was taught Sanskrit and Persian by the raja's personal tutor, Qazi Sadruddin. Neither in his home nor as the darling of a luxurious though enlightened court was there much discipline.

In 1870, when my father was nine years old, Raja Fateh Singh died while traveling in a neighboring state, leaving no son to succeed him. He had wanted to adopt Ajit Singh, who was exactly Motilal's age, as his heir, but there was considerable doubt as to whether the British agent, Captain Bradford, would agree—British agents to princely states often made a very good thing out of an adoption by accepting a heavy bribe from some other maharaja who wanted a throne for a favorite younger son.

To carry out his raja's last wish, Nandlal did some fancy footwork. Instead of announcing Fateh Singh's death, he put the body in a carriage and drove madly back to Khetri where the raja "had a sudden fatal illness." By the time Captain Bradford got there Ajit Singh was so firmly ensconced that there was nothing he could do about it—nothing, that is, except to give Nandlal the sack.

So my uncle went back to Agra where he practiced law and soon qualified as a *vakil* before the High Court. When the British transferred the Court from Agra to Allahabad, Nandlal moved the whole family there, which is how we Nehrus came to the place we all regard as home.

It was high time Motilal got some real schooling. He was already a good Persian scholar but he spoke no English, then and even now an essential to advancement in India. Nandlal enrolled him in Christ Church School in Cawnpore, modeled on the lines of the famous English public schools like Harrow and Eton, and staffed by British teachers. Later, he went to Muir College at Allahabad. His academic career was definitely not distinguished.

It was not that Motilal lacked brains. Later he proved himself abundantly provided with them, and he had enormous energy. The trouble was where he applied it—again a lack of discipline. If a thing did not interest him he would have none of it. What he cared about was sports, especially wrestling. And he had a real genius for getting into trouble—and getting out of it. He got around his English schoolmasters almost as easily as he got around his mother. They all liked him and, like her, they made excuses for him and helped him get out of scrapes. At that, his natural brilliance brought him through with respectable marks.

The final act of Motilal's academic life was typical. He went to Agra to take the final examinations for his B.A. Not having studied very hard, and being a perfectionist, he decided that his very first paper was a failure. So he took no more examinations. Instead he spent three days contemplating the Taj Mahal, which, however edifying for his soul, was fatal to his chance of getting a degree. To add to the disaster, his professor furiously told him that his first paper had received a passing mark, and had he continued as well he would have got his degree. The lesson was not lost on Motilal.

Now what was he to do? The law was the obvious answer. Motilal tried it and found his métier. It commanded his interest, and failure at the university spurred his ambition. When he took the examination for a *vakil* in the High Court he topped the list and won a gold medal as well.

Naturally he did not entirely change his ways. Though he practiced law with considerable success as a junior in the office of Pandit Prithvinath, he had plenty of energy left over for the sports he loved, and for dabbling in politics. It took a tragic circumstance to make him concentrate on his career.

Nandlal, whom he regarded both as brother and father, died in early middle age. Now Motilal became the sole support of his own family and also of his brother's widow, five sons and two daughters; for in India we consider ourselves responsible for all the members of our family. Father felt in honor bound to repay Nandlal's love and kindness by seeing to it that the children had the best of everything and were as well educated as though their father had lived. He worked eighteen hours a day, cutting himself off from all other pleasures. When Bansi Dar died ten years later my father took on the support of his family as well.

Nandlal's death was not the first tragedy in my father's life. His mother had arranged a marriage for him when he was very young. His wife bore him a son, but within little more than a year, just as he had grown to love them dearly, both she and her child died. My father, a widower at nineteen, was so badly shaken that he resolved not to marry again.

However, my grandmother made the opposite resolve and she was a most determined lady. The tug-of-war between them went on for several years. Finally, at a family wedding, Motilal saw a beautiful girl of thirteen to whom he was strongly attracted.

Swarup Rani Thussu was an enchanting child with a fair skin, auburn hair and hazel eyes. She was as delicate as a flower. Her family were Brahmans who had come from Kashmir more recently than we, and were very orthodox. She remained true to her faith all her life.

My grandmother lost no time in arranging the marriage her son desired. Mother came to the Nehru house as a bride at the age of fourteen, but according to our custom, the marriage was not consummated until she was seventeen years old. In fact, my mother and father were not even allowed to be alone together. Once Father slipped into Mother's room just to talk to her and try to get to know his bride a little better. My grandmother caught them and packed Mother off to her family for another two years.

Meanwhile the tremendous effort my father was making began to pay off. My brother, born in 1889, was the son of a comparatively poor man. Eleven years later, my sister Nan was born the daughter of a well-to-do family, and I was born in 1907 into a house of great luxury. Father's success was due to hard work, legal knowledge, especially of the Hindu laws of inheritance, and imaginative application of his knowledge. But what counted perhaps more than any of these things was his personality, full of enthusiasm, humor and surprising patience with difficult clients. Most important of all was his reputation for absolute integrity. The first big opportunity he got was being retained in the complicated inheritance case of the enormous Lakhna estate in 1894. The case dragged on for thirty years, though Father finally won it for his client.

At first, the whole family were crowded into a house in the old part of Allahabad. Then they moved to 9 Elgin Road, in what was called the "Civil Lines," a suburb where English and Eurasian families lived in handsome houses. Finally, in 1900, Father bought the great house where I grew up, and named it Anand Bhawan.

It was a huge, rambling, one-story brick house, painted white, built around a central courtyard with a fountain that played every evening and bright tropical flowers that were changed according to the season. There were verandahs all around the outside of the house, facing out on a walled park or compound big enough for a little girl to get lost in. There were wonderful gardens in which English flowers—gladioli, chrysanthemums, delphiniums and a formal garden of roses—bloomed beside the gaudy flowers of India: deep red poinsettias, pink and yellow hibiscus, and masses of bougainvillea. In the spring, the jakaranda trees were like tall fountains of vivid blue blossom, contrasting with a tree we called Flame of the Forest, afire with bright orange-colored flowers. Brighter even than the flowers were the birds—parrots, myna birds, tiny green-and-yellow coppersmiths, and dozens of others. They woke you at first light with their noisy greeting to the dawn.

The house had an immense drawing room where Father gave big parties for his British friends and various maharajas whose legal business he handled, as well as for many eminent Hindus and Muslim friends. There were more than a dozen bedrooms. Father and Mother each had a suite of rooms with their own verandahs. Her rooms were filled with delicately carved Indian furniture and divans covered with gay cushions; while his were crowded with Western furniture in the somewhat dubious taste of turn-of-the-century England. Schooling, ambition and inclination made Father a great anglophile at this time, and he tended to copy the worst as well as the best of English culture.

Like many an English manor house, Anand Bhawan came equipped with a ghost. Though she became known as the Nehru Ghost, she was none of ours. Legend said that a previous owner had drowned his wife in the swimming pool, the reason she haunted that part of the house. Though I never saw her myself she scared some of the young men of the family; not only the youngsters but my older cousins who, because of their European education and Father's training of skepticism about other-worldly phenomena, were supposed to be proof against such things. They described a shadowy figure clothed from head to foot in white. She was never vicious but sometimes made appealing gestures to them which they did not understand.

20

The nearest I ever came to her was when I encountered my cousin Brajlal Nehru, who was the father of the present Indian Ambassador to Washington, coming along the corridor from the pool. He was shaking and white as parchment. I ran up to him and said, "Are you all right? You look ill!"

In a harsh voice he said, "I've seen her. Don't touch me! I don't know what might happen to you."

Father made his first trip to England in 1899. He had a splendid time there, entertained by various notables and taken to the Strangers' Gallery of the House of Lords to watch Parliament in action. Naturally this hospitable reception confirmed his English tastes. From that time on, until he joined Mahatma Gandhi's National Movement, all his clothes were made in England—though the story that he sent his shirts to be washed in London is nonsense.

We have a picture of Father taken at this time in his formal cutaway coat of English broadcloth and gray striped trousers, with a stiff shirt, high collar and black satin tie. His rather full face is adorned with a handle-bar mustache—which he soon cut off. Though it is obviously a posed picture, there is the beginning of a smile on his lips and his big brown eyes hold a glint of laughter, as though he found the whole business deliciously funny.

When Father returned from England there was quite a tempest in the orthodox Hindu community. In those days a Hindu who traveled in Western lands was thought to be defiled, and had to go through a purification ceremony called *prayashchit*. Father refused to go through this "tomfoolery." The more liberal of his Hindu friends accepted him, but the strictly orthodox, including some of my mother's family, considered him an outcast. Father took it all good-humoredly. He said to one of my uncles, "I know you feel you will be polluted if you eat at my table, but it won't hurt you to drink a whisky-and-soda with me."

Despite this humorous approach, the situation had its serious side and brought on a diatribe from Father on the caste system. He wrote: "My enemies will find me a tough nut to crack. I know what your *biradare* [community] is and if necessary, in self-defense, I will ruthlessly and mercilessly lay bare the tattered fabric of its existence and tear it into the minutest shreds. [But] so long as H and the others of his ilk howl and bark I will pass them by . . . in contemptuous silence. . . ."

In the end it was his son who ripped "the tattered fabric" of caste.

Father made another trip to Europe in 1900, and this time he brought back an automobile. He was the first Indian in Allahabad to own one, and perhaps the first in all India. Naturally this monster also caused great resentment among the orthodox. They looked upon it as "the machine of the devil," and were scared stiff every time he went out in the car. The roads he was going to travel were cleared, for fear he would run over someone. Father took great pride in this.

Soon after he moved to Anand Bhawan, Father imported an English tutor for his son, Jawahar. My brother never went to school in India. Up to that time he had an English governess and "a dear old Pandit who was supposed to teach me Hindi and Sanskrit." My brother was much under the influence of our mother, who spoiled and loved him, as did our aunts, who told him beautiful stories from the Hindu epics *Ramayana* and *Mahabharata.* Munshi Mubarak Ali charmed him with tales from the Arabian Nights and stories of the revolt of 1857.

Bhai admired Father tremendously—from afar—but was rather afraid of him. In his autobiography he wrote: "He seemed to me the embodiment of strength, courage and cleverness above all other men . . . and I treasured the hope that I would grow up to be rather like him. But much as I admired and loved him, I feared him . . . I had seen him lose his temper with the servants and beat them, while I shivered with fright mixed with resentment. . . . His temper was indeed an awful thing and I do not think I ever came across anything to match it. . . . But fortunately he had a strong sense of humor also, and could control it (if necessary)."*

Bhai was used to seeing Father drink his whisky-and-sodas, but the first time he saw him drink a glass of claret, he ran to Mother screaming, "Father's drinking blood."

The tutor's name was Ferdinand T. Brooks. He was a good classical scholar and an ardent Theosophist, who had been recommended by Father's friend, Mrs. Annie Besant, then the leader of that movement. Mr. Brooks soon acquired a paramount influence over Bhai, so much so that when my brother was thirteen, he asked

* *Toward Freedom* (New York: The John Day Company, 1941), p. 21.

my father's permission to become a Theosophist. Father, who once had veered that way under the influence of the founder of the cult, Madame Blavatsky, and who never took religion seriously, merely laughed and said, "All right." So Bhai was initiated into the Society of Theosophists by Mrs. Besant herself. It did not take.

The more lasting contribution made by Mr. Brooks was inculcating a love of English classics in his pupil: Alice's delightful adventures in Wonderland; *Kim* and the *Jungle Books* by Rudyard Kipling, that poet of the imperial dogma; Scott, Dickens, Thackeray, H. G. Wells and Mark Twain; and such current novels as *The Prisoner of Zenda,* the Sherlock Holmes tales, *Three Men in a Boat,* and Du Maurier's *Trilby* and *Peter Ibbetson.* For true adventure there was Fridtjof Nansen's *Farthest North.*

Mr. Brooks also rigged up a little laboratory where Bhai could conduct simple experiments in physics and chemistry. My brother was always tremendously interested in science and the development of modern technology. He was especially keen on aviation, and he told me of his avid interest in the flights of the Wright brothers and the pioneer aviators of France and England.

Father was determined that his son should have the best education the world afforded, and this to his mind was English. In 1905 he went to England again to put Jawahar in Harrow. This time he took my mother and my sister Nan, who was five years old. Having deposited his son in the care of Doctor Joseph Wood, the Headmaster of Harrow, he took the rest of the family on a whirl around the continent and returned to Allahabad bringing with him Miss Hooper and a huge Renault limousine. Before leaving Europe, he wrote an immensely touching letter to his son in which he said: "In you we are leaving the dearest treasure we have in this world, and perhaps in other worlds to come. . . . It is not a question of providing for you as I can do that, perhaps in a single year's income. It is a question of making a real man of you, which you are bound to be. It would be extremely selfish—I should say sinful—to keep you with us and leave you a fortune in gold with little or no education. . . .

"I never thought I loved you so much as when I had to part from you. . . ."

23

3

"the cobra is dead"

Soon after my parents' return to Anand Bhawan another son was born to them. The baby boy lived only long enough to engage their hearts and died at the age of one month. Two years later, in November 1907, I was born. Though Father tried never to show any difference between sons and daughters and, unlike most Indians, gave them equal educational opportunities, I may have sensed his disappointment. Perhaps that is why I was such a tomboy, always trying to outdo my cousins at their own sports—cricket, tennis, swimming—instead of being a nice, feminine little girl like my sister.

I was supposed to be the ugly duckling. My sister was always beautiful and won people's hearts with easy charm. I was not as fair as she, and I overheard snatches of conversation between my mother and aunts saying what a pity it was that I was not handsome like my brother and sister. That made me very shy among strangers and a little sad even in the family. Father helped to put me right.

I remember going to my father's room one Hindu New Year's Day, a very different thing from the Western New Year. I must have been about five years old and I was all dressed up in a long skirt down to my ankles, and a pretty embroidered blouse with a little scarf draped over my shoulders. I was wearing a child's necklace and a few bangles that had been given to me. Father took no notice of me and went on shaving. I stood there in my new clothes and said, "Father, do you think I'm very ugly?"

He looked over his shoulder and said, "No, darling. How did you get that idea?"

"Well do you think I am as good-looking as Bhai or Didda?"

24

Father turned around then for the first time and picked me up in his arms and kissed me. And he said, "Whoever told you that story or wherever you heard that, believe me it's quite wrong. You don't have to be beautiful to be smart. I can't say whether you'll grow up to be beautiful or not, but in my eyes my Choti Beti is a very lovely little girl and I think she is going to be a very bright little girl." Then he gave me another kiss and set me down.

That was the best New Year's Day.

In spite of all our relations living at Anand Bhawan I had a rather lonely childhood. My brother and sister were so much older, and even though some of my cousins were my age, Miss Hooper's strict regime was an obstacle—though I managed to dodge it quite a bit of the time by purposely getting lost in the compound or in the great, rambling house. In addition, I had the horses and dogs and other pets. At the peak, Father had twenty-two horses in the big stables. Heaven knows how many dogs were in the kennels, ranging from the hounds he used for hunting—a sport he dearly loved—to house pets and the Great Danes who roamed the house and grounds at will.

When I was three years old he gave me the little white pony on which I learned to ride. The first tragedy of childhood was going out to the stables one morning and finding my pony dead of snakebite.

There was a pair of delicate little deer—they were no more than three feet high—that I loved and lost when one of them hanged himself on the rope by which he was tethered and the other died of loneliness. There were also rabbits and white mice, which I soon got rid of; and the family cobra, who lived beyond the swimming pool in the wood-and-coal-storage room. He could go in and out to the garden at will.

I was strictly forbidden to go near that room, but had no idea why. One day I was walking alone in the garden, probably trying to escape Toopie, when I suddenly heard a swishing noise. Then I saw a huge cobra glide out of the house. He passed quite close to where I stood trembling, unable to move; and taking no notice of me, he disappeared into the garden. I ran wildly into the house. Father had just come home from court. He saw my hysterical condition and asked me what was the matter. Pulling myself together, but still trembling all over, I said very carefully, "There is an enormous cobra who has just come out of the storehouse."

He took me in his arms and said gently, "There's nothing to fear. I know about the cobra but your mother won't allow it to be killed because it is inauspicious to kill a cobra unless it attacks you, especially a king cobra. He's always going in and out of the house. He won't harm you."

After that I saw the cobra many times but my fear of him, and of all snakes, simply disappeared.

Miss Hooper had a difficult time trying to make me into a proper English girl, for I was very willful and rather wild. When I was particularly bad she would lock me in the bathroom until I apologized. Since stubbornness is also a family trait—and I have all the bad ones—I often held out until quite late and missed my supper. (Not that I minded so much. Supper was so boring.)

The person who frustrated Miss Hooper most in her attempt to make me an English lady was my mother, who wanted to make a good Hindu out of me. In addition to taking me to the temples she insisted on another rite which horrified Toopie, and me as well.

Allahabad, which was formerly called Prayaga, is one of our most holy cities and Anand Bhawan stands on holy ground. According to the *Ramayana*, King Rama returned to Prayaga from his exile and met his younger brother Batrata, who had ruled as his regent, on the very spot where the fountain played in our courtyard.

But Allahabad is especially holy because there the sacred rivers, the Jumna and the Ganges, meet and flow together for a space without mingling, the clear green of the Jumna contrasting with the Ganges' muddy current. There was a third river, the Sanaswa, which has disappeared. Each year in January tens of thousands of pilgrims from all over India come to bathe in their waters, and in my teens my mother made me go with her to immerse myself in those icy, sacred rivers.

Mother insisted on using certain ancient Indian beauty preparations on my sister and me. Every morning she applied to our faces, arms, shoulders and chests a paste made of dried orange peel ground up and mixed with fresh cream, which was left on for ten minutes and then washed off with warm water. It was supposed to remove blemishes and to be good for the skin. I used it myself for years after I grew up and finally gave it up because it is so difficult to make in an apartment. When the orange skins dry they become very hard, and must be powdered by grinding them with a stone on a concave bit of rock. I tried it once with a blender; the blender broke.

A nightly ceremony was painting *kohl* around the eyes of my sister and me. Mother made it by sticking an almond on a fork and burning it, while holding a silver spoon over the flame. The black stuff that accumulated on the spoon was *kohl*. This was not done for beauty but because it was supposed to be good for our eyes. When we woke in the morning our faces and pillows were an awful mess. I still use *kohl* but I buy it in Indian beauty shops.

From Mother, I absorbed Hindu culture, the beautiful and terrible myths and legends of my native land, just as my brother had done. In this, she was ably assisted by my aunt, whom I called Bibi Amma. She was Mother's sister, and her husband had drowned when she was only eighteen. Orthodox Hindu widows had a very sad life. They could never remarry, no matter how young they were, and they always dressed in mourning white. They wore neither jewelry nor makeup, nor were they supposed to eat tasty food or join in any festivities. Instead they had to devote themselves to religion and good works. Often they became unpaid servants in the houses of relatives. Sometimes I think that suttee (the custom of a widow flinging herself on her husband's funeral pyre) was kinder than the dreary life the widows led.

Bibi Amma held fast to all these ancient customs. She never ever ate with the family but cooked all her own meals alone. She came to live with us and take care of Mother who became ill after the death of my little brother and was always thereafter a semi-invalid. Bibi Amma was utterly devoted. My mother became to her not only a sister but the child she never had; and she was a second mother to me. I loved to go to Bibi Amma's room and listen to her tell the ancient tales of India over and over again, and also eat the delicious food she cooked for me on her little stove. Though she spoke no English she had made herself into a fine Sanskrit scholar. Much of the best of my Indian self I owe to my aunt.

Another strong Eastern influence was the Hindu festivals, for which we always wore our Indian clothes. There was the Kashmiri New Year, called *Navoroz*. It does not fall on a given day but, like Easter, is flexible. It always seemed to me a rather nice way of cele-

27

brating the New Year. Just as dawn lightened the sky Mother would come to each of us in turn—nobody was supposed to get out of bed until she came—carrying a big silver tray on which she had put raw rice, wheat, sweetened yogurt, a mirror, a lump of silver and some gold sovereigns, and, of course, *tika*. She went first to Father and put the *tika* on his forehead. Then he would look at the wheat and rice, for prosperity, and taste the yogurt to sweeten the New Year; he kissed the silver and gold, hoping to have them through the coming year, and looked at himself in the mirror before looking at anybody else—if his face was not happy that was bad. We all did the same when our turn came. That day we wore brand-new clothes, and all our relatives came for one meal because Father was head of the family. It was very gay.

Then there was the first day of spring, another moveable feast; and *Holi*, which is a kind of bacchanalia, like Mardi Gras. Everybody is supposed to feel very merry and go mad, especially in the city streets and in the villages where it is celebrated with great gusto. Men and women can flirt as much as they like with each other and the youngsters splash colored water on everybody. At Anand Bhawan all the children of the family gathered and formed teams. We had buckets of colored water and spray guns with which we sprayed each other until we were a colorful sight to see. Then we got cleaned up for lunch.

There was a platform in the driveway in front of our house. On the evening of *Holi* my father used to stand there dressed in an immaculate white *dhoti* and *kurta* (a long shirt). It seemed as though the whole town came trooping up our drive to daub his face with red and purple powder and embrace him. By the time they finished he was a chromatic mess and he loved it. A big buffet table was set up on the lawn and everyone who came was given cold drinks and sweets; they stood talking or wandered around among the trees.

When my brother was Prime Minister he would do the same thing in front of the Prime Minister's House, and all Delhi came to greet him. One day when Jacqueline Kennedy was in Delhi she saw Jawahar standing there almost unrecognizable with a patchwork of color all over his face and white *sherwani*. She exclaimed, "Oh, I must do that, too!" We have a charming picture of her putting *tika* on his forehead and he doing likewise to her.

Divali, the festival of the lights, was another favorite of mine. All the people lighted up their houses with dozens of flickering lamps made of oil-soaked cotton in cups. There were firecrackers for the children, and in the evening the lawns were all lit up and the sky was full of rockets showering down their multicolored stars.

Later, when Bhai and I became very close, I paid special attention to *Bhai Dooj* (Brother's Day). You would go to your brother and put a *tika* on his forehead and a garland around his neck. And he would give you a present. Also, on *Rakshar Bandar,* another brotherly festival, you would make a bracelet called a *rakhi* of skeins of thread with a medallion on it, and tie it around your brother's wrist, which binds him to you forever. In ancient times the man was not necessarily a brother. Ruling princesses or queens of India—of whom there have been many though little is known of them—would send the *rakhi* to a powerful king beyond the borders of their land, and if he accepted it he became their bond-brother, in honor bound to protect them against their enemies. I never failed to send Bhai a *rakhi* each year when we were apart, but I also sent *rakhis* to very dear friends, among them General Daulat Singh, a very fine man, who later became Commander in Chief of our Air Force and was killed in a helicopter crash.

Then there were family weddings: tremendous events at which we girls from ten or eleven years of age on were dressed in Indian finery and loaded with jewels to attract the eyes of mothers looking for brides for their eligible sons. When I reached the age of fourteen, with no matrimonial prospects, Mother made me get up at five-thirty in the morning, take a cold shower and pray to the gods for a good husband. They did not answer for eleven years.

The very height of our wildly extravagant, happy life was my brother's wedding. After we got home from Delhi people poured through the house; and every evening, as was his custom, Father was at home to his friends on his verandah from seven till nine. His roars of laughter echoing through the house gave one a feeling that it was a wonderful world.

When the hot weather came Father took us all, including the bride and groom, to Kashmir. Though I do not remember having been there before it was like coming home to me, as it has been ever since. Father hired a fleet of houseboats on the Dal Lake at Shrinagar, a town from which the Himalayas rise like a stupendous wall to touch the sky with pure white, icy peaks.

The houseboats were very comfortable with three or four bedrooms and baths, a drawing room, dining room, and perhaps a small library. Unlike Western houseboats they had high peaked roofs with over-hanging eaves. Attached to each by a gangplank was a kitchen boat and one where the servants slept; and each had one or more *shikaras,* small boats that looked a little like gondolas, manned by two men to paddle you ashore if you wanted to visit the city. We bought our provisions and flowers from market boats that made the rounds of all the houseboats on the lake.

Life on the Dal Lake was lovely and serene; too serene for Bhai and Father. They decided to take us camping at Pahalgam, which is further up in the mountains at an altitude of eight thousand feet or more. There was no road in those days so we all rode horses up the steep trail that skirted sheer precipices. Mother rode in a *dandi,* a sort of sedan chair carried by four porters. Our tents were pitched in a green meadow on a plateau beside a roaring stream that came right down from the Himalayas, and the air was sharp with the taste of their eternal snows. In the afternoon Father had a cot set up in the riverbed for his nap.

Though we lived in tents it was very luxurious—when you traveled with Father you traveled in style. The tents had wooden floors and there was every imaginable luxury provided by the dozen or more servants we took with us. Bhai had been married little more than a month, but he was not content to remain in camp. He went off with one of our cousins and some porters through the high Zoji-la Pass to explore the lonely valleys leading to Tibet. Roped together they crossed great ice fields seamed by snow-hidden crevasses. Bhai fell into one but the rope held and he was saved. This accident did not deter him in the least. All his life he loved mountaineering and when I was old enough, I joined him in this sport. In his autobiography he wrote of that trip: "I found a strange satisfaction in these wild and desolate haunts of nature; I was full of energy and a feeling of exaltation."

When we returned from Kashmir, Father built a second-floor apartment on Anand Bhawan for Bhai and Kamala. It was complete with a sitting room, dining room, bedrooms and a kitchen, but they took most of their meals with us. So we all continued to live together in one patriarchal family.

In November 1917 Kamala and Bhai had a little daughter whom they named Indira. Both Father and Mother were delighted to have a grandchild, their first, but Mother's joy was shadowed by regret that it was not a boy, to carry on the name. She confided her disappointment to Father who sharply put her right. "You should not talk like that," he said. "You know that I have made no difference between my son and my daughters. I have brought them up in exactly the same fashion with the same amount of freedom. As far as I am concerned I don't care whether I have a grandson or a granddaughter; and in any case this girl is going to be worth more than a thousand grandsons."

Father, as usual, was right.

It was also in 1917 that Toopie fell in love and was married to an Englishman. Though she had been so strict with me, I was very unhappy; for I forgot all the bad things and remembered only the care and love she had given me all my life. However, when she asked me to be a bridesmaid I cheered up. Since all her family were in England, Father gave her away in the Anglican church nearby. It was great fun, but when she had finally gone there was an emptiness.

For a few days I was inconsolable, and then I began to savor the fun of freedom. Father thought that a daughter of his should be educated in the stately way of governesses and private tutors; I wanted to go to school. At first Father would not hear of it. He engaged two or three other governesses and I got rid of them rather easily. So in the end he allowed me to go to an English school in Allahabad. It was a co-educational school run by three old English women. I was the only Indian there.

That left me with no one to supervise me at home. Mother was too delicate to do it; so my sister, who was seventeen, took charge of me. That was the time we became friends. I still enjoy the memory of evenings spent with her in the garden while she read poetry aloud. All the sweet scents and colors of gay flowers and green lawns gave poignancy to the magic words we both loved. Never had we been so close, nor ever would we be again.

31

So, for a few more years, life continued normally at Anand Bhawan, as far as I knew. But I did not realize that Father and Bhai were becoming ever more deeply involved in Mahatma Gandhi's movement for Indian independence. Those were the days of World War I and we Indians were outwardly very loyal to Britain. Mother and Bibi Amma were knitting socks and mufflers for the soldiers—1,200,000 of our best Indian fighting men were in the British army. But beneath the still surface a volcano of discontent was bubbling in India, heated near the flash point by the stringency of British wartime security measures. Later I will try to tell something of the story of the *Satyagraha* Movement and my father's and brother's part in it; but at the time I only had a vague apprehension that the world I knew was coming to an end.

I do remember very well the first time Mahatma Gandhi came to stay with us in Anand Bhawan soon after the war. The excited talk and high expectancy made me realize that some very great man was coming, a man whom my father and brother revered in an extraordinary way.

We went down to the station to meet him in two cars, because we all wanted to go. As the train pulled in my eyes searched the handsome first-class carriages for a glimpse of the great man. Then I saw Bhai and Father greeting a strange person who got out of a third-class carriage. He was small and wizened, and wore only a loincloth and a white shawl draped over his bare shoulders. In snobbish consternation I watched their deferential attitudes as they guided him toward our cars. It was simply beyond my understanding why all this fuss was being made about a tiny little man who came out of the wrong compartment where the servants always traveled.

I did not actually meet Mahatma Gandhi that day, but back in our wing of the house several girl cousins and I were twittering like canaries. Our opinions of our guest were very unfavorable. "Is this the man who is changing all our lives?" we asked each other incredulously. "Is this insignificant person going to make everybody go to prison, and overthrow the British?"

We all agreed it was not possible.

Nor did I change my opinion very quickly. Mr. Gandhi stayed with us for about a week that time. I saw him day after day; I saw people rushing to get him the fruit and goat's milk on which he lived, and I resented it. Why couldn't he eat normal food like everybody else instead of having mashed peaches and goat's milk, although he was perfectly healthy? It seemed to me terribly affected. So I did not get to know him nor did I like him at that time.

Every evening crowds of people came pouring through the gates onto our lawn for his prayer meetings. On one occasion I was standing against a pillar of the verandah looking out at the crowd and wondering what it was all about. Mr. Gandhi came up and pulled my ear and drew me toward him, which was his way of showing affection for a child. He slapped my back and asked me where I had been all these days.

"I've been right here," I answered.

He said, "You must come and talk to me."

"What about?" I asked rather pertly.

"You're grown up," he said, "can't you talk?"

"Yes," I answered, "but I don't understand what's happening."

"Well, we will talk," he said, "and maybe you will understand. Why don't you attend the prayer meeting?"

I had not been to one though I had watched them at a distance from the terrace. In my youthful arrogance I had felt no inclination to join in, nor had I yet succumbed to Gandhiji's enormous spiritual impact. However I was too polite to refuse him, so together we walked to the meeting. I sat near him on the platform where I saw Father and Mother, Bhai and Kamala and many others. The prayer meeting consisted of recitations of verses from our Hindu holy books, and a reading from the Koran and the Bible. The crowd sang Christian hymns I knew and loved like "Abide With Me" and "Lead Kindly Light." Virtually all religions were brought in at one meeting or another because Gandhiji believed that each religion contained one facet of eternal truth.

After the prayers, during which Gandhiji sat cross-legged with his head bowed, he spoke for perhaps five minutes while the crowd listened in utter, breathless silence. Then he stood up and folded his hands in the Indian way, and some in the crowd came forward to bow and touch his feet—which he did not like them to do; others talked to him for a few moments before they all silently drifted away.

One thing I understood, even at that age: To follow Mahatma Gandhi's idealistic way meant giving up all the pleasant things of life. Only by doing this, he believed, only by boycotting English ways, by refusing to co-operate in any way with the rulers of India, could we force them to grant us *swaraj* ("freedom"). Not only that, but all who followed him must pledge their lives and their very souls to his ascetic manner of life and to its ultimate goal.

By chance I happened to be in the room when the final confrontation between Gandhiji and my father took place. In a reasonable tone my father said, "You have taken my son, but I have a great law practice in the British courts. If you will permit me to continue it, I will pour great sums of the money I make into your movement. Your cause will profit far more than if I give it up to follow you."

"No," Gandhiji said. "No! I don't want money. I want you—and every member of your family."

The end of an era for us was signaled in a mystical way. One day a new servant who did not know about the cobra went to the storage room to get wood. Suddenly the snake reared its hooded head. In a panic he grabbed a stick and bashed its head in. The cobra must have been very old because normally it could have evaded him easily. The servant, rather proud of himself, reported his act to my mother. Quite distracted she ran to my father who was working on his verandah. "The cobra has been killed," she said. "Ill luck will come to us."

"My dear," Father said, "ill luck is already here, if you consider it that; for I have joined Mahatma Gandhi. I am going to give away this house and will have to sell all my horses and my wine cellar. We will not be able to live in the way we have."

"Must you?" Mother asked.

"Our son has joined Gandhiji," he replied. "Would you want me not to go with him?"

"No," Mother said. "I am glad you are with your son and we shall all join the movement together. But the cobra is dead...."

Smiling gently, Father said, "Then we'll give him a proper funeral."

So we buried him in the garden with a stone at his head. It is still there.

4

the coming of
Mahatma Gandhi

Father's decision to join Gandhiji's non-violent civil disobedience campaign against the British *Raj* was no sudden thing, nor was it taken easily. He began to be interested in politics thirty-five years earlier in 1885, when the Indian National Congress was formed under the aegis of an Englishman named Allan O. Hume, who had retired after serving the British Government of India for thirty-three years. The first president of the Congress was W. C. Bonnerji. Other prominent Hindu leaders who attended the first meeting in Bombay were Surendranath Banerjea, Badruddin Tyabji, Pherozeshah Mehta, and one who became the Grand Old Man of India, Dadabhai Naoroji. The Congress was conceived as a sounding board to make Indian needs known to her British rulers, and as a first small step in preparing Indian leaders for an eventual, though far-distant, part in the government of their own country.

If the seventy-two gentlemen who met in Bombay, wearing British-style morning coats—no garment devised by man is less suitable for our climate—and mouthing undying loyalty to the British Crown, had realized what they were starting most of them would have turned whiter than their stiffly starched shirts. For if Gandhiji was the spiritual leader of India's struggle for freedom, the Indian National Congress was the political instrument of revolution.

My father, Motilal Nehru, did not attend the first session, but he followed it with intense interest. In 1888, when the Congress met in Allahabad, Father was among the 1,400 delegates. Though its members could still speak of "The merciful disposition of Providence which has placed India under the great British Dominion," it was asserting itself much more strongly. Hume made a fiery speech to the effect that because the government of India refused to take any notice of its suggestions, the Congress should go over its head and try to instruct "the great English nation in its island home," and also the people of India, "so that every Indian . . . may become our comrade and coadjutor, our supporter and, if needs be, our soldier in the great war that we will wage for justice, for our liberties and rights."

This was strong medicine and the British quivered, remembering the Mutiny. Young Motilal Nehru threw his enormous reserve of energy into the work of the Congress to such effect that in 1889 he was made a member of the Subjects Committee along with much older and more distinguished people like Banerjea and Gopal Krishna Gokhale, who became his close friend and ally. When the Congress met again at Allahabad in 1892, my father was the natural choice for Secretary of the Reception Committee. After that, there was a ten-year lull in the Congress proceedings: they met, they talked, they accomplished nothing. Father lost interest and devoted himself to making money.

The viceroyalty of the Marquess Curzon of Kedleston sparked a new resurgence both of imperial splendor and Indian resentment that brought Father back into politics. Lord Curzon was a man of superlatives; he was the youngest, the most magnificent and the most arrogant of viceroys. Though a man of great ability, he had the attitude and taste for splendor of an eighteenth-century English Duke. He was able to gratify these desires because he had married a very rich American. He had a genuine feeling for beauty, and the greatest thing he did for India was to save some of our beautiful ancient temples and other works of art by financing their care and restoration and by putting them under government protection.

Though all India resented his inordinate pride of race and his ostentatious behavior, it was a simple administrative act that fired the spirit of revolt. In 1905, Lord Curzon announced that Bengal would be divided into two parts. From the point of view of administration it made sense; for Bengal with 70,000,000 inhabitants living in vastly different conditions—from the steaming slums of Calcutta to Himalayan villages on the border of Nepal—was an unwieldy unit of government. But in its lack of regard for the feelings of the

Bengalis the proposal was one of those idiotic blunders by which a tactless satrap can undo years of good relations. The people of Bengal reacted with a fury that was shared by the majority of other Indians. Surendranath Banerjea of Bengal said his people had been "insulted, humiliated and tricked."

Since military action was impossible the Bengalis started the first boycott of British goods, hitting the English in their pocketbooks. It was so successful and feeling ran so high that it was worth an Indian's life to be seen going into a British shop in Calcutta. When the Lieutenant Governor of the new province of East Bengal arrived at a railroad station in his domain he had to carry his own luggage because all the porters had mysteriously disappeared.

In 1906, the Muslim League was founded with some assistance from the British. It was intended to give the Muslim community a sounding board like the Congress, which, although some Muslims belonged to it, was predominantly Hindu. British assistance was predicated on the old Roman principle of "divide and rule."

In this agitated atmosphere Father felt obliged to return to politics. He attended the Congress meeting in 1905, and the one in Calcutta in 1906 where the Moderates, who wanted to work within the constitutional framework of British government, and the Extremists, who wanted the Congress to defy England, almost came to blows. In 1907 he took an active part. Father was a Moderate. He thought that by working with the British, India could eventually achieve the goal he envisioned, of Home Rule with Dominion status. At that time he did *not* desire complete independence.

Gokhale was the great leader of the Moderates. When he came to Allahabad in 1907, he received a tremendous ovation. Father met him at the station with our carriage. A crowd of enthusiastic students from Muir College unhitched the horses from the carriage and drew it through streets jammed with cheering people to Anand Bhawan. Partly as a result, Father accepted the presidency of the Provincial Conference of the United Provinces in Allahabad. His address to the opening session was a clear, well-reasoned statement of the Moderate point of view. My brother, writing from England, strongly disapproved. He was already a militant revolutionary.

However, Father used all his growing influence in favor of constitutional methods, and the Moderates succeeded in getting control of the Indian National Congress. As a result of this and certain British concessions, among them the reunification of Bengal, things simmered down after the crisis year of 1907. The Indian scene remained comparatively tranquil—my brother would have said stagnant—until World War I and the return of Mahatma Gandhi.

Such was the condition that prevailed when Bhai came home from England in 1912. Father and Bhai attended the Congress meeting that year. It was a prime example of empty oratory and started a marathon argument between father and son as to how *Swaraj* could best be achieved. The quarrel lasted for seven years, getting hotter all the time, until on occasion they were shouting at each other. But it never affected their love for each other.

The crisis began in 1916 when Mrs. Annie Besant, the grand old lady of Theosophy who was a frequent visitor in our home, founded the Home Rule League to agitate for Dominion status for India. Bhai joined it; Father did not. Almost simultaneously the Indian National Congress and the Muslim League, meeting separately in Lucknow, came to an agreement to work together for Indian self-government. Ironically, one of the chief architects of this agreement was Muhammud Ali Jinnah.

Nourished by Indian resentment of British acts of repression under the wartime Defense of India Act, the Home Rule League swept the country. Stunned by its success, the British Government panicked and interned Mrs. Besant on June 16, 1917. That caused a real uproar. Father, outraged by such unchivalrous treatment of an old lady, promptly joined the League and called a meeting in Allahabad. In an amazingly emotional speech he said: "The Government has openly declared a crusade against our national aims. Let us raise aloft the banner of the Home Rule League, and three hundred and thirty million throats voice forth the motto of Home Rule." The next day he was elected president of the Allahabad Home Rule League and Bhai was elected a joint secretary.

As usual when faced with a united popular outcry, the British made concessions. On August 30, the Secretary of State for India, Edwin S. Montagu, issued a declaration of policy, that of "gradual development of self-governing institutions with a view to the progressive realization of responsible government in India as an integral part of the

38

British Empire." In September Mrs. Besant was released and in October she came to stay with us. Once again Father's horses were unhitched and students drew his carriage through cheering crowds from the station to Anand Bhawan.

These minor concessions again quieted the political scene. Mr. Montagu came to India and many Indian leaders, including my father, conferred with him and the Viceroy, Lord Chelmsford. The result was the Montagu-Chelmsford Reforms of 1918. All India awaited them with high expectations that were dashed by the very meager measure of Indian participation in government they allowed us. However, nothing more happened until after the surrender of Germany in November 1918.

The repressive wartime measures of the Defense of India Act were supposed to end six months after the war. But the British government of Prime Minister David Lloyd George decided that it was "unsafe" to give the Indian people even the small degree of legal protection they had previously enjoyed. In March 1919, Parliament passed the infamous Rowlatt Bill, arming our rulers with "the right to suppress political violence." To us it meant the end of civil liberties in India; and it brought Mahatma Gandhi to the forefront of our fight for freedom.

In 1915 Mahatma Gandhi had returned to India after twenty-two years in South Africa, where he had gone at the age of twenty-five. There, moved by the sufferings of the large Indian colony in Natal and the Transvaal, under the repressive, racist policies of the South African government, he had organized them and led the long fight to ameliorate their condition.

But Gandhiji's way of fighting was like no other man's. For it he had coined the word *satyagraha* which literally meant "truthful effort," though it had religious connotations. The word came to mean passive resistance through civil disobedience. To be willing to die, but not to kill; passively to accept the worst an opponent could do, but never to give in, never to relinquish the ideal that inspired you. This was Gandhiji's way of fighting.

The Indians in South Africa, disciplining themselves to this hard rule, gained the admiration of the world, including England and even the British government of India. After long years of struggle a considerable measure of reform was won from the government of South Africa. When he landed in India, Mahatma Gandhi was already a world figure. The Viceroy gave him the Kaisar-i-Hind medal.

My brother met Gandhiji at the Lucknow session of the Congress in December 1916. Of him he said: "I was simply bowled over by Gandhi straight off. . . . [He] was like a powerful current . . . like a light that pierced the darkness and removed the scales from our eyes . . . like a whirlwind that upset many things. . . . He did not descend from the top but seemed to emerge from the millions of India. . . . It was against this all-pervading fear [of my people] that Gandhi's quiet and determined voice said: 'Be not afraid.' "*

During the war Gandhiji took little part in our struggle for independence. Unlike the Irishman who said, "England's trouble is Ireland's opportunity," his idealistic creed forbade him taking advantage of an opponent's difficulties. He was loyal to Britain and offered to lead an ambulance unit in World War I, as he had in the Boer War.

What drew my brother to him was his concern for the masses, for the desperate condition of the Untouchables. Bhai knew very little at first hand about the terrible conditions in which most Indians existed—"lived" is too lively a word for it—until he came under Gandhiji's influence and went out among the villages to see for himself.

In 1919, when the Rowlatt Bill became law, the Mahatma was recovering from an almost fatal illness. With his extraordinary control of spirit over body he wasted no time on convalescence but immediately launched the *Satyagraha Sabha,* whose members were pledged to disobey the Rowlatt Act, as well as other objectionable laws—to court jail openly and deliberately. The moment he read about it my brother was, in his words, "afire with enthusiasm and determined to join it immediately. I hardly thought of the consequences—lawbreaking, jail-going, etc."†

Father was appalled. All his training, his inclination to compromise and to find a solution within constitutional limits, his veneration for the rule of law with its long tradition handed down the centuries

* From Tibor Mende, *Nehru: Conversations on India and World Affairs* (New York: George Braziller, 1956).

† *Toward Freedom* (New York: John Day Co., 1941), p. 48.

from the Roman Empire to England and on to India, made him distrust *Satyagraha*. Those were the days and nights of the bitterest arguments between father and son, with Bhai, unable to sleep at the thought of going against his father, wandering alone through the grounds in misery; and Father trying to sleep on the floor of his room, to see what it would be like for his beloved son in a British jail.

Contrary to my impression at the time, Gandhiji's first visit to Anand Bhawan in 1919 was not to drag us into his movement. He had come at Father's request. They had long talks together without Bhai present. In the end Gandhiji, who could no more bear to see a family disrupted by his principles than to see men kill for them, did what my father pleaded with him to do, and advised Bhai not to make any rash move that would upset Father. Then everything was changed by the Jallianwalla Bagh Massacre.

On March 31, 1919, in Delhi, and on April 6 throughout the rest of India, Mahatma Gandhi launched his *Satyagraha* Movement with a *Hartal,* a general strike, during which all the people were to pray and fast. Enormous numbers of people took part, and the British government, badly frightened, took severe repressive measures. On April 9, Gandhiji was arrested on his way to Delhi. He was returned to Bombay and set free, but news of his arrest produced numerous riots, the worst of which were in the Punjab. He immediately denounced the riots, called off *Satyagraha* for which, he said, the Indian people "were not yet ready," and went on a three-day fast of expiation.

Brigadier General Sir Michael O'Dwyer, Governor of the Punjab, was one of His Brittanic Majesty's less imaginative and humane satraps. His subordinate, Brigadier General R. E. H. Dyer, was even worse: to an autocratic nature he added stupidity and merciless cruelty. On the day after Gandhiji's arrest, April 10, there was a bloody riot in Amritsar in the Punjab in which three English civilians were killed by the mob. Sir Michael sent General Dyer into the city with a regiment of British troops to maintain order; unfortunately General Dyer's idea of maintaining order was very strange.

First he placed a ban on all public meetings. This was not unreasonable. But on April 13, which was a Hindu holiday, between ten and twenty thousand people gathered in the Jallianwalla Bagh in defiance of the ban—many of them had not even heard of it. The Jallianwalla Bagh was a large vacant depression, a sort of crater, walled in on three sides by tall buildings with a narrow exit in a five-foot wall on the fourth. When the news was brought to General Dyer he lost his head. Visions of the "Indian Mutiny" both frightened and inflamed his mind. This, he thought, was the time to teach the beggars a lesson and nip the imagined revolt in the bud.

Dyer stationed a company of troops on the rim of the Bagh and ordered them to shoot down into the dense, unarmed mass of men, women and children. They had no place to escape. The screaming, hysterical people tried to get away from the murderous fire by rushing to the wall. Dyer directed the fire of his troops upon it, and it was soon buried under dead bodies. According to the General's report his men used almost all their ammunition, firing 1,605 rounds. Hardly a bullet was wasted and some did double and triple duty; for the toll of dead and wounded far exceeded 1,600.*

This began a deliberate reign of terror in the Punjab. The region was placed under martial law and completely cut off from the rest of India. All news was blacked out. British troops fired on crowds in Lahore and throughout the area, and airplanes machine-gunned country villages. There was one street in Amritsar where a young Englishwoman had been attacked during the rioting. British soldiers cordoned it off and for days every Indian who was obliged to go that way was forced to crawl the length of it on his belly. It was all a result of what has been called "the Mutiny Complex"—the Englishmen's pathological fear that 300,000,000 Indians would rise up and massacre them all.

Late in 1919 my brother, traveling from Amritsar to Delhi by train, happened to be in the same car as several British officers. In his autobiography he wrote: "One of them was holding forth in an aggressive and triumphant tone and soon I discovered that he was Dyer, the hero of Jallianwalla Bagh, who was describing his Amritsar experiences. He pointed out how he had the whole town at his mercy and he had felt like reducing the rebellious city to a heap of ashes, but he took pity and refrained. . . . I was greatly shocked. . . . He descended at the Delhi station in pajamas with bright pink stripes, and a dressing gown."†

* An Indian National Congress Committee of Investigation reported nearly 1,200 dead and 3,600 wounded. This may be an exaggeration.

† *Toward Freedom, op. cit.,* p. 50.

British reaction to Dyer's deed was mixed. The government eventually recalled him, but English Tories raised a fund of £50,000 for him and a group calling itself "The Women of England" presented him with a magnificent "Sword of Honor"!

The reaction in India was thunderous. Indeed it is not too much to say that Britain lost her empire at the Jallianwalla Bagh. All factions —Muslims, Hindus, Moderates and Extremists—were united in horror and fury. Father wrote, "My blood is boiling"; and if his blood was in that condition my brother's was like superheated steam. For this was not like other so-called massacres, where troops fired on mobs that were actually attacking them and killed a few people. The unarmed crowd in the Jallianwalla Bagh was trapped and helpless. The killing there was deliberate, cold-blooded murder.

Even so, the Indian leaders did not react with blind fury. Father applied to the government of India for permission to go to Lahore to defend his fellow Congress member Lala Harkishanlal, who with other leaders was being tried for "waging war against the King." When it was refused, he cabled to E. S. Montagu. Mr. Montagu was a man of good will and good intentions toward India. Almost immediately on receipt of Father's cable he ordered the Viceroy to open the Punjab. Father went there to handle the cases, without a fee, of course, and won them all.

The British government sent out the Hunter Committee to investigate the killings in the Punjab, but since it had no Indian members, the Congress formed its own Committee of Investigation. Mahatma Gandhi and my father were members. Working closely with Gandhiji, Father came to know and love him. It was then that he began calling him Bapu (Father), as so many who loved him did. There were no more arguments between Father and Bhai, for Father decided to follow where Gandhiji led.

In December 1919, the Indian National Congress met at Amritsar. Father had been elected president. All the great leaders were present at the Congress including his old opponent, B. G. Tilak, the leader of the Extremists, Mrs. Besant, Jinnah, Srinivasa Sastri, my brother, and, of course, Gandhiji. When Father arrived in Amritsar the station was a seething mass of cheering people. They escorted him through the city in a huge procession. The Muslim League was also holding its meeting in Amritsar and, as the sign and seal of unity, its president Ajmal Khan and Father prayed together in the Golden Temple, the holy shrine of the Sikhs.

Just before the Congress opened, King George V signed a decree of amnesty for all those involved in the Punjab rioting. As expected, this relaxed the atmosphere. Father spoke for three hours at the opening of the Congress giving a complete summary of the terrible events of the year. But, still hoping for a reasonable accommodation with the British, he joined Tilak and Gandhiji in sending grateful messages to King George for his act of mercy.

The great accomplishments of the Amritsar Congress were its expression of unity and the fact that it was there that Mahatma Gandhi's leadership was established and acknowledged.

5
Satyagraha

The year 1920 began quietly. Gandhiji did not immediately renew his *Satyagraha* Movement and, though Father was committed to his cause, he was able to continue the practice of his profession. In one great case he earned a fee of two *laks* (200,000) of rupees. Anand Bhawan continued to function at full tilt with all the horses, dogs, servants and luxury to which we were accustomed.

Do not think that because they were deeply involved in high politics and tragic events, Father and Bhai became glum and solemn. On the contrary their irrepressible spirits and high humor burst out at the least relaxation of tension, and the old house still echoed with their happy laughter, especially when Bhai pulled off what he called a "rag," or practical joke.

The shadow on our lives was Kamala's failing health. Ever since Indira's birth she had seemed frail and easily tired; now she began running a low temperature and feeling miserable. Of course Bhai and Father got the best doctors for her but it was a long time before they diagnosed her illness. Meanwhile they ordered Kamala and my mother, who was also ill, up to Mussoorie in the hills. Bhai went with them.

It was at Mussoorie that Bhai had his first direct clash with the British. It happened that delegates from Afghanistan were there to meet British envoys to settle a little war they had had in 1919. Unfortunately they were staying at the same hotel as my family. Suddenly one evening the superintendent of police called on my brother and asked him to promise not to have any contacts with the Afghans—supposedly because such a dangerous character as Bhai might stiffen their resistance against British demands.

Bhai did not know any of the Afghans or especially desire to, but this suggestion provoked his stubborn pride. He absolutely refused.

45

As a result he was ordered to leave Mussoorie at once. Since civil disobedience had not begun again he obeyed the externment order and returned to Allahabad.

That was the year my sister became engaged to Ranjit Sitaram Pandit. It was not a love match but one of our arranged marriages, though not in the old-fashioned way. Some years before, when my sister was seventeen, Father had arranged a marriage which she refused because she thought herself in love with a young man whom Father considered unsuitable. It caused serious trouble between Nan and Father, and she went to live for a while with Gandhiji and his wife Kasturba Gandhi in his *ashram** on the Sabramati River. Gandhiji worked very hard to bring about a reconciliation between Nan and Father, which took about six months.

Ranjit came into our lives through my cousin Jivan Katju who was his best friend when they were both at Oxford. Jivan wrote to my father telling him what a wonderful chap Ranjit was, with a brilliant future before him as a lawyer, and suggested asking him to Anand Bhawan as a possible husband for Nan. The first I knew of it was one day when I saw a tall, handsome young man getting out of a car with a lot of baggage. A little later as I passed by one of the guest rooms I heard someone singing in a superb voice. Nobody sang at Anand Bhawan as Father had no use for music though I loved it.† I stood and listened enthralled until the singing stopped and the young man who had come in the car came out of the room. In a warm easy way he said, "Hello. I suppose you're Choti Beti."

"Yes," I said, "Who are you?"

"I'm Ranjit Pandit," he answered. "I hope we're going to be friends."

"Why have you come here?" I asked.

"To meet your sister."

"What for?"

"Perhaps to marry her if she likes me."

I liked Ranjit immediately. He was just under six feet tall, very

* An *ashram* is a collection of cottages within a compound usually inhabited by a community of people with some religious interest in common. In Gandhiji's case they were his assistants and special disciples.

† I took piano lessons from my governors and studied Indian music and also the violin.

slim and good-looking. Later I learned that in addition to knowing the law and music, he spoke German and French as well as English and was a fine Sanskrit scholar. He came from a family of Brahmans from Maharashtra, who were very rich. In fact Ranjit had everything, for he was also an athlete, good at tennis, polo and swimming, and an excellent shot. I think my sister really fell in love with him at first sight, and he with her. She was very lovely with a fair skin, large brown eyes and black hair that fell almost down to her waist.

In a thirteen-year-old way I fell in love with Ranjit, too; that is, I hero-worshiped him. We had a wonderful comradeship. Nan was never fond of outdoor things so I was often his companion in sport, riding with him—he taught me how to jump a horse—motorboating on the Ganges, and swimming together in our big indoor pool. Through him I finally got over my fear of the water.

In the evening we all had fun together. There were not any big affairs because the *Satyagraha* Movement had now started, but we had dinner parties and afterward turned on the gramophone and danced. Ranjit loved dancing and was full of song. In his fine voice he sang Western songs, especially opera, and Indian love songs. That was a gay and happy time, though we all knew we were dancing on a volcano.

Ranjit and Nan were married on May 10, 1921, during all the turmoil of that revolutionary year. The date was picked by astrologers as being particularly auspicious, but the fact that it was the anniversary of the "mutiny" of 1857 and that Gandhiji and many other Congress leaders were coming threw the British in Allahabad into a panic. They suspected a deep dark Oriental plot and went around with pistols in their pockets. The old Red Fort was prepared as a refuge for them in the event of a rising.

Father did not allow all this to spoil Nan's wedding. He gave her a hundred and one saris—odd numbers are lucky, so you would never give an even hundred—and quantities of beautiful jewels. She and Ranjit were married around the sacred fire in the courtyard of our house in the old Vedic rite. It was the last great party at Anand Bhawan. (Nan and Ranjit went to live in Calcutta where he practiced law.)

It was at the annual Congress meeting in Calcutta in the autumn of 1920 that the Indian National Congress approved *Satyagraha* or non-violent non-co-operation as its official policy. It was, as the Duke of Wellington said of Waterloo, "a very near thing." Nearly all the great leaders, reacting from the emotion of Amritsar, were against endorsing the Movement. Only Father, who had so long championed the Moderate cause, wholeheartedly backed Gandhiji. There is no question that without his support the motion would have been lost. It was carried by only seven votes. A few people resigned from the Congress, among them M. A. Jinnah, the great Muslim leader.

Immediately on his return from Calcutta, Father resigned from the United Provinces Council and announced that he would not stand for election to the new reformed council. He also wound up his practice, for *Satyagraha* meant absolutely no co-operation with any British institution, and, as I have said, Gandhiji had refused him permission to appear in the courts, even though he could have contributed great sums of money to the cause.

Then Father began to put his house in order. This was necessary because, though Father had made a great deal of money, he had spent it as fast as he made it. He once remarked to a client, "No one can doubt my supreme contempt for money. . . ." It had been his peculiar pride never to save because he felt that this was a reflection on his ability to earn more. Now, as he relinquished all prospect of further earnings, he felt obliged to liquidate everything so that he would have the capital on which to live and support his family.

The horses and most of the dogs were sold; so were the beautiful china and glass and many other lovely things. Father sold most of Mother's jewels with her consent and Bhai sold Kamala's. Many of the servants were let go; the two kitchens became one, and the wine cellar in which Father had taken such pride was also sold. Later he even gave his house away. Our beloved Anand Bhawan was presented to the Congress though we continued to live in it until our new house was built.

Since nothing British must be used, Father put away all his fine English clothes—and so did we all. From that time forth, we all wore *khadi*, the coarse homespun cotton of India. Father's usual costume consisted of a *dhoti* wrapped around his waist, and the long shirt called a *kurta*, with a shawl for his shoulders on cool nights. These gleaming white garments did not detract from, but rather

48

enhanced his natural dignity. With his white hair and nobly formed features he looked like one's idea of a Roman senator.

One thing Father kept. I remember hearing him talking to Gandhiji, the ascetic abstainer whose ideal was an India free from "the curse of liquor and narcotic drugs." Father said, "I have done all these things for you, Bapu, but I am an old man and accustomed to certain ways. Whether you like it or not, I am going to have my two pegs [whisky-and-sodas] before dinner."

However, Father changed to eating mostly Indian food though he liked Western food better. Now instead of having Indian food only on Sunday we had it every day and Western food as a treat on Sunday.

Most of Father's British friends dropped away, either from embarrassment or out of objection to his stand for Indian Independence. Only Sir Grimwood Mears, Chief Justice of the High Court of Allahabad, still came in the late afternoons to share Father's "pegs" and talk of happier days.

There were no more grand European-style dinners, but the house was more crowded than ever with guests. Instead of English officials and maharajas, they were intellectuals and political leaders from all classes. They dressed in khadi and were as simple in their tastes as in their dress, though sparkling with ideas and the intensity of their idealism.

I did not enjoy the changes *Satyagraha* made in my life, though I accepted them with growing ardor. How well I remember my first sari made of khadi! It was a coarse, shapeless thing that felt like sackcloth. In addition, I had to give up the English school I loved so much and return to the dull round of being tutored at home. I had several tutors, one for mathematics, another for English, and so forth. Two hours a day were used learning how to spin; for part of Gandhiji's plan for making India self-sufficient was that we should make our cloth from our own cotton instead of sending it to the mills of England to be woven and resold to us. However impractical this return to cottage industry may have been, it had a strong emotional appeal for the Indian people; and the spinning wheel became a Gandhian symbol of freedom from British economic domination.

49

Another unpleasant, though necessary, change in our lives was that we no longer fled to the hills when the hot weather came down on Allahabad like a suffocating tent. To make life bearable we remained indoors during the noontime hours. All the windows were closed and thick curtains of woven khus grass were hung at the doorways. A gardener walked around constantly wetting them with a hose while another servant worked the punkah, a heavy cloth hung from the ceiling which he pulled back and forth drawing a gentle breeze through the curtains which cooled it by evaporation.

I had changed my eating habits at the time of my sister's wedding in an access of zeal, spurred on by Gandhiji's secretary, Mahadev Bhai Desai, who was horrified to see me downing quantities of meat (which I loved). His sorrowful exhortation on the evils of carnivorousness made me give it up right in the midst of nuptial festivities. Mother was delighted, of course. I remained a vegetarian for three years until I had Christmas dinner with some cousins of mine. I was tempted by a splendid roast, and fell, never to go vegetarian again except in prison when I often could not get meat.

My enthusiasm for *Satyagraha* was but a pale reflection of the tide of emotion that was sweeping India. My brother expressed it when he wrote: "Many of us who worked for the Congress program lived in a kind of intoxication during the year 1921. We were full of excitement and optimism and a buoyant enthusiasm. . . . Above all we had a sense of freedom and pride in that freedom . . . we said what we felt and shouted it from the housetops. What did we care for the consequences? Prison? We looked forward to it; that we would help our cause still further!"*

This tremendous surge of feeling that touched, not only the leaders, but the masses of India, giving them for the first time in half a thousand generations hope and courage and, above all, pride, panicked our alien rulers. They did not know how to combat it. They knew very well how to handle charging mobs with a volley of rifle fire and the chatter of machine guns; but what to do about millions of people who simply and peacefully did nothing at all?

The government's position was further complicated by the fact that the Prince of Wales was due to arrive in November on a "good will tour." The Congress Working Committee, of which my brother

* *Toward Freedom* (New York: John Day Co., 1941), p. 69.

and father were members, declared a *hartal* or strike against the Prince—no one was to go to see him or take part in any of the celebrations. In anguish, the new Viceroy, Lord Reading, cabled the Secretary of State for India that he would have to take action on a "drastic and more comprehensive scale." It was indeed comprehensive.

Mass arrests began in November. Gandhiji's followers welcomed them. In fact people who were *not* arrested would pile into the prison vans, which arrived at the jails with more prisoners than the jailers expected or could handle. The officials were at their wit's ends; what could you do with people like that?

In the midst of all the excitement, the British District Magistrate of Allahabad had the remarkable obtuseness to call on Father and say that the government proposed to use Anand Bhawan for the Prince's visit to Allahabad. Neither Father nor any of our leaders held any ill feeling for the Prince, but obviously this would not do. Father told the Englishman that he had no right to commandeer his house and that he could not have it. The Magistrate was furious and worried. Very courteously Father tried to set his mind at rest. "You need have no anxiety about the Prince's safety," he said. "Our movement is based on peaceful, non-violent means. I can promise you that His Royal Highness will not be harmed."

Incidentally, when the Prince finally came to Allahabad he drove through the empty streets of an apparently dead city. The boycott was more complete than in any other Indian city. Some students painted in big letters on the high wall of our compound NO WELCOME TO PRINCE! The British smeared paint over it before the Prince arrived, but the letters showed through the paint. Father was wild with rage at the students; he might join a *hartal* against the Prince but he was always correct. Such vulgarity infuriated him.

With all our friends going to jail, we knew it was only a matter of time before the police came for Father and Bhai. In the United Provinces the Congress Volunteers were declared to be an illegal organization. Though Father was a member of the Congress he did not then belong to the Volunteers. He immediately joined and his name was put at the head of the roll.

51

On December 6, 1921, police suddenly surrounded Anand Bhawan. A frightened servant told Father that a police officer desired to see him. When he was shown in, the officer saluted smartly and said, "*Adab araj* [I bow to you]." Father returned the salute and the greeting. The officer then presented a search warrant. Smiling, Father said, "Of course you may search this house, but it will take you six months to do it properly."

The man still hung about embarrassed and uneasy. Sensing his trouble Father helped him out. "Have you also a warrant for my arrest?" he asked.

"Yes, sir, I have," the poor chap answered, and produced the warrant.

"I'm ready for it," Father said. "Why did you not serve it all at once?"

By this time the compound was filling with our friends and supporters and the police were getting more and more nervous. Bhai hurried home from his office and was promptly arrested also. Mother and Kamala and I said good-by to Father and Bhai on the steps of Anand Bhawan and they got into an automobile the police had ordered up. Mother was superb. Perhaps she trembled a little but her eyes were dry and proud. Gentle Kamala was visibly fighting back her tears; I was in a raging fury. So they drove away to prison, the first of many times, and for that reason the most dramatic. Later we got quite used to these things.

Father's trial began the next day, December 7, inside the prison; and on that day also four-year-old Indu, as we called Indira, got her baptism of fire in the political wars. The proceedings were, in my brother's words, "farcical." The magistrate was K. N. Knox of the Indian Civil Service, who had been a friend of Bhai's in the local St. John Ambulance Brigade. The government advocate was Justice Banerjea, also an old friend of Father's. Both of them were as embarrassed as only a gentleman can be when forced to do something contrary to his code of friendship. Father, sitting there in his toga-like white garments, with his little granddaughter on his knee, was completely at ease. Indu sat very still with her enormous dark eyes fixed intently on the judge, taking in far more of the proceedings than we believed possible.

Farcical the trial may have been, but it was also dramatic and heart-stopping. Because *Satyagraha* forbade any recognition of or co-operation with the British courts, Father offered no defense. He simply stated his name and very courteously refused to answer any other questions. The charge was that he was a member of the Congress Volunteers. Since his name headed the list of Volunteers published in his own newspaper, *The Independent,* it hardly could be controverted, but just to make sure, the prosecution brought in an illiterate Hindu who was shown the official roll of Volunteers and asked to identify Father's signature written in Hindi. Holding the list upside down he identified the signature which he had never seen and probably could not read.

Very reluctantly and quite red in the face Mr. Knox then sentenced Father to six months in jail and a fine of 500 rupees on the charge of being a member of the Volunteers. Bhai was sentenced to the same penalty on the same day in a different court on the charge of having distributed handbills calling for a boycott against British merchants in Allahabad. They both refused to pay the fine.

They were sent to the district jail at Lucknow. This city was the headquarters of another old friend of Father's, the Lieutenant Governor of the United Provinces, Sir Harcourt Butler. About a year or two before, he had dined at Anand Bhawan. Father had said to him over the champagne, "I may land in your jail some day; will you give me champagne?"

"I certainly will," Sir Harcourt answered.

Though the Lieutenant Governor did not supply champagne he did help to make prison life more bearable for Father. Instead of being confined with criminal prisoners he was put in a small shed about twenty by sixteen feet with Bhai and two of his nephews, Shamlal and Mohanlal; and he was allowed to order meals from outside, have all the books he wanted and write letters. Bhai was utterly devoted in his care of Father, who never before had been without servants. Bhai was valet, cook and housemaid, energetically cleaning up the place every day. When Father fell ill, Bhai was his devoted nurse.

Nevertheless, it was a brave and terrible thing for my father, at his age and habit of life, to go to prison, when even an ardent young man like my brother could say: "No amount of previous mental preparation could prevent the tension and nervous excitement that filled us when first we entered the iron gates. . . . And the eyes turn back involuntarily to take a last good look outside at the greenery and wide spaces . . . at familiar faces that [we] may not see again for a long time. . . ."

Anand Bhawan was a house of sadness after our men left; it seemed as though the life had gone out of it. To add to our distress, because Father and Bhai had not paid their fines, the police came and took things of infinitely greater value to liquidate them. Though we were all boiling with rage we managed to keep our tempers, except Indu. While we stood by, grimly silent, Indu followed them around, her dark eyes snapping with fury. They picked up a fine carpet worth ten times both fines. Indu stamped her little foot and screamed, "You can't take that away. It's from our home and belongs to Mommy and Father." Then she flew at the police inspector. We had to drag her away. When he heard of it, Bhai was afraid she would hate the British forever.

That was a strange childhood Indu had. From the time she was three or four she heard nothing but talk of politics. Though she did not understand all that was said, her sensitivity made her intensely aware that something vitally important was happening. She became serious and intense. She used to sit very quietly listening to the discussions. How much she retained and how much she did not, I cannot say, but over the years, as she sat in a corner, intent on the talk, she must have absorbed some of the ideas—forming what you may call her philosophy. As some people have said, she has a political strain.

It showed itself even at four or five years old. Instead of playing childish games, she used to gather a group of servants together, or if they were too busy, she would line up her dolls and make political speeches to them, exhorting them to work for *Swaraj* and practice *Satyagraha.* She had the words and at least some understanding of their meaning. In one sense she was never a child.

I remember that one evening some years after this time, when she was eight or nine years old, I saw her standing on the railing of our house clutching a pillar with one hand, the other raised high.

She seemed to be muttering something, so I went up to her and asked, "What in the world are you trying to do?"

She looked at me solemnly with her round little face ringed by jet-black hair and her dark eyes burning, and said, "I'm practicing being Joan of Arc. I have just been reading about her, and some day I am going to lead my people to freedom just as Joan of Arc did."

6
father founds the
Swaraj party

Though almost all the Congress leaders and some 30,000 of the
rank and file were in jail, Gandhiji was still free. Because of his
worldwide reputation as a great spiritual leader the government
had not dared to touch him. A few days after Father and Bhai were
sent to prison Gandhiji invited Mother, Kamala and me, together
with some of our relatives, to come to his ashram on the Sabarmati
River at Ahmedabad and attend the Congress meetings. Kamala
brought Indira along. We traveled third class, I suppose as a gesture
of simplicity as we were not yet so poor. It was a trying but exalting
experience. Sitting on the hard wooden seats in the stifling railway
carriage for hours on end was agony for my delicate little mother
and for Kamala who had not been strong since Indira's birth. Their
fortitude amazed me, but it was all part of the tremendous morale
of the time. I had not realized how deep and strong were the faith
and love the Indian people had for Gandhiji. Because they knew we
were going to see him and that we were fighting at his side, they
took us also into their hearts. At every station crowds of people
pressed around our compartment filling it with flowers and food.

When we reached Sabarmati Ashram, Gandhiji welcomed us
warmly and asked gravely for news of Father and Bhai. Then someone showed us to our rooms. The ashram consisted of a number of
cottages close by the banks of the river. The central house was
occupied by Mr. and Mrs. Gandhi and some of his close associates;
several families lived in each of the other small cottages. We slept
in a sort of students' hostel. Mother had a room to herself; the rest
of us slept on the floor in one large room.

That was my first taste of the ascetic life of a follower of Gandhiji. At four o'clock on those cold December mornings we got up and attended Ghandiji's prayer meetings, held at dawn on the banks of the Sabarmati. Then we bathed ourselves and had breakfast. The food was completely tasteless; whatever we had was just boiled, without any of the condiments we were used to—not even salt. Then, except for Mother who had a young boy to help her, we did our washing in the ancient Indian way, pounding it on stones in cold water. It is no joke washing a sari of thick khadi, which in those early days was terribly coarse. Later we got much better at weaving it. (While he was in prison in 1922, Bhai sent home 10,576 yards of yarn, writing, "It took me a considerable time to spin it chiefly because I tried to spin fine yarn. Spinning coarse yarn does not interest me." Even in prison Bhai remained a perfectionist.)

Despite the hardships of the life, our stay with Gandhiji was a wonderfully uplifting experience. I, who had sneered at his prayer meetings three years before, would not have missed a single one of those beautiful moments in the dawn on the riverbank, nor a single meeting of the Congress, watching Gandhiji, the saintly figure of the prayer meetings, metamorphose into an astute politician without losing his integrity. It was the beginning of a new life for me.

That absolute Gandhian integrity almost caused a rupture between him and my father and brother a few weeks later. The Indians' high enthusiasms for the Movement, combined with British repression, began to cause a few incidents which could not be described as non-violent. Then, in the remote village of Chauri Chaura in the United Province, the peasants attacked a police station and burned it. In the riot twenty people were killed including four policemen who were burned in the flaming building.

Gandhiji was deeply shocked. He decided that his people were not yet sufficiently disciplined for non-violent non-co-operation and again stopped *Satyagraha,* except for the boycott on British goods. He decided to concentrate on the "constructive" program, the spinning wheel, communal unity and the abolition of Untouchability.

When Father and Bhai heard of this in their prison, they were exasperated and filled with gloom. To stop civil disobedience just as the tide was surging high was, they realized, to doom the Movement, for the present at least. Bhai pointed out that if every such break in discipline would result in calling off *Satyagraha* it could never achieve anything. Human nature could never be so perfect as to avoid all violence in a clash of people against a government, and he also pointed out that even if discipline were perfected, a cynical enemy could always hire people to start a riot, and then blame it on Gandhiji's followers. Later, in the 1930's, Gandhiji recognized this point as being well-taken and announced that the Movement would not again be stopped because of minor rioting.

From prison Bhai wrote the Mahatma what the latter described as "a freezing letter," and received a sorrowful reply detailing all Gandhiji's reasons for his action. And it may well be that he was right and Bhai wrong; for Gandhiji had an uncanny sensitivity for the feelings of the Indian masses. He instinctively knew just what they thought and how they would act in given circumstances, and he foresaw that in their present emotional condition Chauri Chaura was not an isolated incident but the precursor of bloody revolution which would have betrayed everything that Gandhiji believed in.

This was not the only difference of opinion between my brother and Mahatma Gandhi. Bhai, committed to the Socialist school of thought, considered Gandhiji's Rousseau-like idea of returning India to a primitive cottage-industry economy as pure fantasy. He went along with it because he recognized its value as a symbol and inspiration for the Indian people, but he firmly believed that the cure for India's economic ills was more, not less, industrialization. He knew that no large country could exist in the modern world without employing all the machinery of modern life.

In addition, Bhai had a personal fondness for modern inventions. He wrote, "I have always liked big machines and fast travel." And he delighted in modern gadgets. In 1948, when he was Prime Minister of India, someone gave him his first electric razor. He was so fascinated by it that at a dinner party in his house on York Road he sent for the razor and demonstrated it to his guests by shaving himself at the table.

Another thing that troubled Bhai was Gandhiji's deeply religious emphasis, though in the exalted mood of 1921 he was almost caught up in it. He wrote: "I came nearer to a religious frame of mind in 1921 than at any other time since my early boyhood. Even so I did not come very near."

What bothered my brother, beyond the nagging thought that religion had been used so often to exploit the masses, was that it tended to divide people. Not Gandhiji's religion, which was an idealistic blend of the truths of all religions, a true spirituality; but the fact that others in his camp used religious phrases to strengthen dogmatic ends. He wrote, "I used to be troubled sometimes at the growth of this religious element in our politics, both on the Hindu and Moslem side. I did not like it all. Much that the Moulvis and Maulanas and Swamis and the like said in their public addresses seemed to me most unfortunate. . . . The religious twist that was given to everything prevented all clear thinking. Even some of Gandhiji's phrases sometimes jarred upon me. . . ."*

In short, Bhai recognized that in India religion was not a unifying but a divisive influence. He feared it as such, and he was right; for it brought about the fatal division of India and Pakistan. At the same time he realized that: "[Gandhiji] was a great and unique man, and a glorious leader, and, having put our faith in him, we gave him an almost blank check, for the time being at least."

Soon after Gandhiji stopped *Satyagraha,* Bhai was released from prison, on March 3, 1922. The British had discovered that there was no law on the books against distributing pamphlets calling for a *hartal.* Of course, Bhai immediately started working for the Movement again. As he had been doing ever since 1920, he went out among the villagers, talking to them about the Movement and learning about their needs. Despite her slight fever, Kamala often insisted on going with him. She never took her temperature and indeed she could not take proper care of herself when she was traveling around by train and car. She was very shy at first with the crowds of people but later she started making speeches and going to the villages on her own when Bhai was in prison. She carried on and let nothing upset her.

Bhai was always tremendously moved and encouraged by his reception in those small, impoverished places, where the peasants, scratching the arid soil with wooden plows, had only the ambition

* *Toward Freedom* (New York: John Day Co., 1941), p. 77.

to raise enough food to keep themselves and their families alive. When Bhai talked to them he made them want something more, made them think of freedom from foreign rule and domestic serfdom. As they responded to his words with new hope and courage, he gained self-assurance in the knowledge that he could sway the masses with his oratory. Though he said himself that he never could feel one with the crowd, but was always aware of another self looking over his shoulder, he did feel a sort of communion with them, the power of his words going forth and reflected back in their emotion, forging the bond which is the basis of power in a democratic society.

Bhai was also the very active in promoting the boycott on foreign cloth. Most of the cloth merchants of Allahabad had formed an association pledged not to deal in foreign cloth, but several of them broke the agreement and my brother organized picketing of their shops.

On May 11, Bhai went to see Father in the jail at Lucknow. As he was leaving he was arrested, taken back to Allahabad and tried for "criminal intimidation and extortion" in connection with the picketing. Refusing to plead either guilty or not guilty he was convicted and sentenced to eighteen months' rigorous imprisonment. He had been out of jail only a little over two months.

Even before that, the Viceroy and Mr. Montagu, pressed by inflamed British opinion and the conservative press, had finally decided that Gandhiji, too, must be dealt with. On March 10, 1922, he was arrested and sentenced to six years' imprisonment on the charge of "sedition." With the great leader muzzled and Bhai also in prison, the National Movement lost impetus. Meanwhile Father came home to us in June, having served his full term. Bhai was again released ahead of time, in January 1923.

Father was starting a new political venture. The Government of India Act of 1920 embodying the Montagu-Chelmsford reforms had provided for some measure of responsibility in the reformed provincial councils and the newly enlarged Indian Legislative Assembly. Father, still hopeful of accomplishing something within the legal framework, felt that since *Satyagraha* had been called off, Indian leaders should run for election to the councils and the Assembly if only for the purpose of obstructing the proceedings and "carrying the good fight into the enemy's camp." He and C. R. Das formed the Swaraj party for this purpose.

Superficially, Father and Mr. Das seemed an odd couple; for Das was extremely impulsive and emotional while Father was level-headed and restrained, and, in his public appearances, always calm. They did have many heated arguments, for Das was moved by emotion, while Father refused to be drawn into what he called "rabid sentimentalism." But the arguments always ended amicably.

The first meeting of the Swaraj party was held at Anand Bhawan. Its formation caused a violent split in the Congress between those who favored changing their policy to permit entering the councils, who were known as "Pro-Changers," and those who opposed this, called "No-Changers." My brother did not take sides, but acted as a mediator to keep the split from becoming permanent. Partly as a result of his efforts, at the Congress meeting in Delhi in September 1923 a compromise was worked out permitting members of the Congress party to stand for election if they could do so in good conscience.

Father and Mr. Das published the Manifesto of the Swaraj party on October 13, 1923, and began to electioneer. In spite of the very short time before the November elections, the Swaraj party did amazingly well. In the provincial councils, they won an absolute majority in the Central Provinces; and Das put together a coalition in Bengal that obliged Governor General Lord Lytton to invite him to form a ministry to run that part of the provincial government which the Government of India Act so permitted.

However, the important thing was the Indian Legislative Assembly. This was not a real parliament or responsible government, since its acts could be nullified by a stroke of the Viceroy's pen, but it maintained the forms of a parliament and was both a sounding board and a national arena where different parties could test their strength. Some members were appointed by the government but most of them were elected. A certain number of seats were reserved for communal (religious) minorities—both Bhai and Father objected to this as fostering divisiveness; the remainder were open. At the polls the Swaraj party elected over forty members. By forming a coalition with M. A. Jinnah, the Muslim leader, and Madan Mohan Malaviya, leader of the Moderates, Father secured a majority in the Assembly, and was elected leader of this coalition. They consistently defeated the Government party, which was made up of the appointed delegates and those Indians willing to go along with the British. Naturally, this did not force the government to resign as it would do in a real parliament, but it made things very difficult for them.

For six years Father was thus the leader of His Majesty's Loyal (more or less) Opposition. In that time he not only won the admiration of his own countrymen but the respect of the British as well. Sir George Rainy, a member of the Viceroy's Council, wrote of his "exquisite fitness of attire which symbolized the clean fighter and the great gentleman, and that impressive face, deeply lined and careworn, on which character and intellect were so deeply imprinted. . . . The quickness of his intellect, his skill in debate, his adroitness as a tactician and his strength of purpose rendered him a formidable adversary. . . ."

Father sometimes took me to Delhi with him when he attended meetings of the Assembly. I was now sixteen and acted as his hostess at the dinner parties he gave for his associates in his rented house there. I also enjoyed attending meetings of the Assembly, and I can testify, though perhaps less impartially than Sir George, to the great impression he made when he rose to speak, dressed in his immaculate white khadi with his Gandhi cap worn at a jaunty angle. Friends and opponents alike listened intently to his quiet, logical speeches.

Meanwhile Bhai was in and out of trouble again. In September 1923, immediately after the Delhi Congress, he went to the princely state of Nabha, purely as a tourist. He was arrested and charged with all sorts of desperate deeds, and spent two weeks in jail before he was released, oddly enough, by the intercession of the Viceroy, Lord Reading, who did not want any inflammatory incidents to upset the comparative calm that was settling over India. If the government jails were unpleasant, those of the princely states were indescribable. In his noisome cell in Nabha, Bhai caught typhoid fever, which nearly killed him and laid him low for many months.

Gandhiji, who was in Yeravda prison, had an attack of appendicitis and an emergency operation. As a result, his sentence was commuted by the Viceroy and he was released on February 5, 1924, probably less from humanitarian reasons than because Lord Reading did not want a martyred messiah on his hands. No sooner had Gandhiji recovered his freedom than he spoke strongly against the Swaraj party, whose members, he felt, had defected from the pure principle of non-co-operation. This brought him into an unhappy conflict with my father.

Gandhiji was at Juhu on the Arabian Sea near Bombay. In April, Father rented a tiny cottage near the beach and we went there with Bhai and Kamala. It was a wonderful change from Allahabad, and it was delightful to watch Bhai playing in the sea like a dolphin and running up and down the beach while his body got lean and hard and his gaiety bubbled over.

However, the main purpose of the trip, which was to convince Gandhiji that the Swaraj party was on the right course, failed completely. After nearly two months of long private talks with Bhai acting as moderator and C. R. Das coming down to help, Father and Gandhiji were as far apart as ever. Father, rightly I think, felt that his presence in the Assembly was of great value to the ultimate success of the movement for Indian self-government. Gandhiji maintained that since the British ruled by violence, to have any connection with a government institution such as the Assembly was to be part of "an evil thing" which would contaminate its members and corrupt the principle of non-violence.

In spite of this sharp disagreement on basic principles they remained devoted friends and, although Gandhiji had the power to sway the Congress against the Swarajists, he did not bring about a direct confrontation but permitted Father and his associates to dominate the Congress.

That was the year that a Muslim leader, the famous Maulana Muhammed Ali, was president of the Congress and Bhai was its general secretary. In December, Gandhiji himself became president of the Congress, which Bhai said was "in the nature of an anticlimax, for he had long been the permanent super-president." Gandhiji insisted that Bhai again become General Secretary.

When the British authorities accused the Swaraj party in Bengal of acts of anarchy, raided their offices and arrested Subhas Bose, Gandhiji generously rushed to their rescue. It was then that the breech was completely healed. The Mahatma reached a compromise agreement with Father and C. R. Das, according to which non-co-operation was suspended, except for the boycott on foreign cloth. Thus the Swaraj party became an instrument of the Congress.

The following June, when we had managed a little vacation at Simla in the hills of the Punjab, a telegram came telling us that C. R. Das had died suddenly. Father was completely stricken. He sat unmoving with his head bowed in grief for a long time. Thereafter for as long as it existed Father alone led the Swaraj party.

During all this period Bhai was working for the Congress party with no salary. Even though he and Kamala were living at Anand Bhawan and had few expenses, he was very unhappy at being dependent on Father for money. He had long discussions on the subject with Gandhiji, who advised him that if he felt that way he should take time off from public service and get a job. Father would not hear of it. He pointed out the immense importance to the country of the work Bhai was doing, and that he and Kamala spent so little on themselves—they wore simple clothes, and Bhai always traveled third class on his constant political trips—that their support was no burden on him at all.

Father still had considerable means though he had refused to take any new cases. I remember one client who came with a *lakh* of rupees in cash hoping that the sight of the money would tempt him. Father looked at it frostily and said to me, "Well, Beti, do you think I should take it?"

I hesitated only long enough to sense his feelings, with which my own were in full accord; then I said, "No, Father, I don't think you should."

He gave my hand a quick squeeze and said to the client, "I'm sorry, but I cannot take your case. You see even my daughter knows it would be wrong."

However, now that non-co-operation had been canceled, there was no reason why Father should not practice and he began to take a few cases. But in spite of this easing of his finances, in his argument with his son Father ran into Bhai's stubborn pride, and the discussion continued until it was settled by an unhappy event.

7

in the western world

A son had been born to Kamala and Bhai in September 1924; but instead of joy there was great sorrow, for he only lived about a week. In addition Kamala was very ill, and her trouble was diagnosed as tuberculosis. In those days that was close to being a death sentence. After over a year, in which she slowly got worse instead of better, the doctors declared that her only chance was to go to Switzerland where the air was pure and sunny, and where the leading experts on her disease might be able to help her. Father and Bhai were willing to do anything to save her and so it was decided. Bhai and Kamala and Indira, who was now nine years old, sailed for Europe in March 1926, on the same ship with my sister Nan and her husband, Ranjit Pandit, who were going on a long-planned holiday.

Father badly needed rest and change and he planned to sail in June to join Bhai and Kamala, taking me with him. I was tremendously excited. But in May the blow fell. The great Lakhna inheritance case—Father's first big one, begun in 1894—came up for final adjudication. It was one thing to refuse new clients, but loyalty and gratitude combined to make Father feel he must finish what he had begun thirty-two years ago. He canceled his passage. I was plunged into despair.

However, my father was a very extraordinary person, for an Indian father, or any other for that matter. He said I could go to Europe alone, because I could be of great help to Bhai with Kamala and Indira.

The night before I was to leave was long and trying. First my mother took me to her room. Sitting there amid her divans and delicately carved furniture, the very essence of old India, she begged me not to go. Every tradition and instinct of her orthodox Hindu soul opposed the idea of a girl of nineteen going off alone and unchaperoned to lands which she undoubtedly considered Godless and probably barbaric. To tempt me she said that if I would remain only a week more in India she would arrange for me to become engaged to one of the young men whom she had in mind for me. She ticked them all off on her fingers. All of them I had known, some since childhood. I told her that I did not want to marry any of them and that I was determined to go, although in my heart I was a little frightened at the prospect. She pleaded with me for two hours using every weapon of religion, respect and love. But despite my quavers, I held firm.

As I came out of her room my father's valet was waiting to intercept me with the message that Father wanted to see me. I thought, Not again!—I can't go through any more! But I had to go.

I fairly stalked into his room and before he could say a word I burst into a tirade. "Look, Father," I said, "if you're going to give me another lecture I'd rather not go at all. Mother has been talking for two hours, begging me not to go or at least to get engaged before I do. I'm sick and tired of listening to all this. So whether you like it or not, I do not wish to have another lecture thrust on me, and I will not go abroad if I have to listen to one."

Father looked at me over his glasses with that charming quizzical smile of his, and he said, "Why do you jump to conclusions?"

"I'm so fed up," I answered.

He said, "Now, darling, sit down and don't interrupt."

So I sat on the edge of the straightest Victorian chair I could find with my back stiff with resentment and all he said to me was, "I only want you to bear one thing in mind. You have the gambling spirit. You are going to be alone on a ship that takes seventeen days to reach Italy. Do not play cards aboard ship, because I am not going to pay your debts.

"And secondly," he said, "I want you to remember your duty to us, and I want you to be, as you always have been, frank and

66

straightforward with me. Promise me that you won't do anything about which you cannot write me."

I promised him, not knowing what I was in for, because there were often times when I was away that I wanted to do things, to go out alone with young men, to gamble—he was right about me there—and to do other things he would not approve of. But I always remembered Father sitting there so generous and so liberal, making it possible for me to go, and throughout my two years abroad I don't think I ever broke my promise to him.

Bhai met me at Naples and took me to some of the Italian cities I had read about: Rome, Florence, Milan and other smaller places on the way to Geneva. With my background of Western education they were both familiar and strange, like meeting a long-standing friend of one's family with whose picture one is familiar. I was enchanted and thrilled, the more so since, with his knowledge and, above all, his enthusiasm, Bhai was the perfect guide. We really became friends on that trip, for he was no longer my awesome big brother busy with great affairs, with time only to pat me kindly on the head. He was an ideal companion, sharing his thoughts with me and delighting in my pleasure at the beauty of those ancient sunlit buildings of Italy. I had never been so happy.

Finally we reached Geneva. I loved Switzerland with its cool, invigorating air and snow-topped mountains, though I did not love it quite so much as Kashmir. Fine as they are, the Alps are only a reminder of the Himalayas; they never equal their overpowering, dramatic impact.

Bhai's little flat delighted me because I had never before lived in anything so small. Kamala was taking treatments in Geneva and lived at home. Bhai told me that she had not improved as much as he had hoped, and I must take care of her and the flat, and cook for them. That meant starting from scratch, for I had never cooked before except to dabble in doing some of our exotic Indian dishes. I managed somehow. Luckily I had studied French, but how little practical use my irregular verbs were I only learned when I went to market with our maid Marguerite. It sounded like an entirely different language from that spoken by my British teachers in Allahabad.

Indira was with us, too, until the time came for her to go to the good boarding school at Bex in which her father had entered her. There she learned to speak the excellent French she has kept ever since. Her education was, to say the least, sporadic, because of all the places her father and mother lived. Naturally, she did not have an English governess as we did, but she picked up English because all of us at Anand Bhawan spoke it at least as much as Hindustani—even after Father joined the Movement. And she always had a good mind and that intense, unchildlike concentration that enabled her to master any subject and make the best of what each school had to offer.

As soon as I had settled in, Bhai gave me a French dictionary, a map of Geneva and some tram and bus tickets, and told me to get out on my own. I was rather nervous, but I soon became very independent, and proud of it.

I studied French with a delightful Swiss girl and then Bhai arranged for me to go to the International Summer School. That was a great experience, for I met people from all over the world. Many of the leading statesmen of Europe, who came to meetings at the League of Nations, lectured there. One day Albert Einstein drifted into a lecture room so quietly that at first no one knew he was there. But that unforgettable face and lion's mane of graying hair could not long go unnoticed, and when he was discovered there was an uproar in which the poor lecturer was quite forgotten.

A little later Einstein came to my brother's flat. I was too overpowered by his towering intellect to do more than mumble, "How do you do?" but Bhai engaged him in a rapid and interesting conversation. When the great physicist shyly smiled at some quip of Bhai's I began to feel completely at ease, though I never got the courage to talk to him.

Bhai also took me with him to call on Romain Rolland in his villa at Villeneuve not far from Geneva. They had a great deal in common, for the great French author had written a biography of Mahatma Gandhi, though he had not yet met him. Once again I played the quiet mouse—not my accustomed role.

Bhai never could be still a moment. He was forever rushing off to meetings in different European capitals, and he told me that if I learned typing and could act as his secretary he would take me with him. So I learned to type and after that I often went along.

It was interesting to see Bhai growing in ease and authority as his knowledge of the world and, particularly, its economic problems expanded under the influence of the liberal leaders from many nations whom he met. Ever since his return from England, in 1912, he had lived within the closed circle of Indian affairs, concentrating on the ultimate goal of our independence, thinking of little else. Though it was caused by the unhappy circumstance of dear Kamala's illness, it is not too much to say that his long stay in Europe was an essential element in his education for the great role he was to play.

Naturally Bhai was a magnet for all the Indian exiles in Europe. To me they were legendary figures whom I regarded with a certain awe. But my brother only pitied them because they had been left so far behind by onrushing events that they seemed to him figures of futility, like half-forgotten ghosts that only materialize when someone happens to remember them.

As autumn came on, it was evident that Kamala's health was not improving. On the doctor's recommendation Bhai decided to take her to a sanitarium at Montana-Vermala high in the Alps near Bex, where Indu was in school. It was a small town, hardly more than a village, and when the deep snows came we seemed cut off from the world. The strangest thing to me was the silence at night, a stillness so dense that it was like a curtain of white velvet—it is always noisy in India.

Bhai and I went in for skating and skiing. He has written about how clumsy he felt flopping all over the slopes before he learned the art of it, but that was just my perfectionist brother. Because of his natural timing and the superb control of his body his Yoga exercises had given him, he learned very quickly. Soon he was skimming over the snow, a slim, graceful figure, glorying in his swift passage. I did rather well also, which was another bond between us. The next summer we went mountaineering and climbed halfway up Mont Blanc.

However, nothing but prison bars could keep Bhai in one place for long. With Kamala well cared for, we had more freedom of movement. In December he went to Berlin, at that time in its postwar decadence of hopeless poverty and the extravagant night life of the black-market profiteers. The city was also heaving with an underground swell of discontent and was a meeting place for the exiled revolutionaries of the world. Naturally Bhai sought them out. From them he heard about the meeting of the Congress of Oppressed Nationalities to be held in Brussels in February 1927. He immediately wrote home suggesting that the Indian National Congress should take an official part in it. The Congress agreed and, just as he hoped, appointed him its official representative. He took me with him to Brussels.

That was a dramatic and fascinating experience. Many of the delegates were men whose names I had heard and whose deeds I had read of in the literature of the worldwide struggle against imperialism. There were Africans, Arabs and Singhalese, liberal leaders from the East Indies and a large delegation, headed by Madame Sun Yat-sen, from the Kuomintang. (The Kuomintang, at that time, was sweeping all before it in China and had not yet split into the opposing factions headed by Chiang Kai-shek and Mao Tse-tung.) Of course, the radical parties of most European nations were represented, as well as British and American liberals. And, I regret to say, so were the imperialists, who slipped their spies in, in the guise of delegates. In his autobiography, my brother mentions one member of the French Secret Service who admitted attending the meeting in blackface. Bhai himself was an object of acute suspicion to the imperialists. The British Secret Service, which my brother said was "the best in the world," was following him around Europe.

Naturally I was thrilled to meet and listen to the men who were carrying on the same fight as we were in all parts of the world. And I was very proud of Bhai who made two of the best speeches before the Congress. When the League Against Imperialism was formed at the Brussels meeting, Bhai was made a member of its working committee. This experience brought his sympathies even more strongly on the side of the Communist-oriented Third International, as opposed to the Second International, which was going along with outmoded Fabian socialism. He favored the Third International even though, as he says, "The Communists often irritated me by their dictatorial ways, their aggressive and rather vulgar methods and their habit of denouncing everybody who did not agree with them."

I made other trips with my brother: to Paris—I loved that gay and beautiful city at first sight—and to London, whose famous streets and buildings I knew from books, and adored, and whose theater I thoroughly enjoyed. But the British people left me cold.

It was in London that we first met Krishna Menon, who was to become my brother's close friend and advisor, some say his evil genius. Menon, who had been studying law, was running an organization called the India League, which was composed of friends of India. He had a few Indians and many English men and women working under him and with him. While we were fighting for our independence, they tried to keep the British public informed of our version of what was happening by issuing pamphlets and brochures, and sometimes making speeches. Throughout the years, Krishna Menon was head of this organization, giving it completely selfless service.

We met him in the tiny office of the League, a terribly gaunt young man with black hair, dark burning eyes and a great eagle's beak of a nose—a very intense person. But, contrary to general opinion, he had a keen though wicked sense of humor. Part of his fascination for my brother was that they could laugh together.

At the time we met him, he was very poor and lived miserably, but I believe he found virtue in so doing. Many years later I came to London when Krishna Menon was High Commissioner to Great Britain of independent India. He had bought a beautiful white mansion at 9 Kensington Palace Gardens (known as "millionaires' row") with green lawns, tall trees, and flower gardens, as an embassy residence worthy of a great nation, but he did not move in. He still lived in a little room which was also his office in India House. There was a single bed in it, an armchair and a desk.

Menon had all sorts of idiosyncrasies which increased with age. He would eat virtually nothing, but drank countless cups of tea. When he would come to stay in the Prime Minister's House in New Delhi, when I was acting as my brother's hostess, he wanted tea and more tea, and grilled tomatoes on toast—I got very bored watching him eat grilled tomatoes.

He also retained a puritanical prudery. When I was staying with him in India House when he was High Commissioner, his secretary rang me up and said, "The H.C. wants to know if you would like to go to the theater with him."

"What is the H.C.?" I asked.

"The High Commissioner, of course."

"Yes, I would," I answered.

"What would you like to see?"

I had been going to the theater with friends and the only play left that I wanted to see was *A Streetcar Named Desire* starring Vivien Leigh. The secretary gasped, "Oh, not that!"

"Why not?"

"The H.C. can't go to a play like that," she said.

"Well then, he can just get me tickets and he needn't come," I said, "or he doesn't even have to give me tickets, I'll go."

She said she would check and Krishna Menon came on the phone. "I hear you want to see a scandalous play," he said.

"I don't know whether it's scandalous or not until I see it."

He then said he'd see about it.

The next day the secretary said the H.C. would take me himself, but he made sure to ask quite a party, including a rising star of the Labour party, Patrick Gordon Walker, whom I knew well.

When we had seen the play even Krishna Menon said, "I don't see what all the fuss in the newspapers was about."

My brother was a little like Menon in his attitude about spending money on himself. Traveling with him was exciting but not very comfortable. Though Father was willing to make him a generous allowance, he felt a moral obligation to live as simply as possible. We always used public transportation or walked—what miles I walked through half the art galleries of Europe and then long city blocks home! Sometimes when I was ready to drop, I would say, "Oh, Bhai, can't we take a taxi?" And he would answer, "Of course, Beti, but if we do we can't afford to go to the theater tonight."

So we walked.

In the summer of 1927, Kamala was much better, and Father came to Europe at last. Retired or not, a revolutionary though he might be, he was the same *grand seigneur* in his manner of traveling. Suddenly we were going first class, with chauffeured limousines to meet us, and staying at the *grande luxe* hotels. I remember going into one in England where the old porter said to me, "Did I hear the name Nehru, Miss?"

72

"Yes," I said.

"A long time ago a gentleman named Nehru stayed with us," he said. "He had a lovely wife and a young son who was going to Harrow."

Rather touched, I said, "This is the same gentleman and the slightly bald younger man with him is the little boy who went to Harrow."

I must admit I reveled in luxury after my brother's Spartan regime. All of us, including Kamala, went to Paris and on to Berlin. There Father and Bhai received an invitation from the Soviet government to attend the celebrations in Moscow in honor of the tenth anniversary of the Russian Revolution. Father did not want to "waste time" in going, but Bhai was very keen to see the face of the new world that he considered the hope of mankind. Both Kamala and I wanted to go, too.

The long train trip over the endless plains of Poland and Russia was uncomfortable and exhausting. When we reached Moscow, we were put in an enormous suite in the Grand Hotel which was far from luxurious. All the plush and gold furniture of czarist days had been hidden under coarse slipcovers because the Communists scorned bourgeois trappings. It was bitterly cold, and I could not even get a hot bath, though Father succeeded by making a tremendous fuss.

To Father, Bhai's brave new world looked grim and drab. He saw the seedily dressed people in the streets, the poorly stocked shops, and the dilapidated streetcars and sparse motor traffic. The whole Communist theory was contrary to his way of thought and everything his eyes beheld confirmed his opinion. Even the habits of Russian officialdom under Stalin were repugnant to him. When he was given an appointment to meet Foreign Minister Chicherin at four o'clock in the morning he exploded. So furious was he that finally, as a great concession, the hour of the meeting was advanced to I A.M.

On the other hand, Bhai, looking backward into the tortured Cossack-and-knout history of the Russian masses and forward toward the goal of a just and plentiful social order, saw things differently. To him it was heartening that in so short a time the Russians had come so far. He looked into the faces of the poorly dressed people in the streets and saw the inner glow of a quiet determination to bear all suffering and sacrifice for the sake of an ideal.

One thing impressed us all, and that was the Russian prisons. We had some experience in that line, though for myself so far only as a visitor to my father and brother. The prison we inspected was probably a showplace; nevertheless it was a good one. Only the sentry outside had a gun; inside the guards were not armed at all. The cell doors were left open and the prisoners circulated freely. Some of them were listening to radios they had made themselves, others were musicians practicing on their instruments for the prison orchestra, while some worked in the carpenter shop. It was surprisingly clean.

When we left Russia after only four days even Father was glad he had been there, though he still opposed the whole system. Bhai was more firmly convinced than ever that communism was the hope of the world, though not necessarily the Russian kind. He believed that each nation must develop its own variety of communism according to its character and economy. He hated the violence and tyranny of the Bolsheviks, as he still called them, but he approved their goals. He believed that communism in India should use other means, though always within the Marxian framework.

He wrote: "Russia apart, the theory and philosophy of Marxism lightened up many a dark corner of my mind. History came to have a new meaning for me. The Marxist interpretation [made it] an unfolding drama with some order and purpose . . . behind it. In spite of the appalling waste and misery of the past and present, the future was bright with hope. . . . I was filled with a new excitement. . . ."

And still my brother was not inclined toward, never really believed in, Gandhian non-violence, for he wrote: "Reformism is an impossible solution of any vital problem. . . . In India only a revolutionary plan could solve the two related questions of land and industry as well as almost every other major problem before the country."*

For all of these long thoughts my brother was never a member of any Communist party. He would have been a terribly bad Communist; for he could never have accepted a party discipline that made him act or speak contrary to his conscience, or even keep his mouth shut if he felt truth needed saying.

* *Toward Freedom* (New York: John Day Co., 1941), p. 230.

8
salt from the sea

Bhai thought he had been away from India far too long. Soon after our trip to Moscow he, Kamala, Indira and I sailed for home leaving Father to wander around Europe for several more months. It was good to be home, good to hear the great discordant symphony of Indian noises: the many bells—from the tinkling sound of the hawker with his barrow of wares to the boom of the big temple gongs; the constant chatter of people talking, as they seem to do all night in India; and, best of all, the grand chorus of our birds which awakened us as they greeted the dawn.

Father came home in midwinter and immediately resumed work on the new house which was to replace Anand Bhawan. It was only a hundred yards from our old home, in the same big compound. When he gave his old house to the Congress, Father changed its name to Swaraj Bhawan (Freedom House). Because he could not imagine living in a house by any other name, he called the new one Anand Bhawan, and so I shall henceforth call it.

It started off to be a relatively small house that could be run economically, but Father was constitutionally unable to do things in a small way. He was in effect his own architect, for though he engaged one, the poor man had very little to do except to try to reduce Father's flamboyant ideas to the practical possibilities.

The house grew and grew, on paper at first, and then in bricks and mortar and marble. And it caused another argument between Father and Bhai.

"Why do you have to build another mansion?" my brother asked logically. "You have just given away one big house and the idea was to live in a hut or something."

"You can go and live in a hut right across the road there if you like," said Father. "But I'm not going to live in one!"

So our new house rose in considerable splendor. It was two stories

75

high, built of light-gray painted brick, with deep, shady verandahs circling both floors. Graceful stone columns supported the roofs of the verandahs which were guarded by lacy white balustrades. Their floors were pink terrazzo reflecting a rosy glow on the gray walls. The flat roof was also balustraded and from it rose a pagoda-like summerhouse with a white dome. There was also a raised second deck like a lookout or captain's bridge, with a flagpole from which flew our national flag.

Inside, the house was cool and spacious. In addition to Father's office, the drawing room and dining room, Father and Mother had rooms on the first floor. My room was on the second floor where there was a suite for Bhai and Kamala. Indira also had a room and bath, and there was a guest room. We moved in in 1929.

Although, like the first Anand Bhawan, this one was built on holy ground, the seers warned Father that it was an unlucky place for a house and the owner would not live long. Naturally he paid no attention, but unhappily they were right.

As soon as he came home, Father gave me my first car—a Citroën. Of course I enjoyed it, but after about a year I talked a young man I knew into buying it for nearly twice what Father had paid for it—I never could resist driving a good bargain. Then I said to Father, "I have no car and I need one to get around."

Generous beyond anyone I have ever known, he gave me a beautiful Armstrong-Siddeley, painted bright red. I loved it madly and bought myself a bright red sari of very fine khadi to match it. I felt very dashing.

But Father could still be stern. A certain young man was seeing a great deal of me. After a while Father noticed his continual presence and asked me who he was. "He's a prince of someplace," I answered airily. "He comes to play tennis, and he writes me three or four letters a day. In fact, he's in love with me."

"Well," Father said, "he's not coming from tomorrow on."

"Why not?"

"No daughter of mine is going to marry a prince," he said. "It's all right for me to handle their cases, but I know what they're like, and I'm not going to allow you to marry one."

"You can't, you can't stop me," I said. "I am grown-up now and you can't tell me what I can do and what I can't."

76

The danger-light came on in Father's eyes and he said, "You'll never be grown-up enough, mind you, for me not to be able to thrash you if I feel like it."

I stopped seeing the prince.

However, in another test of wills with Father, I won. A new Montessori children's school was starting up in Allahabad. I had studied the Montessori method in Rome and Florence, so when I applied for the job of teaching, I got it. Father was horrified by the thought of my working for pay. "I won't have it," he said. "It's all right for you to teach the children if you want to, but not for money. I am perfectly capable of supporting you. I give you everything you want, and if you take money from these people it will reflect on me."

There again was the same argument he had had with my brother: that peculiar pride of his in being the *pater familias* on whom we all depended, stood in the way of my having even that much independence. This time Bhai came to my rescue and talked Father into letting me take the job. I kept it until our cold war with the British heated up again.

The moment he got home, Bhai plunged back into politics. He again became the secretary of the Congress, mainly, he said, to keep the Moderates from getting control. The Swaraj party had split while we were in Europe, but Father was still a member of the Assembly and a powerful figure in the Congress. He wanted to work for dominion status.

But a new *élan* had risen in India while we were away. The long period of stagnation following the outbursts of 1919–21 had ended, and the spirit of revolt was seething beneath the surface. Bhai was the yeast that made it rise. In a hundred fiery speeches all over India he preached the doctrine of complete independence. So radical was he that even Gandhiji protested that he was moving too fast, and Father was terribly worried. My father was trying to keep a united front among all parties, and he feared that if my brother had his way there would be a drastic split between the more conservative elements and the radicals led by Bhai and Subhas Chandra Bose. Again our house was divided and tension built between father and son. When Father's rival for the leadership of the remnant of the Swaraj party, Srinivas Iyengar, formed a radical new party called the Independence for India League, Bhai and Bose became its secretaries.

One thing on which my father, brother and Gandhiji were all in agreement was anxiety over the rise of communal, or religious, bitterness in India. In the days of Mogul Emperors, and even under British rule during the nineteenth century, there had been virtually no ill will between Muslims and Hindus. They had worshiped separately; but they had lived together, worked together, and, in the Indian Army, fought together as one people. In modern times the peak of Hindu-Muslim co-operation had been the agreement between the leaders of the Congress and the Muslim League to work together for Home Rule at Lucknow in 1916.

From that time forward, relations between them had steadily deteriorated—to the advantage of Great Britain, and the misfortune of India. We believed that the British fanned the flames of mistrust and enmity as part of their divide-and-rule policy; even though Lord Irwin, when he became viceroy, made a moving speech for religious tolerance. Whatever the cause, bitterness increased throughout the years and erupted in communal riots and killings and ever growing violence. This was the main reason for my brother's dislike of organized religion. Perhaps his lack of sympathy with it led him to underrate its power over the masses.

In February 1928, soon after our return to India, the Simon Commission arrived in Delhi to look into possible changes in the constitution which the British had graciously imposed on India in 1919. The Commission took its name from Sir John Simon, a liberal Englishman and a lawyer of great repute. It consisted of eminent members of Parliament of both parties, including a young Labour member named Clement Attlee. There was not a single Indian on the Commission.

Indians of all shades of opinion reacted furiously to the fact that another constitution was to be rammed down our throats by an all-British commission. Once again, by lack of elementary tact, the British did for us what we could not seem to do ourselves: they unified India. Radicals, Liberals, and the Muslim League under Jinnah, joined in a resolution to boycott the Commission. Father, speaking in the Assembly, expressed their point of view when he

said, "I have the honor of knowing Sir John Simon. . . . I have myself described him as a very big man . . . but the Indian people will
not surrender the right of self-determination to the biggest man in
the world."

The Simon Commission was boycotted. When the members came
to Lucknow, the capital of the United Provinces, a hundred thousand
people massed around the railroad station carrying black flags, and
banners inscribed SIMON GO BACK. Bhai was in the forefront of
the crowd when the mounted police charged it with swinging
batons and *lathis* (long sticks weighted at the end). He was beaten,
bruised and covered with blood—an injured arm pained him at
times throughout the rest of his life.

Father, Mother and I were enjoying a quiet afternoon in Anand
Bhawan when someone telephoned us about Bhai's injuries. My
parents were frantic with anxiety. Father said we must go at once
to Lucknow. He found our chauffeur had gone home for the night
so I offered to drive them. The measure of Father's love for Bhai
was that he accepted my offer, though with great misgivings. I was
thrilled, and brought the big, shiny Delage limousine he had
bought on his recent trip to Europe, up to the front door. Father
and Mother got in, and I set off on the two hundred and some-odd
miles over narrow, twisting roads to Lucknow. I was confident and
drove fast and, I think, well. At least I got them there safely; and,
on arrival, I had won my father's admiration—which was a great
thing for me. We found Bhai pretty badly battered, but very proud
of having proven his courage and manhood.

As a result of the boycott and a great upsurge of popular feeling
evinced by strikes, riots and—contrary to Gandhiji's principles—
outbreaks of violence and acts of terrorism throughout India, the
Simon Commission accomplished nothing. Their eventual report
became a mere footnote to history.

At the very height of the feeling, in December 1928, the Congress met in Calcutta. Once again Father had been elected President
and we all went to Calcutta with him. Determined to show the
British that they considered Father their duly elected chief, the
Congress and the people staged a magnificent reception. We rode
from the station in an open carriage drawn by white horses ridden
by young postillions. We were surrounded by a smartly uniformed,

mounted bodyguard of members of the Congress Volunteers, commanded by C. Subhas Bose. The big house that had been taken for us was covered with flowers, flags, and bunting in our national colors, and was guarded by Volunteer cavalry. Every time Father went out they formed a guard of honor, with Bose in full regimentals riding ahead in a pilot car. Finally Father said to Bose, "Please call off the guards. I am in no danger and would rather go quietly by myself."

At the Congress an oratorical battle took place between Father and his son. The older man spoke for moderation and the acceptance of dominion status; Bhai flamingly championed a declaration of full independence. It was only by calling in his last reserve, Mahatma Gandhi, who though ill came to Calcutta to support him, that Father was able to achieve a compromise in the form of a vote for the so-called "Nehru Report" which demanded full Dominion status. If this were not accepted by the British Parliament within a year the Congress would then demand independence. Later, Jawaharlal Nehru was named President of the Congress which was to meet at Lahore in the Punjab in December, 1929.

Tension continued to rise throughout 1929. Ironically, that was the year the government of India finally moved into its capital city of New Delhi. In 1911, Lord Hardinge had moved the capital from Calcutta to Old Delhi because it was closer to the center of India and had a far better climate. Immediately after World War I, the British had started building New Delhi in the tawny plain beyond the old city, undeterred by the lesson presented by the tombs of the Mogul Emperors scattered over the plain. It was a reckless display of the magnificence of the Empire. Huge buildings of red sandstone trimmed with white stood on broad avenues lined with shade trees and green open spaces. There was the Assembly building with its perfectly round chamber, the state buildings, and handsome residences for high officials. Crowning it all, at the head of the wide King's Way,* was the Viceroy's House, or rather palace. It was built in neo-classical style with an interminably long, pillared façade whose center was surmounted by a golden dome. The dome hung above the Durbar Hall, with its glittering

* Now called the Raj Path.

chandeliers, crimson and gold draperies, and magnificent throne for viceroys yet unborn.

The extensive gardens were a happy combination of East and West, with mirror pools on which lotus flowers floated, feathery flowering trees, green lawns and formal beds of sweet English flowers. It was a house that any nation could be proud to own as the residence of its Head of State, and is one thing for which we can be grateful to the British.

The new Viceroy was Lord Irwin,* the beau ideal of an English aristocrat, slim and very tall—six feet five—and incredibly elegant, despite the wooden hand he wore on his withered left arm. Always a little aloof, calm and courteous, he had a surprisingly flexible mind considering his upbringing. Even those who fought him, like Gandhiji and my father and brother, admitted that he had great integrity; and he was deeply religious. When Gandhiji was told that Lord Irwin prayed before making any important decision, he smilingly said, "What a pity God gives him such bad advice."

It was his other councillors who gave the Viceroy bad advice, the old India hands and the military men with whom he was surrounded. In addition, although the Labour government of J. Ramsay MacDonald had come to power and the Secretary of State for India, Sir Wedgewood Benn, was far better than his ultra-conservative predecessor, Lord Birkenhead, British public opinion went on an anti-Indian rampage. The debate in the House of Commons in October 1929 was so vitriolic that it was evident that any large concessions to Indian opinion would bring MacDonald's shaky government down. The Viceroy's hands were tied. There would be no question of dominion status by 1930.

However, in October, the Viceroy took what he considered the ultimate step toward conciliation and called the Indian leaders to Delhi to discuss a possible round-table conference leading to eventual Dominion status. Father was there and Bhai went too, though unwillingly. Gandhiji went, of course, for, without him, there would have been nothing. There were representatives of other Indian points of view. All parties finally agreed on a formula envisaging Dominion status as the basis of the conference. Except for Subhas

* Later the Earl of Halifax, British Foreign Minister and wartime Ambassador to the United States.

Bose, they all signed the agreement—Bhai only after strong persuasion from Father and much heart-searching. "A bitter pill," he called it.

The agreement never had a chance. Such an uproar now broke out in England that the government had to backwater. Indian opinion was infuriated by the imperialistic speeches of such Conservative leaders as Birkenhead, Winston Churchill, and Lloyd George.

It was under these conditions that the Congress met at Lahore. Again our people recognized the importance of pageantry. Jawaharlal Nehru, the new president, rode to the meeting on a white horse, followed by a cavalcade of young men; and very handsome he looked, slim and easy in the saddle, wearing tight trousers and a sherwani made of white khadi, and the Gandhi cap above the burning intensity of his eyes. Father gave the *gadi* of the presidency to his son, the only time on record that such a family transfer of power took place in a democratic parliament.

Bhai pushed his program through with ease and oratory. Though they knew that each vote was "a farewell to ease and comfort, to domestic happiness, and the intercourse of friends, and an invitation to lonely days and nights in prison," the Congress declared almost unanimously for complete independence and set January 26, 1930, as Independence Day.* They also approved the renewal of *Satyagraha.*

On the bitterly cold morning of January 1, 1930, under the deep blue Indian sky, tens of thousands of people gathered on the banks of the Ravi River, while Bhai solemnly read to them our Declaration of Independence, which echoed the great American Declaration of 1776, with a definite Gandhi-Nehru twist:

We believe that it is the inalienable right of the Indian people, as of any other people, to have freedom to enjoy the fruits of their toil and to have the necessities of life. . . . We believe also that if any government deprives people of these rights and oppresses them the people have a further right to alter or abolish it. The British Government has not only deprived the Indian people of their freedom, but has based itself on the exploitation of the masses, and has ruined India economically, politically, culturally, and

* Now called Republic Day.

spiritually. We believe, therefor, that India must sever the British connection and attain *Purna Swaraj* or complete independence. . . .

We hold it a crime against Man and God to submit any longer to a rule that has caused this fourfold disaster to our country. We recognize, however, that the most effective way of gaining our freedom is not through violence. We will therefor prepare ourselves by withdrawing as far as we can all voluntary association from the British Government. . . . We therefor hereby solemnly resolve to carry out the Congress instructions issued from time to time for the purpose of establishing *Purna Swaraj*.

Ten times ten thousand voices gave the pledge and roared, "Swaraj *Ki Jai! Nehru Ki Jai!* (Long live Independence! Long live Nehru!)"

On January 26, 1930, this scene was repeated all over India as the declaration was read to vast crowds in the cities and to small gatherings in countless villages. Millions of Indians pledged themselves to our struggle for freedom. Congress members of the Assembly and the provincial councils immediately resigned.

Bhai was riding high. He has described himself as a little intoxicated by the adulation of the crowds that gathered wherever he went and that came by thousands in pilgrimage to Anand Bhawan. They were all over the verandahs and jamming the grounds so that we knew hardly a moment's peace, and Bhai was forever dashing out to address them. The Indian press went flat out, loading Bhai with extravagant praise, and people addressed him by such magniloquent phrases as "*Bharat Bhushan* [Jewel of India]" and "*Tyagamurti* [O, Embodiment of Sacrifice]." He got a little pompous, but his sense of humor held up well. He wrote, "Sometimes I felt an almost uncontrollable desire . . . to stick out my tongue or stand on my head. . . ."

Kamala and I played our part in keeping his feet on the ground. When Bhai came down to breakfast we bowed deeply and asked how the Jewel of India had slept, or if the Embodiment of Sacrifice would like some bacon and eggs. Even little Indu joined in the game. Bhai blushed and smiled sheepishly.

Though my brother was the current hero of India, everyone from the sweeper at the crossing to the Viceroy in this three-hundred-room house in New Delhi knew that Gandhiji was the man who would decide on the next step. Gandhiji himself did not yet know his plans. When on January 18, our great poet Rabindranath Tagore asked him what he intended to do, he said, "I am furiously thinking night and day, and I do not see any light coming out of the surrounding darkness."

Suddenly the light came. The salt tax was the most hated of all Indian taxes and weighed most heavily on the poor. In a letter to the Viceroy, Gandhiji announced that on March 11 he would begin *Satyagraha* by breaking the Salt Laws. It was an inspired move, typical of Gandhiji in its sure appeal to the Indian masses, having a combination of materialistic and spiritual motives. In my brother's words, "Salt suddenly became a mysterious word, a word of power."

On March 11, after morning prayers, Gandhiji left the Sabarmati Ashram at the head of seventy-eight disciples and close associates, to walk to Dandi on the Arabian Sea two hundred and forty miles away. Wearing his loincloth and shawl and carrying a long staff, he strode along at his usual brisk pace that left much younger men exhausted. Peasants sprinkled the road ahead to lay the dust and strewed green leaves on it. People came for miles to kneel by the roadside as Gandhiji passed by, and every house was decked with our national colors. Everywhere men and women joined the marchers, while the whole world watched the Mahatma's progress, and Indian morale rose like a rocket.

Father and Bhai went to Ahmedabad for the meeting of the Congress committee that planned the *Satyagraha* campaign, and made arrangements to replace the officers who were sure to be arrested. Then they drove to Jambusar where Gandhiji was encamped with his pilgrims. After talking half through the night they stood and waved as Gandhiji led his people down the road in the sunrise.

When they got back to Allahabad my father and brother began intensive training of the Volunteers, not to fight—they had no arms —but to make them more efficient in their own work and in handling large crowds. Kamala and I joined up. In the interests of mobility we dressed like boys, with tight-legged trousers, knee-length *kurta* shirts and Gandhi caps.

Gandhiji reached the seacoast on April 5, 1930 with his unarmed army, now several thousand strong. All that night they prayed, and at dawn on April 6, the anniversary of the 1919 *Satyagraha,* Gandhiji led them down to the sea. There, the ascetic Mahatma, who had not tasted salt for six years, walked into the ocean, and then returning to the beach symbolically gathered some salt left by evaporated seawater.

That was the signal. All the pilgrims began making salt by boiling seawater in kettles or pans. Soon, from every Indian city and village along thousands of miles of coast, people rushed to make salt from the sea. Inland it was a little more difficult. As my brother said, "We knew precious little about making salt." But we all read up on it, and collected pots and pans and succeeded in making some pretty dreadful stuff which we auctioned off at high prices. It was a little like the Americans and their fight against the English tax on tea, except *they* could not very well make tea.

The British, appalled by the unforeseen enormity of the Movement, did not wait long to crack down. The leaders were arrested. Vallabhbhai Patel went first, on April 7. They took Bhai on April 14, tried him in jail, sentenced him to six months for breaking the salt laws, and took him to Naini Prison just across the Jumna River. He wanted to appoint Gandhiji in his place as president of the Congress, but when the Mahatma refused, he appointed Father, who accepted. Gandhiji was arrested shortly after midnight on May 5 and sent to Yeravda Prison in Poona.

My father was beginning his last illness. Doctor M. A. Ansari, who had examined him in March, described his condition as "very unsatisfactory." He wrote to Gandhiji that "The continuous anxiety and strain which he has recently undergone . . . had caused a fresh exacerbation of asthmatic attack, and had placed a further strain on his dilated heart. He could hardly walk or even perform ordinary movements without losing his breath. As you know he has been running an erratic high blood pressure. . . ."

Against all advice Father went into action as president of the Congress, apparently triumphing over his failing heart and lungs by sheer willpower.

9
"he will live long"

With Bhai in prison and Father busy directing the Congress campaign
it was up to the women to represent the family in the active phase of
the Movement. As mass arrests began this same thing was going on
all over the country; for the first time, Indian women came out of
their traditional seclusion to stand beside their men in the front lines
of our struggle for independence.

My sister Nan and her husband had returned from Calcutta to
Allahabad to take part in the Movement. She joined us, while Ranjit
acted as secretary to a Congress committee. She and I worked all day
directing the Volunteers, attending meetings, and picketing merchants who sold English goods. More extraordinary, my delicate little
mother, who had always been cared for like a china doll, came out in
the blazing sun and hundred-degree heat to march in the picket lines.

And Kamala! Kamala, whose fatal disease had returned, was the
most active of all. She became the best organizer, the most intrepid
marcher and the leading spirit of the women of Allahabad, up at
5 A.M. to drill volunteers, on the picket lines at eight.

One day I found our house full of children from about ten to
fifteen years old; the girls were dressed like the boys in khadi trousers
and *kurtas*. They were chattering like parakeets. Indu was organizing what she named the Monkey Brigade to take part in the Movement. As she said, "I wanted to join the Congress, but they told me
I'd have to wait until I was eighteen. So I got mad and said, 'I'll have
my own organization.' "

The name was an echo of the Hindu legend about the time when
Rama's wife, Sita, was held prisoner by the Demon Ravana on the
island of Ceylon. The Monkey God Hanumana called all the
monkeys of India to the rescue. They formed a living bridge, hands
grasping tails, from India to Ceylon. Sita walked over the bridge in

86

safety to rejoin Rama in the jungle abode of his exile. Ever since then, monkeys have been honored by the Hindus; and it is as sinful to kill one as to kill a sacred cow.

Indu's Monkey Brigade grew to several thousand children. At a mass meeting she could not make her voice carry to all of them so she used "human loudspeakers." She'd shout a sentence and a boy or girl in the crowd would turn and bellow it to those further back and so on. Her executive ability at the age of twelve or thirteen was remarkable. Though we laughed at her Monkeys at first, they proved very useful. They took over jobs like addressing envelopes, making flags, and cooking. When they marched in processions waving flags and making a lot of noise, the police would not touch them.

This immunity made them good for carrying messages between officials of the Congress and the Volunteers, unnoticed and unsuspected because they were children. They could even get through to the outer doors of the jails and when they saw someone going in, whisper a message to be delivered to a prisoner. And they gathered intelligence. Policemen sitting outside their station houses talking about their orders and plans would take no notice of some kids playing hopscotch in the street, never thinking they were acting as tape recorders.

But do not think it was all deadly serious business. The Monkeys had great fun planning their coups. It was like a glorious but dangerous game of hide-and-seek played for high stakes. Nor was Indu overly solemn. She was now a lithe and leggy teen-ager dedicated like her father to freedom for India, and with his abounding vitality. Sarojini Naidu, poetess and Congress leader, who was our great friend, referred to Indira in a letter to my brother as being like, "Atalanta, fleet of foot with sunrise in her eyes."

My brother was thrilled by the news of our activities. He wrote from prison, "By the time I come out I expect to find the women running everything."

Oddly enough I was the first of us to be arrested. On November 11, some members of the Youth League of which I was secretary were to be tried; and with my cousin, Miss Shyama Kumari Nehru, who was a lawyer, I went to Magistrate Bomford, whom I knew well, for a permit to attend the trial. His office was full of our placards and our national flags captured from the demonstrators, and he was in a very harassed state of mind. When I asked him for the permits he burst out, "I'm sick and tired of you and your like upsetting everything. Why the hell don't you get married?"

"I will when I want to," I said.

"Child marriage was not such a bad idea," Bomford groaned.

"Are you going to give me the permits or not?"

"I'm fed up, but here they are."

I drove Shammie to Malaka Jail for the trial in my Armstrong. It was the usual cut-and-dried affair with the boys offering no defense. We waved good-by to them as they were taken off to prison. As we started to leave a police officer came up with a warrant for the arrest of Shammie and me—evidently Bomford had really had it. We were tried right then and there; I, on the charge of attending an illegal meeting some weeks before, and Shyama for some other illegality. We were convicted and sentenced to one month's imprisonment or a fine of 100 rupees, which, of course, we refused to pay.

While we stood waiting I could see my beautiful little car parked outside the window. Quietly I dropped the keys down the front of my blouse. As they were taking us off a policeman asked for my keys. Straight-faced I said, "I've lost them."

I was allowed to send Father a note by a friend, saying I was sorry. Then they locked us up in separate cells. It is a grim feeling when a steel door clangs in your face; yet I was only half scared—and half elated at becoming one of the company elected to suffer for India. Most of all, I worried about Father who I knew was dying and who had asked us to try not to get arrested.

Some hours passed, so slowly that I wondered how one could stand it for a whole month. Then a door clanged and footsteps came along the cell block. A matron opened the door. "Someone to see you."

It was a Singhalese boy named Bernhard Aluvihari, who was a great friend of mine. He looked terribly upset. "I can't stand seeing you here," he said, waving a hundred-rupee note. "I'm going to pay your fine."

"You must not," I told him. "It's against our pledge."

"You can't stop me," he said.

It was true; I could not. He paid the fine and I was released. Someone had already paid Shammie's fine. We came out in the night and there was my beautiful little car. I dropped Bernhard off at his lodgings and drove home. The house was dim with only a light or two. Father had already gone to bed, but Mother was sitting up reading the *Ramayana*. She did not greet me with any great enthusiasm. "Your father heard someone was going to pay your fine," she said. "He is very upset. You had better see him first thing in the morning."

I got up early and went to Father as he was having his morning tea. "What are *you* doing here?" he asked.

"Someone paid my fine."

"I know. Who was it?" he said angrily.

"I don't know," I lied.

"Look at this," he said, showing me the newspaper. There were banner headlines:

MISS KRISHNA NEHRU—
UNKNOWN PERSON PAYS FINE?

PANDIT MOTILAL NEHRU'S STATEMENT. "I have just heard that some unknown person has paid the fine of Rs. 50,* inflicted on my daughter Krishna this afternoon. . . . If my information is true the unknown person has done the greatest disservice to me, to my daughter and to the country. His name cannot long remain a secret. And if my countrymen have any regard for me . . . I hope they will look upon him as my deadliest enemy and that of the country, and treat him as such."

"That's how I feel," Father said when I finished. "Now who was it?"

I still said I did not know, but Father was not easily put off. He guessed that it was Bernhard.

Poor Bernhard. He got no thanks but instead the words that he was not welcome at Anand Bhawan. Years later I saw him again in Ceylon, and found that he had shared digs with my husband, Raja Hutheesing, at Oxford.

In spite of my ignominious release I was a bit of a heroine among my friends. If I was inclined to get puffed up, Bhai soon put me right.

* Father was wrong, it was 100 rupees.

89

In a note from prison he wrote: "I understand you are getting caskets and addresses . . . surely a few hours in jail do not deserve an epic. Anyway, don't get a swelled head, or perhaps it's better to have a swelled head than no head at all."

To return to important things. Back in June, I had gone to Bombay, the stormiest city, with Father and Mother and Kamala. Father received a tremendous reception. But we also saw some terrible attacks by police on peaceful Congress processions; horses charging and the sickening crack of *lathis* on bare skulls. When we came back to Allahabad, Father was utterly exhausted. He planned to go to Mussoorie for a short rest on July 1. In the early morning of June 30, he was arrested while still in bed and taken to join Bhai in Naini Prison just across the Jumna River.

The government had suddenly declared the Congress Working Committee an illegal body, so that any or all of its members could be taken at will. As fast as they were arrested other patriots were appointed to take their places. Kamala, too, was given this great honor.

In prison Father was quartered in a small barracks with Bhai and two old friends, Narmada Prasad Singh and the Mohammedan Congress leader, Doctor Syed Mahmud. In his exhausted condition it was very difficult for him, even though we were allowed to send his food in from Anand Bhawan. The four men occupied four tiny cells in a separate barracks and, as the monsoon was on, the roof leaked in the torrents of rain. At night it was difficult to find a dry spot on the narrow verandah* on which to put my father's cot. He had frequent bouts of fever.

Bhai nursed him devotedly. Father wrote to me: "Please tell everyone that I am quite well now. [This was not true.] Hari [his valet] would do well to take a leaf out of Jawahar's book. From early morning tea to the time I retire for the night, I find everything I need in its place. . . . It has never become necessary to ask for anything which had so frequently to be done at Anand Bhawan involving a fair amount of shouting. . . . Mahmud lends a helping hand but the chief burden falls on Jawahar. . . . I wish there were many fathers to boast of such sons. . . ."

* Later the government widened it especially for him.

In August, Father and Bhai were asked to go to Poona to confer with Gandhiji in Yeravda Prison, for peace talks arranged with Lord Irwin by Doctor Tej Bahadur Sapru and M. R. Jayakar. When they consented, the government provided a special train. Though its schedule was secret, the word-of-mouth telegraph alerted the people and great crowds cheered them through the stations en route.

At Yeravda, Colonel Martin, the superintendent, courteously asked my father what kind of food he would like. "I eat very light, simple things," Father said. He then outlined menus from morning tea to dinner.

The superintendent was aghast. As Bhai said, "Very probably at the Ritz or the Savoy it would have been considered simple."

Three days of conferences with Gandhiji, Sapru and Jayakar resulted in a statement of the conditions under which they would call off Civil Disobedience. These were not acceptable to the Viceroy, so nothing came of it. But Father never recovered from the strain of those meetings. When next we saw him in Naini Prison, his face was swollen and he seemed very ill although he laughed and cracked jokes in his old way. In September his condition was so bad that government doctors, as well as his own, recommended his release. Weak as he was, Father telegraphed the Viceroy that he wanted no special favors. Nevertheless, Lord Irwin, who was both humane and intelligent enough not to want a dead martyr on his hands, ordered his release.

Mother, Nan and I took Father to Mussoorie for treatment— Kamala remained in Allahabad for her work on the Congress Working Committee. The cool, high air had a wonderful effect. When Bhai, having served out his sentence, arrived with Kamala for a three-day visit, they thought Father had turned the corner.

Bhai was only out of jail eight days. During that time he started a tremendous new campaign against the government. At meetings with thousands of *kisans* (peasants) he organized a movement against paying land taxes that spread throughout India. The government could not wait to clap him back in jail again; they also took Ranjit Pandit. On the first of January, 1931, Kamala was imprisoned. Bhai wrote, "I was pleased, for she had so longed to follow many comrades to prison."

91

After Bhai's rearrest, Father flung himself into the work of the Congress, for a few days seeming to triumph again over his illness. But it was not for long. When he went to see his son on visitors' day at the jail, Bhai was shocked by his appearance. "His face was even more swollen. He had some little difficulty in speaking and his mind was not always clear. But his old will remained and this kept the body and mind functioning."

On January 26, 1931, Lord Irwin revoked the illegality of the Working Committee and released many of the Congress leaders in a gesture of amity and the hope of making the second Round Table Conference in London a success—the first one had failed owing to the fact that no official Congress representative attended. Father was in such bad condition that Bhai was released a few hours earlier than the others. He came home with Kamala and Ranjit. Gandhiji was freed from Yeravda Prison on the same day. He arrived at Anand Bhawan the next night. Father lay awake waiting for him, and as Gandhiji slipped silently into his room he smiled and seemed comforted.

Now all the Congress leaders who were free came to Allahabad, as did many more of Father's old friends. All day long we had an unending stream of visitors. The house, verandahs and lawn were crowded with them, talking in hushed tones. Father, sitting in an easy chair "like an old lion mortally wounded . . . but still very leonine and kingly,"* received them two or three at a time. Knowing they had come to say farewell he would occasionally say something witty to relieve the funereal gloom.

Seeing so many of the Congress there, Father proposed that a Working-Committee meeting be held at our old house next door. "Decide India's fate in Swaraj Bhawan," he said, "and let me be party to the honorable settlement of the fate of my motherland. Let me die, if die I must, in the lap of a free India."

The meeting was held, and though Father was too ill to attend it, he received the committee members once again. Then most of them left, but Gandhiji remained. He and Father had many serious talks and some light ones; for when Father thought things were getting too solemn he'd make a joke. He was as meticulous as ever about his

* *Toward Freedom* (New York: John Day Co., 1941).

92

clothes, and hated to have the least spot on them. This amused Gandhiji, who never worried about material things. One day Father, who had been lying still and apparently asleep for a long time, suddenly asked for a drink. Gandhiji, sitting next to his bedside, put his hand on Father's arm and said, "Motilal, you should not think of earthly things like drinks. You should recite the *Gita* and try to think of unworldly, spiritual things."

With a flash of his old skepticism Father said, "I leave unworldly things to you and my wife. While I'm still on earth I will be earthy."

Another day Gandhiji and Mother and I were sitting by Father's bed. He seemed to be in a coma, but he suddenly roused and said mischievously to the Mahatma, "Bapu, if you and I happened to die at the same time, you, being a saintly man, would presumably go to heaven right off. But, with due deference, I think this is what would happen: You would come to our River of Death;* you would stand on the bank and then, most probably, you would walk across it, perhaps alone or maybe holding on to the tail of a cow. I would arrive much later. I'd get into a fast new motorboat, shoot past you, and get there ahead of you. Of course, being very worldly, I might not be allowed into heaven—if there is one."

Gandhiji laughed at the mental picture Father had conjured up. My dear mother was shocked, as she had so often been before, by her husband's unorthodox humor.

Father got steadily worse though we had three of the finest doctors in India attending him. Besides Doctor Ansari, they were Doctor Jivraj Mehta and Doctor B. C. Roy. They could do nothing. His poor face swelled until his eyes were almost closed, and he constantly coughed up blood. Early in February the doctors decided that he should go to Lucknow for deep X-ray treatments which were unavailable in Allahabad. Father did not want to go. He knew that his time had come and he wanted to die at Anand Bhawan which he loved so much. The doctors, true to their Hippocratic Oath, insisted and appealed to the Mahatma. Father finally yielded to Gandhiji's persuasion.

We took him to Lucknow in an automobile on February 4, and stayed at the Kalakanker Palace. It had been a long and exhausting

* Like the Styx of ancient Greek belief.

ride for Father, but the next morning he seemed better and we began to hope again. We were all there, Mother, Bibi Amma, Nan and Ranjit, Bhai and Kamala, and Gandhiji.

In the afternoon Father grew much worse; his breathing was so difficult that he had to have oxygen. That evening we sat on the stone floor of the corridor outside his room waiting, and praying; it was terribly cold. Finally, one of the doctors came to me and said that Father was asking for me. When I went into the room he appeared to be unconscious. The doctors told me to sit behind him on the bed and give him support as he was more comfortable sitting up. Then they left us for a little while.

After a few moments Father stirred and seemed to be groping for something. I bent forward to ask what he wanted. He could not speak but with great difficulty tugged at my arm; and sensing what he wanted I carefully moved around to sit facing him. He took my face between his poor swollen hands and drawing me to him he kissed my face all over as though in a last farewell. I sat trembling with the effort of holding back my tears. Then feeling my control going, I gently tried to slip away from his embrace, but he still held me with surprising strength. As though he knew that I was close to collapse he rallied all his strength to whisper, "My Choti Beti, you must always be brave. That's how I have taught you and you must not let me down."

Then he relaxed and unable to bear more I propped pillows behind him and fled to fall sobbing in Kamala's arms. Afterward I sat on the floor outside his room with the others shivering with the cold and misery.

Perhaps I dozed for suddenly there was Bibi Amma telling us he had gone. Bhai and Mother were with him. The rest of us filed into the room. Jawahar sat holding his father's head in his lap, his lips trembling and eyes filled with unshed tears. Father's serene face was even more beautiful in death than in life; his noble features increased in majesty. Each in turn touched his feet but only his children kissed him.

Gandhiji came in last and after touching Father's feet stood looking down at him as though contemplating the ultimate mysteries. Then he went to Mother who, almost prostrated, sat in a corner supported by Bibi Amma. Putting his thin arm gently around her he said, "Motilalji is not dead. Men like him never die. He will live long."

All India, even his enemies, mourned Motilal Nehru. His body covered by masses of brilliant flowers lay in state, at first in Lucknow. Gandhiji sat by him for hours; so did Mother, tiny and forlorn as though the will of life had gone from her. Bhai, looking ten years older overnight, stood on the other side of the catafalque while thousands of people passed by and hundreds of thousands tried to get near enough to pay him homage. Then Father's body, covered with our orange, green and white national flag, was put in an automobile. Jawahar sat beside it, and Ranjit drove while Hari, his valet, sat at Father's feet. A huge Indian flag flew from the car.

Kamala, Nan and I went ahead, followed by another car with Mother and Gandhiji. The roads were lined deep with people all the way from Lucknow to Allahabad. As we approached our home the crowds were so dense it seemed impossible to get through, but somehow they made way for us. We came through the iron gates of Anand Bhawan. I looked up to see the tall flagpole on the roof from which our national flag always flew defiantly high; it was at half-mast.

Mother and Gandhiji did not arrive immediately and we worried and wondered. When they finally came we learned that our chauffeur had been weeping so hard that he missed the road and our big Delage limousine turned over in a ditch throwing Mother and Gandhiji out. Miraculously they were only badly shaken.

Father lay in state again at Anand Bhawan until evening when he was taken in a tremendous funeral procession down to the sacred rivers. We all followed his body, hidden beneath a pile of beautiful flowers with only his face uncovered, through the gates of Anand Bhawan. In the dusk on the riverbank, Jawahar, rendering the last melancholy service of a Hindu son to his father, took a flaming torch and lit the pyre of sandalwood.

10
Lucknow
central
prison

My brother had no time for mourning. The day Father died, the Indian members of the first Round Table Conference landed in Bombay. Srinivasa Sastri, Sir Tej Bahadur Sapru and M. R. Jayakar hurried directly to Allahabad for the funeral ceremonies. The next day they met with Gandhiji, Bhai and other members of the Working Committee to give an account of the Conference. From what they said it was evident that very little had been accomplished. However, the consideration with which the British had treated them gave them hope that a second proposed Round Table Conference would accomplish something—Sastri, Sapru, Jayakar, were incorrigible optimists.

After two days of discussion someone proposed that Gandhiji should write to Lord Irwin and ask for an interview and have a frank talk with him. Bhai opposed the proposal; but Gandhiji, who liked to meet those who disagreed with him face to face accepted the suggestion.

"Dear Friend": he wrote to the Viceroy. "As a rule I neither wait for outward prompting nor stand on ceremony, but straightway seek personal contact with officials whenever I feel such contact is needed. . . . But somehow or other in the present case I have missed the guidance of the Inner Voice.

"But I have received suggestions from friends whose advice I value that I should seek an interview with you. . . . It was felt that, before the Working Committee took any final decision, it might be better for me to meet you and discuss our difficulties with you. I therefore ask you, if you are willing, to send me an appointment as early as may be possible. . . .

> I am,
> Your faithful friend
> M. K. GANDHI

Lord Irwin's affirmative reply flashed back immediately. On February 17, Gandhiji walked five miles from Doctor Ansari's house where he was staying in Old Delhi to the Viceroy's House and that famous meeting. The fact that it took place at all made the British Tories livid. Winston Churchill expressed their feelings in his thunderous style: "The nauseating and humiliating spectacle of this one-time Inner Temple Lawyer, now seditious fakir, striding half naked up the steps of the Viceroy's palace to parley on equal terms with the representative of the King-Emperor." That was the sort of thing Lord Irwin had to combat in his honest attempts to reach agreement with the Indian leaders.

Gandhiji did not "stride up the steps," but was ceremoniously escorted by two gorgeously uniformed troopers of the Viceroy's Guard through a side door. Lady Irwin noted that almost all the servants found some reason to be on hand for a glimpse of the Mahatma. It must have been quite crowded as there were over seven hundred of them.

Lord Irwin and Gandhiji hit it off at once. So different in background and appearance, the formally dressed Viceroy towering like a telegraph pole over the small figure in his loincloth and shawl, they each appreciated the good will and sincerity of the other. Their sense of humor was also in accord. Once Lord Irwin asked the Mahatma if he would like a cup of tea. "Thank you," Gandhiji said producing a little paper bag out of his shawl. "I will put some of this salt in it to remind us of the famous Boston Tea Party." They laughed together. When Sir Cecil Griffin, who disliked Gandhiji, asked Lord Irwin if the Mahatma had been "tiresome," the Viceroy remarked, "Some people found Our Lord very tiresome."

A few days after the meetings began, Bhai received a telegram summoning him and the other members of the Working Committee to New Delhi. He went with serious misgivings. Gandhiji was making progress in his talks with the Viceroy. Sentence by sentence an agreement was hammered out. The Working Committee conferred each day with Gandhiji but the negotiations were definitely in his hands. On the evening of March 4, 1931, in a meeting that lasted until after midnight, they came to an agreement which became known as the Delhi Pact. As Gandhiji started off alone on his long walk home the Viceroy said, "Goodnight, Mr. Gandhi, and my prayers go with you."

My brother has told how he and the other Committee members waited up until almost two o'clock. When Gandhiji came in, clutching the Pact, they read it anxiously. Speaking for the Congress, Gandhiji had agreed that an official representative would attend the Second Round Table Conference and that meanwhile Civil Disobedience would be "discontinued." The Viceroy recognized that the discussions in London would not preclude eventual Indian independence, but limited Home Rule of a federated India was envisioned for the present. As a symbolic gesture Indians who lived near the sea could be allowed to make salt. The Civil Disobedience prisoners would be freed.

What shocked my brother, who had not previously seen it, was Article 2, stating reservations or safeguards "in the interests of India," that included British control of "defense; external affairs; the position of minorities; the financial credit of India; and the discharge of obligations."

This was not independence or even real Home Rule, he thought; this was the same old leading strings, the end of his plans for the socialization of India's economy. It was surrender, making all the brave words and sacrifices in vain. Yet there was nothing he could do; for a word had been given, a compact ratified, and it was unthinkable to repudiate Gandhiji. In his "great emptiness" Bhai thought of Eliot's lines, and it seemed that his world was ending with a whimper.

The next morning he walked with Gandhiji in the dawn and felt "a little soothed." The Mahatma pointed out that the Pact was "provisional and conditional," and that he had told the Viceroy that complete independence remained India's goal. Bhai saw clearly that there was no middle way for him. Either he must break with Gandhiji and denounce the Pact, or accept it and work wholeheartedly for it. This he reluctantly decided to do. The Delhi Pact was formally signed that morning after breakfast.

While he was still in New Delhi, Bhai wrote me a letter that was typical of his generous nature:

Betty darling,

I seem to be hung up here indefinitely. . . . I had hoped to get a clear week to settle . . . our domestic affairs. So far the whole burden has fallen on Father and all of us were relieved by his loving care of a host of difficulties. His amazing love for his children enveloped us and protected us, and we lived freed in a large measure from the care and anxiety which most people have to face. . . . We have to do without him now, and as every day passes I feel his absence more and a terrible loneliness takes hold of me. But we are children of our father and have something of his great strength and courage. . . .

I have not been able to examine Father's papers yet. But he probably has not left a will. . . . Technically, in law, I suppose I am the heir of his property. But my own inclination is against inheriting property or at any rate living on inherited or unearned increment. . . . But [because of my public service] it would not have been Father's wish that I turn to making money now.

In any event, however, I can only consider myself as a joint sharer in Father's property; the other sharers being Mother and you. I am not including Nan as she stands in no need of money. I would like you, therefore, to consider yourself as an equal sharer with Mother and me of Father's property. Indeed Mother and you are the real sharers. I am a trustee for the family property. . . .

Look after Mother and yourself.

Your loving brother
JAWAHAR

After setting the machinery in motion to stop Civil Disobedience, Bhai came home to us. He looked utterly spent from those terrible two months which had seen Father's death and what he considered the appeasement of the British; and he suffered what he called "a

99

little breakdown in health." Yet when Gandhiji asked him to move the resolution ratifying the Delhi Pact at the special Congress meeting in Karachi, he agreed to do so. Mother, Kamala and I went with him, and heard his emotional speech which moved everyone present.

There was no question about it; the Pact was popular in India. As our people came home from prison there were great rejoicings. Gandhiji was at the height of his popularity, acclaimed by enormous crowds wherever he went. India looked to the future with high hopes.

After the Congress meeting Bhai desperately needed a rest. He could not get one in India, for wherever he went people pressed in upon him with national and even personal concerns. So he and Kamala and Indira went to Ceylon. It was the first and the last real holiday they ever had together. The peace of that scented languorous island flowed through Bhai's soul. The magnificent welcome given him by the Singhalese restored his faith in the ultimate triumph of his ideals. He wrote to me: "I felt suddenly that it was the glory of India and her great fight that they were honoring and we were just the poor symbols and embodiments of that glory. . . . Today it is a proud privilege to be an Indian. . . ."

They returned by way of southern India, landing at Cape Coromin, its farthest tip, and visiting many of the princely states like Travancore, Mysore, and Hyderabad on their way north. Everywhere Bhai was received with courtesy and honor even though the maharajas hardly agreed with his politics.

As soon as he got home Bhai plunged back into politics. In spite of the truce, the country was heaving with unrest. The peasant-farmers were desperate. They had been hard hit by the great depression that had started in the United States and spread like a black plague sickening national economies around the world. Bhai, sympathizing deeply with their wretchedness, did nothing to calm them; rather he inflamed their anger.

Meanwhile a new viceroy, Lord Willingdon, had succeeded Irwin. He earned the distinction of being the most unpopular viceroy of the century. Though my brother maintained that it mattered not who the viceroy was, while the strings were pulled from London, it did help to have one who was courteous and sympathetic to the Indian point of view, if only because, as the man on the spot, he could advise our distant rulers of our real feelings. Lord Willingdon was none of these things.

Gandhiji was appointed by the Congress as its only representative at the Round Table Conference. My brother traveled with him from Simla, where he had been conferring with Lord Willingdon, to Bombay. On August 29, Gandhiji sailed on the *Rajputana* with eighty-seven other Indian delegates representing all sections of Indian opinion, including twenty-three maharajas, rajas, and nawabs who represented themselves. All the other delegates traveled first class; Gandhiji and his little entourage traveled third, sleeping on the open deck, for ten pounds apiece. As he said good-by to my brother, even the ever-hopeful Mahatma was doubtful. "There is every chance of my returning empty-handed," he said.

That is just what happened. From the monumental Aga Khan, presiding over the proceedings, to the least of the Untouchables, every one of the other eighty-seven delegates thought only of their particular faction, and each demanded separate electorates. Gandhiji alone represented all of India. Under such conditions the conference ended in chaos. When Gandhiji returned to India on December 28, 1931, Indira greeted him with a letter from her father telling him that Jawahar had been arrested on his way to meet him in Bombay and was again in prison.

At a huge meeting of peasants in Allahabad on October 23, my brother had inaugurated the "No Rent Campaign," advising the peasants not to pay rent to their landlords unless the government of India adopted suitable measures to relieve their distress. The campaign spread through the United Provinces like a forest fire. The provincial government struck back by promulgating an ordinance making it a crime to incite the peasants to refuse to pay rent, and serving an internment order on my brother, forbidding him to leave Allahabad or take part in any political activity.

True to his fiery way of inviting trouble, Bhai wrote to the district magistrate who had issued the order saying that he had no intention of obeying it, and that he was going to Bombay on December 26 to meet Gandhiji. On the morning of December 26, he boarded the Bombay Mail. Shortly after leaving Allahabad the fast express ground to an unscheduled stop, and police took my brother and his Muslim companion, Tasadduq Sherwani, off the train. Bhai said, "The superintendent who arrested us on that Boxing Day morning looked very glum and unhappy. I am afraid we had spoiled his Christmas.

"And so to prison."

On January 4, 1932, Bhai's trial took place in Naini Prison. He was sentenced to two years' rigorous imprisonment and a fine of 500 rupees or six months more if he did not pay it.

On that same day Gandhiji was arrested; so was the President of the Congress, Vallabhbhai Patel. The Congress and all its committees were declared illegal organizations; and thousands more were arrested, so many, that soon all the jails in India were filled up and large temporary camp-jails were built. The new Conservative British Government had decided to stamp out the Indian National Congress.

With Bhai and most of the other leaders in jail, we women took up their work though we knew that in the present mood of the government we would not last long. Dear Kamala had paid the price of her activity at her husband's side and was prostrate in Bombay, grieving that she could not take part in the Movement. Nan and I and our mother went to work with all our strength and enthusiasm. We visited the nearby villages, encouraging the peasants to hold fast against paying rent, and we began picketing boycotted merchants again. In mid-January we were served with an injunction against taking part in any *hartals,* processions or meetings. Independence Day, January 26, was only two weeks off and a great meeting was planned for that day, so we laid low.

The outdoor meeting was the largest held in Allahabad up to that time. Stretching as far as we could see from the platform, white *dhotis* and Gandhi caps and rainbow clusters of saris rippled with the movement of a crowd whose attention is not yet fixed, while the noise of their chattering seemed likely to make speaking impossible. Yet when Mother was introduced and stood at the tall microphones they were silent and still as though frozen.

That was one of the most extraordinary things. A tiny, fragile Hindu lady, born to the luxury and seclusion of strict orthodoxy, suddenly became a revolutionary orator. Her fiery speech swayed and roused the vast crowd to a peak of high emotion voiced in their wild, shrill shouts of "Swaraj *Ki Jai!* Nehru *Ki Jai!*"

Then the *lathi* charges began. Amid confusion and the cracking of heads, the police broke up the meeting. Many people were arrested then and there. Somehow we managed to get Mother safely back to Anand Bhawan. My sister and I were a little disappointed that we had not been arrested.

We need not have worried. The next morning at 9:30 the police car arrived. While the anxious servants huddled in the hall, Nan and I were told we were under arrest. The inspector was, as usual, courteous and rather embarrassed, and gave us time to collect our things and say good-by to Mother and Bibi Amma. Then he drove us to the district jail where we found many of our women friends. They were all cheerful and excited and our mood matched theirs.

We were signed in, weighed and given a cursory physical examination. Then we were taken inside the prison. It had no special women's quarters, as female prisoners were only held there until tried. One yard was set aside for them. Our fellow prisoners, apart from our comrades, were mostly thieves, professional criminals and prostitutes with the usual diseases. We were locked up four to a cell.

It was one thing to be a cheerful martyr in the high excitement of being arrested for love of your country, and quite another to spend night after night in a filthy cell full of insects crawling about the grim walls. For several nights we could not sleep, lying there imagining that some slimy thing would crawl over our bodies; nor was it all imagination—they did. Then we got sensible and cleaned the whole cell out every night before going to bed. The reassurance this gave us, and sheer exhaustion, made us sleep at last.

Every morning we were routed out early for the English superintendent to inspect us and make sure no one was missing. One day two of us were rather late for the lineup. As soon as he saw us the superintendent shouted "Hurry up! Hurry up! I can't wait here all day; there's a tennis tournament I want to see and you're holding me up in this unpleasant place."

I shouted back. "We find this filthy place even more annoying than you do. Why shouldn't you miss the tennis one day when we have to miss it every day?"

One thing that made it bearable was that Mother came to see us every day of the three weeks we were there.

According to the government's custom of not allowing dangerous prisoners like ourselves to go to court, we were tried in jail. We sat all in a row in one of the offices and, as our names were called out, we answered to them and then refused to make any defense. We expected to get at most six months.

Nan was called first. After the mumbo-jumbo to make it all legal, the magistrate, speaking in a low, embarrassed voice, condemned her to a year's rigorous imprisonment and 500 rupees' fine or three months more if she did not pay. It was a stunning blow. I felt my stomach turn over, but Nan only looked stony-eyed, and I hope I did, too, when my turn came to receive the same sentence.

We spent four more days in the district jail; then, in the night, we were moved to Lucknow Central Prison. We arrived there on an icy winter morning. The high grim walls towering over us tightened our hearts, as we realized what it meant to be shut away from the world for a whole year; but we clung to the tattered fringes of our courage. A matron showed us to our barracks, and told us the rules, the last one being: "You are free to walk about the yard, but you will be locked up at 5:30 P.M."

That shook us badly.

We looked at our bleak little cell. It was more forlorn and colder than the bare dirt yard on which its barred door opened. There were no walls, only bars, and the only protection from wind-driven rain was a piece of canvas rigged over the bars. It flapped loose in a wind and we would huddle in one corner all night trying to keep dry, but we were always soaking wet in the morning. Luckily it does not rain much in northern India in winter, only during the monsoon. There was not even a cot in the cell though we got cots later, for we were Class A prisoners—Classes B and C had to sleep on the floor.

Out in the yard the other prisoners were sitting around or washing their clothes at the tap. Some of them smiled at us and others stared sullenly. The six saris we were allowed were dirty and we decided to wash them. We had been given small pieces of soap, and we took our clothes to the single tap, soaped them, and pounded them on a big rock that was under it for that purpose. It was no easy thing to handle the thick khadi when it was soaking wet.

Monday was parade day. Our cell doors were unlocked at five in the morning as usual, and from then on there was a great scurry of preparation. By eight we were all lined up in our cleanest clothes with our aluminum mess plates shining—the matron saw to that. The superintendent was thorough and very courteous. On our first parade he asked us if we had any complaints or wanted anything. When he came to me I said, "Yes, I want to study so I would like some French and Italian books, a book on shorthand, three dictionaries, and a couple of novels." I was perfectly serious for I did not know we were only supposed to have six books at a time.

Equally seriously the superintendent said, "Wouldn't it be better if I asked the authorities to put in a small library for you? Then you would have more choice."

I caught a flash of humor in his eyes and said, "That would be lovely if it's not too much trouble for you. You see I don't want to waste my time here just spinning yarn. I hope you do it soon."

I did get my books but it took two months.

The food was awful. Being Class A we had a choice of European or Indian (vegetarian) diet. We chose European, but the meat was all bones and not much at that. Finally, we asked if we could cook our own meals. Permission was granted, so we cooked on a little coal-burning stove. The matron took it away every afternoon at five-thirty along with our knives in case we should feel like committing suicide. Except for our much older cousin, Mrs. Uma Nehru, all the others were orthodox Hindus who objected to our eating meat in the barracks, so we cooked it out in the yard at noon, and had a cold supper in our cell much later as we could not eat at five-thirty.

Washing ourselves was a problem. The other prisoners did not seem to mind sitting out in the open yard by the tap and pouring water over themselves from a jug; but somehow we could not get used to bathing in public. So we got permission to carry the cold water in buckets to a small unoccupied cell, and washed there. We could bathe as often as we liked, at least twice a day in summer.

We were allowed visitors once every two weeks; how we looked forward to those days! But sometimes no one came, for nearly all our family were in jail, and poor Mother had to visit my brother and Ranjit as well as Nan and me. Then we heard she had been badly wounded in a *lathi* charge, and we were frantic with no news of her until she came again, battered and bandaged up, but delighted with her honorable wounds.

Mother told us that she had been in a procession in Allahabad during National Week—April 6 to 13—commemorating Jallianwalla Bagh and the other Punjab massacres. The procession was halted by police and someone brought her a chair. She sat on it in the middle of the road at the head of the column. People taking care of her were arrested and led away. Then came the *lathi* charge. Mother was knocked out of her chair and hit repeatedly on the head with canes. She lay unconscious in the dusty roadway with blood flowing from the wounds in her head. After the street was cleared she was picked up by a police officer who took her in his car to Anand Bhawan.

That night the rumor ran through Allahabad that she was dead. The city rose and, forgetting about non-violence, angry mobs attacked the police. There was a great riot and shooting in which people died. My brother in prison wrote, "The thought of my frail old mother lying bleeding in the dusty road obsessed me, and I wondered how I would have behaved if I had been there. How far would non-violence have carried me. Not far, I fear...."

Had I been there I would not have thought of non-violence at all; it is not in my nature.

My only visitor outside of the family was a Muslim girl, who was a dear friend. She had a difficult time getting a pass because only near relations were supposed to come; but somehow she got around the superintendent. She brought me the nicest present I got in prison, a bottle of nail polish. We put it on then and there, and it gave my morale a tremendous lift. When I came back to the barracks some of the women were shocked—according to them nail polish was not suitable to our dedicated simple life. But I did not care, and got great pleasure from my bright red nails in those gray surroundings.

So our life went on for days and months. Sometimes Nan and I were terribly dull and lonely, missing the people we loved. Oddly enough, at other times we were quite happy and contented, working, reading and discussing life and philosophy and, of course, politics. I studied my shorthand and Nan dictated to me for practice. She read a great deal and wrote innumerable letters, most of which were never sent, as we were strictly limited as to how many we might mail. In those long days, we were very close to each other.

During the summer monsoon I came down with malaria. Through nights of burning fever, followed by cold sweats, while we all cowered behind the flapping canvas to keep dry, Nan and the others nursed me and pulled me through. But if there is anything more wretched than being in jail, it is being *sick* in jail.

Being more gregarious than Nan, when I felt well enough I made friends with some of the other prisoners, many of whom were quite young girls. One told me she would get out of jail and live with some man until he threw her out. Then, if she could find no one else, she would deliberately break some law so she could come back and have food and shelter.

The one I remember best was a dear, pretty, tragic young girl named Bachuli. When I had won her confidence I asked her why she was in prison. She answered, "For murder." It seemed incredible; the child was only about sixteen. "Why, why did you have to murder someone?" I asked.

"I murdered my husband," she said, and told me her story. She had been married at fourteen to an older man who treated her with abominable cruelty, beating her, half-starving her, taking sadistic pleasure in her pain and terror. Finally one night, after giving her a terrible thrashing, he fell asleep with nothing on but a silk handkerchief around his neck. Bachuli crept up to him and twisted it with all her strength. He woke up shouting and struggling but with the strength of terror she continued to twist the handkerchief until he went limp. "I half expected him to wake up and give me another thrashing," she said. "But he did not, and I lay there beside him unable to move. That is how someone found us in the morning.

"So I was tried and convicted. I was too young to be hanged. I got life imprisonment. That is all."

That is all. She seemed to take it as a matter of course, as something the fates had willed. Her story and those of many other young girls I met in Lucknow Prison made so deep an imprint on my mind that when our time of freedom and power came at last, I had myself appointed a magistrate of the Juvenile Court of Bombay and devoted myself to helping children like her.

"You will not forget me in the great world outside?" Bachuli asked when I was finally leaving the prison. "They tell me people outside don't like to remember convicts."

"I won't forget you," I said. And I never have.

A year passes even in prison. With the extra sentence for not paying our fines, less time off for good behavior (though I had behaved as badly as I knew how) we were actually there for over thirteen months. When our time was up they took us back to Allahabad and turned us loose. When we drove up to Anand Bhawan in a taxi it was dark; for Mother was with Kamala in Calcutta. Lights went on and servants clustered around us. Soon the house filled up with relatives and friends, all talking at once; their chatter made me dizzy and confused after the subdued sounds of prison. Hari came to ask what we wanted done with the suitcases of clothes we had brought back from jail. "Burn them," I said violently. "I never want to see those things again!"

So much had happened in that lost year that I never did catch up. We had only snatches of news that our visitors told us. We knew, of course, that the government had seized Swaraj Bhawan, which the Congress had been using as a children's hospital, and closed it. Daily we expected them to take our own home from us.

We had also learned of Gandhiji's famous fast in Yeravda Prison that breached the barrier against hte Untouchables for the first time; but now I heard the details. Fasting was Gandhiji's most effective technique for bringing men to reason and compromise. He had done it first in South Africa to bring strikers and mill owners together; and several times in India, usually to stop violence either by his own followers or communal rioting which he abhorred above everything. As the aura of his saintliness grew, his fasts became ever more effective; for the whole world watched and the pressures on those who opposed him became intolerable.

The occasion of his fast in Yeravda Prison was a change proposed by the British Cabinet to the Constitution of India that would grant separate electorates to the "Depressed Classes": the Untouchables. The British government was completely baffled by the objection to it on the part of the great champion of the poor, but Gandhiji explained it logically in a letter to Sir Samuel Hoare, Secretary of State for India: "I should not be against even overrepresentation for the

Depressed Classes. What I am against is their statutory separation, even in a limited form, from the Hindu fold so long as they choose to belong to it." In other words, having a separate electorate would set the Untouchables apart. All his life Gandhiji had fought against the "bar sinister," the division between the higher castes and the *Harijans* ("Children of God"), as Gandhiji called them. He was prepared to "fast unto death" rather than have this bar written into the Indian Constitution. The fast was more against the leaders of the Hindu community than against the British.

Gandhiji began his fast on September 20, 1932. Though he had survived twenty-one-day fasts, and would again, by the fourth day he was near death. The effect in India was terrific. All the Hindu leaders who were not in jail came to Yeravda to confer with him. Doctor B. R. Ambedkar, leader of the Untouchables, was holding out for a separate electorate, but even he could not withstand the pressures. On the fifth day, a suffocatingly hot afternoon, Ambedkar came to Gandhiji, but they could not agree. That afternoon Chakravarti Rajagopalachari and Sapru came up with a compromise giving the Untouchables weighted voting for a limited time. Ambedkar agreed. Gandhiji agreed. The British government, ready to agree to almost anything rather than have the Mahatma die on its hands, cabled its acceptance. Gandhiji sipped a glass of orange juice.

My brother did not altogether approve of Gandhiji's fasts. To him they "smacked of revivalism" and he wondered if with their strong connotations of religion ("the enemy of clear thinking") they were the right method of pursuing political objectives. But he had to admit that this one had an extraordinary effect. The political result was not important; had it been only that, Gandhiji would not have risked his life for a trifling concession. But the fast triggered an enormous upheaval, "a magic wave of enthusiasm," that swept through the Hindu community. During those five days hundreds of temples were opened for the first time to Untouchables; caste Hindus fraternized with them in the streets and sat beside them on benches reserved for Untouchables. Brahmans dined publicly with scavengers and street cleaners. My orthodox mother announced in the newspapers that she had eaten food given her by an Untouchable; tens of thousands of Hindu women followed where she led. It was not an end to Untouchability, but it was a wonderful beginning of an end.

11

my marriage

When I came home from jail our family was scattered. Bhai had been transferred from Naini Prison to Bareilly Jail; and when the hot weather came, he was sent to Dehra Dun Prison in the foothills of the Himalayas, to Dehra Dun where young Jawahar had been met by his father and a gay cavalcade of cousins, on his return from England in 1912.

When I went to see Bhai there, the prison was so full that he lived alone in an old lock-up outside the actual walls but within the prison compound. In his room was a very beautiful little statue of Buddha which he had acquired in Ceylon. Unreligious though he was, my brother got great comfort from the serene features of the man who became a god to hundreds of millions of people. Bhai also liked to read the New Testament, for he revered Jesus Christ—as a man, not as God.

During all his terms in jail Bhai strenuously maintained his schedule of exercises, keeping fit for the work ahead. In Dehra Dun, the place he was kept was so small there was no room to walk, so in the morning and the evening he was allowed to walk up and down outside the gate under guard. This was a precious privilege for him, for he could look at the towering Himalayas freshly clad each morning in new coats of snow. Even during the monsoons he walked there in tropical downpours.

Prison is harder on some people than others. Gandhiji, with his spiritual self-sufficiency minded it little, if at all; so long as he could read and spin, and meditate and pray he was content. He called his prison "Yeravda *Mandir* [Yeravda Temple]." But to a man of action like my brother, confinement was torture that he could only bear by the most stringent mental and physical discipline. The only time I ever saw him break was when Nan took her children to see him. When his little three-year-old niece climbed lovingly on his shoulder it was too much. He wept.

As I have said, Mother was with Kamala in Calcutta where she had gone to have treatments, so Nan and I went there first. We found Kamala so much better that in about a week we all came back home to Allahabad. Then at Mother's suggestion I went with Nan to see her children and Indu who were in a boarding school at Poona. To get there we went to Bombay and then took a train that climbed up through the Western Ghats, those superb hills southeast of Bombay, to the town, which itself is lovely with a good climate, fine houses and beautiful gardens.

Bhai and Kamala had sent Indu to school there when they came home from England, and it was ideal for children whose parents could not be with them. Nan's three little girls, Chandalekha, Nayantara (who was called Tara) and Rita were very young—Rita was only three. I think that this made prison much worse for Nan than for me, though she was very brave about it.

We stayed in Poona for about a week, and went to see Gandhiji in Yeravda Prison. Then we took Nan's children to Bombay. It was there that I met my future husband.

There was a party for Nan one night at the home of one of Ranjit Pandit's relatives—he was still in jail. When I came in, several young men gathered around me asking questions about prison life and treating me like a heroine, which I minded not at all. The only man who took no notice of me was a very elegant young fellow who was sitting in a corner by himself. His indifference rather piqued me and I asked my hostesses' son to bring him over and introduce him. The son said, "Oh you won't like him; he's very difficult."

That was no more than the truth—I can never say I was not warned; but I said, "Never mind, bring him over anyway."

So I was introduced to Raja Hutheesing. He stood there very tall and thin with a pipe in his mouth. In an extreme Oxford accent he said, "Are you very proud of yourself? Do you think you did a great thing by going to prison?"

My Nehru temper was near the flash point, but I only said, "Well, no. I've only done what others have done. I *am* proud of having played a part in my country's struggle for freedom."

Then as I began to boil I added, "What have you been doing while we have all been in prison? Having a good time, I suppose."

"You think so?"

"Yes," I said, "I don't think you are any good because this is the time you should be working for your country; not just sitting around or even working or studying. You should give everything else up as so many students have done in India."

He said, "I don't agree with you, and what is more I don't think you're a heroine."

That was an odd way to begin a courtship. I never thought I would see him again; but he called up the next day to ask me to lunch and I went.

Raja always claims that this was not the beginning. Though I have no recollection of it, he says that he met me at his uncle's house in Delhi in 1924 when I was there with Father for the Legislative Assembly. At seventeen I was very thin—about ninety-five pounds. My black hair fell to my knees and when it was piled on my head it made a towering confection of which I was rather proud. Raja says, "You looked like a golliwog, and I decided to marry you that evening."

We had several other dates and some deep discussions, mostly about books and communism, before I went home to Allahabad. Raja was quite different from the sarcastic, superficial dandy I had thought him at first sight—that evening, I believe, he was putting on an act for my benefit. He was sensitive and somewhat of a mystic, more Indian and less Western than I, despite the Oxford drawl. I liked to look at his hands with their long sensitive fingers. He was, I found, a very gentle person.

From Anand Bhawan, I went with Nan and her children to Mussoorie, from which we could visit Bhai in Dehra Dun Prison. Raja and I wrote to each other, and in August I decided to go again to Bombay. There I spent most of my time with Raja. We went to cinemas and for long drives in his car. We talked endlessly about books, about authors, about imperialism and socialism and communism; but never about anything personal. I knew he must like me but it rather irritated me that he would lecture me for three or four or five hours a day and never so much as try to hold my hand.

Then one morning I saw headlines in the paper that said my mother had been taken very ill with pleurisy and was in the hospital. I telephoned Raja breaking our date for that evening and telling him I was taking the night train to Allahabad. He was very understanding and sweet.

Just before my train was due to depart, Raja appeared in my compartment. Rather breathlessly he said, "The newspapers always exaggerate things; your mother can't be as sick as they say. Now if you will get off the train I can get a special license and we can get married in three days; and then you can go home."

Never in all the days we had been together had he said anything about marriage or even loving me. I was completely astounded; my mouth probably dropped open. Then I rallied myself. "I'm very sorry but I have to leave," I said rather sharply. "And I do not want to get married by any special license. My brother is in prison and I want to have his consent and my mother's."

So he jumped off, and the train went on. But I knew I was going to marry Raja.

When I reached Allahabad I found that Mother was very ill indeed, and had been taken to Lucknow for treatment. She was so sick that the government released Bhai a little ahead of time from prison, and we all met in Lucknow. For days we could think of nothing but Mother's illness. Then, as she began to get better, I thought of Raja again.

Nan was the first person I told. Knowing Raja she was very sympathetic and promised to prepare Bhai for the news. Then Bhai sent for me in a rather paternalistic fashion—after all, he was the head of the house—and cross-examined me.

"I hear you are contemplating marriage, my little Beti," he said. "What do you know about the young man?"

"Nothing at all," I answered.

"What does he do?"

"He is a barrister, just starting to practice."

"What are his people like?"

"I haven't the faintest idea."

Bhai was getting cross, but he kept his temper yet a while. "Has he any brothers and sisters?"

Again I looked blank, and felt like kicking myself for not having asked Raja a few obvious questions.

"I understand he went to Oxford," my brother said with a great show of patience. "What college?"

"I don't know," I said.

"You call him Raja, but his initials are G. P. What's his real name?"

Terrified, I whispered, "I don't know."

Absolutely livid Bhai said, "This is preposterous!" And stalked out of the room.

I had to agree that it was indeed preposterous. Feeling very sad and stupid I wrote to Raja asking for the vital statistics. He sent me a huffy reply couched as a dossier:

MY CREDENTIALS

Name:	Gunottam Hutheesing
School:	National School and Gujarat Vidyapith
College:	St. Catherines, Oxford.
Inns at Court:	Lincolns
Degree:	B. A. in Politics, Economics and Philosophy.
Clubs:	None
Profession:	Barrister at Law.... May enter politics.
Hobby:	Armchair lounging with pipe. Indulge in the habit of thinking—quite uncommon with most people.
Games:	Played cricket years ago—do not play anything now.
Character:	Am considered conceited and selfish.
Views on Marriage:	Believe in giving complete freedom to anyone who has any and wishes to preserve it.
References:	None.
Future prospects of a brilliant career:	None.
Financial responsibility:	Tolerable. Can afford to live in moderate comfort. Certainly not in great affluence.
FINALLY:	This is an application—a presumptuous one, maybe—to ask Miss Krishna Nehru to agree to be married to the above person in October, 1933.

This document amused me because I knew how annoyed its author must be. Poor Raja had worse to come. Bhai hurried off to Bombay to look him over and then conferred with Gandhiji. The Mahatma knew Raja's family but wanted to look him over, too, so he sent for Raja and put him through a rigorous examination. He must have passed, for Bhai invited him to Lucknow to meet Mother.

This was a delicate business, for Raja was a Jain. This ancient sect was founded in about 500 B.C. by a teacher named Mahavira. The Jains do not believe that the universe was created by a personal god but that it grew according to natural law. However, through the centuries they came to worship their founder as a god, as well as some twenty-four saints; and, like all religions, Jainism became encrusted with strange shibboleths, rituals and dietary laws. They are passionate advocates of non-violence.

Dear orthodox Mother had always hoped I would marry a Kashmiri Brahman. Liberal as she had learned to be in politics, the thought of her daughter marrying a man who not only was not Kashmiri, but not even a Brahman, upset her greatly, so their meeting in a narrow white hospital room in Lucknow was in the nature of a confrontation.

Raja had led an extraordinarily sheltered life, almost unacquainted with suffering. He could not stand pain of any sort: he could neither stand it himself, nor look on others who were suffering. When he saw my mother, still very beautiful, lying in a big hospital bed with the sadness of the sick in her expression, his large brown eyes grew moist with compassion. Always soft-spoken, his voice and attitude were so gentle that Mother loved him immediately.

When after a few moments he left the room, Mother said to me, "You know you are going to marry a saint."

"How did you find that out in fifteen minutes?" I asked briskly.

"Well, you've got a bad temper," Mother said, "and you don't show any feeling for people who are suffering. But look at how he reacted."

It was quite true. We were used to Mother being delicate, but Raja, who had not expected to see anyone so ill, had been obviously quite undone.

Naturally, Mother gave her consent.

Fortunately my marriage took place during one of the lulls in India's struggle for freedom. Gandhiji had once again called off *Satyagraha,* and the British were letting people out of prison instead of putting more in. So my family was together again.

The person who was most delighted with my engagement was Kamala. She liked Raja the very first time she met him. She had always loved me dearly, more as a daughter than as a sister-in-law, and I think she had almost given up hope of my ever marrying, because I had refused so many offers; so she was thrilled that I had, at last, chosen someone whom she and all the family liked.

Though she was far from well that autumn of 1933, Kamala took enormous pains with my trousseau, and saw to all the details of the wedding. The one thing that upset her was that our family had very little money left. Nearly all her jewelry, and Mother's, too, had been sold; there was not much left for me. But still she gave me part of what little jewelry she still had; and Mother gave me a little of hers. It was Kamala more than anyone else who made my wedding a gay and happy occasion.

I was married at Anand Bhawan on October 20, 1933, at nine o'clock in the morning by civil registration because, since I was a Brahman and Raja a Jain, no Hindu ceremony would have been legal at that time; also, Mother was still very weak and could not endure a prolonged ceremony. Kamala always hoped that we could have a religious rite later, but we never did.

I was more annoyed by the fact that I had to wear khadi, but it was not the type of khadi I had when the Movement began. I wore a peach-colored sari made of gossamer-fine, hand-spun cotton with a broad gold border, and I wore a little jewelry. I had wanted to be married in my father's bedroom, but nobody would agree to that, so the big sitting room was decorated with bright flowers and ribbons, and ashoka leaves were hung on the doorway through which I entered, because that tree is supposed to be very auspicious.

When Bhai came upstairs to take me down, he thought I did not look much like a bride, for I had no pearls in my hair, or the other jewels that are usually worn. He took a rose from a vase and stuck it in my jet-black hair and said, "Well, now you look better." Then he took me downstairs.

116

Raja was waiting there in his Indian clothes, a fitted sherwani over a *dhoti* with a Gandhi cap. I don't like that costume at all, but I must say he looked very elegant in it. Mother was reclining on a chaise longue; the others were standing. Raja and I said the usual things that are said at a civil marriage and signed the book. It was very different from my brother's and sister's marriages; but life was very different. Nan had a hundred and one saris in her trousseau; I had thirteen. She had diamonds, emeralds and pearls in matched sets of necklaces, rings, bangles and earrings: I had the scraps that my mother and Kamala's kindness found for me. There were no sacred fire and chanting priests. But they were not needed, for as things turned out it was a good marriage.

Raja's mother was too ill to come from Ahmedabad, but his brothers, Surottam and Shanti came, and some other relatives, among them his uncle, Kasturbhai Lalbhai, a leading industrialist, who was very fond of Raja.

A strange thing happened at the wedding. We signed the documents and shook hands with the registrar. Then my brother put his arms around my husband and me. Suddenly Raja was missing. I looked around and saw him bent double touching his uncle's feet. Then he tugged at my sari wanting me to do so, too. I had told him I would not, but with all his relatives' eyes on me, I gave in, and very awkwardly and abruptly touched his uncle's feet. Raja brought up his brothers and sister and I had to do it again and again. By that time I was getting mad so, though it is not our custom, I made Raja touch the feet of my entire family, beginning with my mother who was still lying on the chaise longue, and Bibi Amma. He took it for granted and did it naturally and gracefully.

Bhai told the Hutheesings that they were invited for lunch, and there would only be members of our family. Their faces were a study when they found there were a hundred and fifty of us.

After lunch Raja and I went to the house Bhai had taken for the Hutheesings in Allahabad. There was more foot-touching and when it came time for our traditional return to my family home, the Hutheesings loaded me with jewels, more even than Nan had, until I looked like an overdecorated Christmas tree. I arrived at Anand Bhawan, glittering and rather elated.

Bhai was waiting on the porch. As Raja and I got out of the car, he put his arms around me and kissed me. Then he held me off, looked me up and down, and said, "Darling, you look awful. Take off all those dreadful diamonds and things."

Feeling very unhappy I said, "But I've never had any and I rather like them."

"That is not the point," Bhai said sternly. "They're too ostentatious; just take them off. We don't do that sort of thing." Perhaps he had forgotten his own wedding and radiant Kamala as she left the Nehru Wedding Camp.

"At least let Mother see them," I begged. "They might make her feel happier."

Bhai consented, and I went up to Mother's room where there was still a trained nurse on duty. Though she was still so ill, she looked me over minutely, mentally appraising everything, as Indian women do. Then she smiled and said, "Darling, I am glad you have not married somebody who is dreadfully poor."

I said, "I really don't know what he is." And at that time I did not, though I had never seen so many diamonds and pearls and emeralds. In any case my brother made me take most of them off as soon as I came downstairs. In their place he hung garlands of yarn which Gandhiji had spun and sent to Raja and me. We had dinner with the immediate family and then I went back to Raja's temporary home.

A day or two later we went by train to Ahmedabad. Throughout the journey Raja kept telling me rather nervously how very orthodox his family was, until he made me nervous, too. We arrived at five o'clock in the morning and drove to an enormous, old-fashioned Indian house with curlicues and minarets and dozens of windows with every light blazing. Raja took me upstairs and I saw his mother lying in bed, as my mother had been, although she looked ever so much larger under the bedclothes. But she had a very gentle face and was in great pain.

She was, I found, a most remarkable woman—whatever Raja's family has today is entirely due to her achievements. His artistic, brilliant father died young leaving absolutely nothing. At the age of thirty-two, Raja's mother found herself with six children to support, and not even sure of their next meal. She went around to all her relatives and friends of the family borrowing money. Though they thought they would never see it again they let her have it. She set up four looms in the big backyard of her house and went into the textile business. She was told she could not succeed unless she learned English, so she learned English, while bringing up six children and managing the looms. She had no knowledge of business, but she had the gift or talent or common sense, or whatever it is that succeeds in business. The four looms grew into a small factory, which in turn grew great. She paid off her astonished creditors and was able to send her second son to the London School of Economics, and when Raja was ready, she sent him to Oxford and the Sorbonne and Heidelberg, and the Inns of Court.

My mother-in-law was a very strong-willed woman. I soon found out that we had many things in common. She was very difficult and I was, too. We had lots of arguments, and in all the years—she lived until 1961—she would never take a meal in our flat in Bombay because we were meat-eaters; though she would have a cup of tea. But we grew to love one another, and when she was dying she kept asking for me, even if I left the room for a few minutes, even though her own children were there to take care of her.

The Hutheesings were indeed a very orthodox, pious family. They even have their own temple which Raja's grandfather had built. It was big and very beautiful with much lacy stonework, and delicate spires; and from its building the family got its surname. (Many Indians did not have last names until the mid-nineteenth century.) The story goes that my husband's grandfather owned some land which the British used as a polo field. One day he said, "You can't use this field any longer. I am going to build a temple on it."

"You must not do that," they protested. "Where will we play polo?"

"You must find some other place. This is my land and I want to use it."

He started building, and each night the British would come and knock down whatever the workmen had done by day—all day the workmen built and all night the British broke it up. Finally the old man got really angry. He hired the men to work night and day and build a wall so high and strong that it could not be knocked down. Then even the British Resident (governor) gave up. Using the Gujurati, which he knew well, the Resident said to Raja's grandfather, "I shall call you 'Huth-ee-singh' because you are like a stubborn lion." The old gentleman liked that, and took it as his family name.

The most difficult thing about my first visit to Ahmedabad was the food. My brother had warned me, "Do you think you can put up with their food?"

"What's food!" I said gaily. "I'm in love."

The orthodox Jains are strict vegetarians; nor do they spice their food as much as we do; the vegetables seemed tasteless to me. I was used to bacon and eggs, toast, marmalade and coffee for breakfast, and could not stomach tea and a lot of Indian sweets at that hour. In addition, the Jains never eat after sundown, which meant they had dinner about five o'clock in winter; we Nehrus never dined until nine. In that first six weeks I was near starvation. Once I sent the servant I had brought with me from home out with orders to get me some eggs and smuggle them into the house for me. He walked the streets all day and could not find a single egg in that city of Jains and Buddhists. I weighed ninety-eight pounds when I married Raja; and when he finally took me home to Anand Bhawan I weighed eighty-two.

I spent most of those six weeks in Ahmedabad, all dressed up in gold-bordered saris and covered with jewels, receiving the Hutheesings' friends who came to look Raja's bride over. As I was finally leaving I got another shock. My mother-in-law said, "Which of the jewels do you want to take with you?"

"Just those you gave me, that I wore at my wedding," I said.

She looked aghast and said, "But they do not belong to you."

"Why don't they? You gave them to me and I have been wearing them all this time."

"Because they belong to the family and, in a joint Hindu family we share everything."

Then she and Raja explained that in that old-fashioned kind of joint family everything they had was owned in common: the factory, the house, the investments, the jewels, everything belonged in the common pot. "But you can borrow the jewels any time you want to," my mother-in-law said.

"If they're not mine I don't want them at all," I answered.

So I did not have any big jewels, because I could not bring myself to wear something that was not really mine. When I did get a few jewels of my own, I chose sapphires. Few Indian women will wear them because they are considered unlucky. But I love them and they are lucky for me; I never feel quite right unless I am wearing a sapphire.

Among the beautiful letters I received on my marriage the one I treasured most was from Gandhiji who also sent two garlands of yarn he had spun himself to be hung around the necks of Raja and myself. The letter said:

My dear Krishna:

You are now going to be reborn, for marriage is a sort of rebirth, is it not? Your sister, Swarup . . . persuaded her husband to go and settle down in her old province, but there is a great deal of difference between Swarup and you, and I do not think you will try to take Raja away. Besides, Raja is a Gujurati who will not easily leave his homeland. So I hope you will make Gujurat your home, or maybe Bombay. My only wish is that wherever you are you may be happy and add lustre to the already bright name of your illustrious parents.

I regret very much I am unable to attend your marriage, so I shall have to content myself with sending you my blessing.

Your BAPU

Everyone seemed worried that I would drag Raja away from his homeland to live in my northern country. Vallabhbhai Patel even wrote me from Nasik Prison cautioning me against doing so. How strong-minded and willful they must have thought me! I had no intention of doing anything of the kind.

Raja and I began our married life in Bombay where he practiced law before the High Court. Fortunately our first years were passed during a comparatively peaceful time. Gandhiji had called off mass civil disobedience and inaugurated what he called Individual *Satyagraha,* which meant that selected leaders would refuse to obey the laws. Naturally, my brother was one of the first of these—he was violently opposed to discontinuing mass civil disobedience—and he landed in jail again in February 1934. Gandhiji himself had temporarily lost interest in *Swaraj* and was devoting all his heart and soul to his work for the Untouchables. Without his inspired leadership and with Bhai in prison, the Movement lost momentum and almost sputtered out.

After being in jail in Calcutta, where the climate plus his confinement made him lose weight and become quite ill, Bhai was sent again to Dehra Dun. On a cold and somber day Raja and I went there with Kamala to see him. Not yet recovered, he looked terribly thin and careworn. Kamala and I were much upset, but the effect on Raja was far worse. He had never been to a prison before and the sight of Jawahar looking so pale and sad in his drab little cell, with a cot, a few books, and a spinning wheel in one corner, completely unnerved him. When we returned to our hotel, Raja went straight to his room and lay on his bed for hours staring at the ceiling in unseeing misery.

Soon after this visit, Kamala's disease flared up again. All through this period she had ups and downs, slight improvements that brought hope to us all, followed each time by a worse relapse. For a few days she was so ill that Bhai was temporarily released from prison to be with her. When she recovered somewhat, he was sent to Naini Prison close at hand. Then her doctors ordered her to Bhowali in the hills, and the authorities thoughtfully transferred Bhai to Almora Prison where he was allowed out occasionally to visit her in her room at the sanitarium. Indu was also in Bhowali, having left school to be with her mother.

Meanwhile, after living with Raja's family in their house in Bombay for several months, we took a little flat of our own on Warden Road. I loved it, and we were very happy there. I was expecting my first child, who was born on February 1, 1935. He was the first boy, who lived, in our immediate family since the birth of my brother forty-five years before. Naturally there were great rejoicings. My brother sent me a telegram from Almora Prison: CHEERIO GET WELL SOON AND BRING THE HOWLING INFANT HERE FOR DISPLAY AND CRITICISM LOVE JAWAHAR.

Kamala wrote ecstatically from her sanitarium and added, "Bring him here for me to see."

I named him Harsha, which means "joy," and is also the name of an ancient king of Kanauji; and as soon as he was old enough to travel—my friends said it was much too soon—I took him to Bhowali to show him to Bhai and to Kamala. So he had his first glimpse of a prison at the age of six weeks, which is rather early even for a Nehru.

When I brought Harsha into the room in the sanitarium where Kamala was lying in her bed, she instinctively stretched out her arms to take the baby, who was big and fat and healthy. Then suddenly she drew back. With tears in her eyes she said, "No. I don't want him to catch my disease."

This aroused such a storm of love and sorrow in my heart that I wanted to just fling him into her arms, and I said, "Oh, I couldn't care less!"

But she refused to touch him, and lay there beaming and smiling all the time in her joy for me and delight in my son.

That was the only time she ever saw him; for soon afterward the doctors ordered her to go to Badenweiler in the Black Forest in Germany. And we did not see her again.

Kamala died in Lausanne on February 28, 1936. Indira, who had accompanied her to Europe, was with her, and so was Bhai, who had been released from prison on September 4, 1935, when the government learned that Kamala was dying. Three days later my second son, Ajit, was born in Bombay; but all the joy he might have brought me was drowned in my sorrow.

Bhai was truly bereft. He blamed himself that his preoccupation with India's struggle for freedom had kept them so much apart and robbed Kamala of years of happiness they might have shared. Not that Kamala ever expressed such a thought; she was as dedicated to *Swaraj* as he. It was the price that leaders of men and those who love them must pay, and she would not have had it otherwise. But to Bhai, in his sorrow and loneliness, it seemed too high a price.

He had Kamala cremated in Europe and brought her ashes home with him. Though Indu would have been a great comfort to him, he unselfishly decided not to embroil her yet in the bitter struggle that he knew would engulf him again on his return to India, for in his absence he had been elected president of the Congress for the second time. So he took her to England, where he put her in the Badminton School in Bristol, and came home alone.

12
the coming
of war

Bhai was President of the Congress in 1936 and again in 1937, a somewhat unusual thing. Those were stormy sessions, less on account of British interference than because of a sharp division of opinion between the Indian leaders. The Simon Commission and the Round Table Conferences which had labored so mightily had at last brought forth a mouse in the form of the Government of India Act of 1935. This provided a federated central Government of India, which Bhai called "A fantastic affair . . . [it] tied up feudal and autocratic states [governed by maharajas] with semi-democratic provinces, and was intended to perpetuate the British imperialistic structure." In fact it was so ridiculous that it was never put into effect.

However, the Act did give the provincial legislatures a certain degree of responsible government. The usual safeguards, or dictatorial powers, were reserved to the provincial governors, but it was agreed that they would only be used in cases of dire emergency. My brother characterized the Act as "a new charter of slavery." He firmly believed that only a duly elected Indian constituent assembly should frame a constitution for India. He worked for this throughout all the years, steadfastly refusing to accept any constitution that bore the label "Made in England."

Bhai's presidential speech to the forty-ninth session of the Congress at Lucknow in April 1936 was a strong plea for socialism as the hope of the future for India—a position with which a majority of its members disagreed. He then reviewed the darkening international situation with fascism triumphant in Germany and Italy, and Mussolini's legions conquering Ethiopia, while Japan waged war in Manchuria and northern China. Finally, he denounced the new Government of India Act, but recommended that Congress candidates run for office in the elections to be held under the Act early in 1937. However, he ended with an impassioned plea that, if elected, the Congress candidates refuse to accept office. His stern creed allowed no compromise and no co-operation with our alien rulers.

Though they had elected my brother their president—and even re-elected him for the next session—the majority of the Congress were opposed to his no-office plan. They wanted Congress candidates to run and form provincial governments if elected. Bhai fought this motion bitterly in the Congress and in the Working Committee, and often thought of resigning because of the bickering and dissension between the different factions. He wrote: "A sense of suppression and frustration grew, and I became a solitary figure in public life, though vast crowds came to hear me and enthusiasm surrounded me." It was at this time that he received a letter signed by conservative members of the Working Committee like Rajendra Prasad, Rajagopalachari, Vallabhbhai Patel and J. B. Kripalani, threatening to resign if he continued his support of the Socialist Left. Gandhiji intervened to straighten things out and Bhai loyally campaigned throughout India for Congress candidates, though he refused to run for office himself.

In that campaign, he rushed up and down our land from the northern frontiers to the southern seas, buoyed up by excitement and the enormous enthusiasm of the people, in a feat of endurance that surprised even him. He took microphones, amplifiers and generators with him and addressed a dozen or more meetings a day, from a few score people in the villages, to crowds of a hundred thousand or more in the great cities. In all he reckoned that he traveled 45,000 miles, spoke to 10,000,000 people and greeted several million more in passage.

This tremendous activity was a wonderfully good thing for Bhai, taking his mind off the loss of Kamala and giving him new knowledge and insights into our huge country and its tremendous variety of people. He called it "a voyage of discovery."

The result of the election was a triumph for the Congress candidates who won majorities in seven out of eleven provinces. Then came another great row in the Congress as to whether the successful candidates should accept office and form provincial governments. Bhai was against it as before, and again he was overruled. The Congress people agreed to form provincial governments on the understanding that there would be no interference from the Viceroy or the provincial governors. Later, two governors did try to exercise their "reserve powers." The elected ministries threatened to resign, and the governors backed down.

My sister also played a great part in the campaign. She was now well known in Indian politics by the name of Vijaya Lakshmi Pandit and had served as Chairman of the Municipal Council of Allahabad. I have forgotten to mention that when a Hindu bride comes to her new family she is given a new name. For example, Raja's people called me Manjari which means orange-blossom. The name is highly unsuitable to my character, so I stuck to Krishna. However, my sister did not like her own name, Swarup, and thought it most suitable when the Pandits called her Vijaya Lakshmi which means Goddess of Victory.

Victorious she was in the election and was made Minister of Local Self Government and Public Health in the new government of the United Provinces, or Uttar Pradesh as we call it now. She thus became the first woman minister ever to hold office in India, and the second in the whole British Empire.* She and Ranjit, who had also been elected to the provincial legislature, moved to the capital of the United Provinces, Lucknow, where we had been imprisoned so long. It was quite a switch from our former barracks to the big office of a minister of state, which Nan redecorated with her usual good taste.

When my brother's second successive term as president of the Congress ended in 1937, he had no desire for another. In fact, with his delicious sense of humor, he wrote an anonymous article for the *Modern Review* in which he pointed out the dangers of giving Jawaharlal Nehru too much power. It ended with the words, "Let us not spoil Jawaharlal by too much adulation and praise. His conceit is already formidable. It must be checked. We want no Caesars!"

* Margaret Bondfield, Minister of Labor in Ramsay Macdonald's government, was the first.

He signed the article "Chanakya" and no one but Indira knew he had written it.

After retiring from the presidency, Bhai took a somewhat less active part in politics. He badly needed a rest and went on a trip to Burma and Malaya but, as he remarked, it was no vacation. Tremendous crowds greeted him everywhere and there were innumerable luncheons, dinners and meetings he was forced to attend. However, like all his journeys, this one gave an insight into the condition and thinking of the peoples of other countries that was immensely valuable in the years ahead.

Early in 1938 we were, for a wonder, all together again at Anand Bhawan. Bhai settled in, temporarily forgoing his restless journeying about the land. Nan came with her three girls from Lucknow. I brought my sons from Bombay. Only Indu was away at her school in England. Mother, who had been very ill after suffering two strokes, one in 1935 and another in 1936, seemed stronger and quite gay, perhaps because of the unusual circumstances of not grieving over one or another of us suffering in prison.

One evening we had a very merry dinner and sat around afterward chatting. Nan was taking a night train to Lucknow so Mother decided to remain up until she left. At about eleven o'clock it was time for Nan to go. Mother moved forward to kiss her, but suddenly crumpled. Bhai, with his cat-quickness, caught her before she fell, and we carried her to her bed; she was unconscious before we laid her gently on it.

The hastily summoned doctor told us that Mother had suffered a massive stroke and had only a few hours to live. Stunned by the suddenness of it, we sat beside her bed with Bibi Amma all through the night, listening to her labored breathing, hoping she would regain consciousness if only for a moment to say good-by. About five o'clock in the morning she seemed to fall into a quiet sleep. Bhai, bending over her, whispered, "She has gone."

I went to break the news to Bibi Amma, who had gone to her room to pray. At first she could not seem to believe that the little sister whom she had brought up and always thought of as her child could die before she did. When she finally understood, unlike most Indian women of her time who beat their breasts and cry aloud, she became stony-eyed. Calmly she told us how to make all the arrangements for the funeral and saw to everything. We covered Mother with gay flowers. How terribly tiny she looked, but how beautiful with her wrinkles smoothed away by the gentle hand of death.

Tens of thousands of people gathered around our home at the news of Mother's death. Bibi Amma and Nan and I did not go to the cremation for we could not bear to watch it. While Bhai and all the servants went down with her to the sacred rivers we three stood on the portico with a host of relatives watching the cortege pass through the gates. Then Bibi Amma went into the big empty house and stood in the doorway of Mother's room looking sadly at all the familiar things. Putting my arms around her I said, "Bibi Amma, please go and lie down for a little while."

She looked at me and said, "Go have a bath, dear."

Instead I begged her to have some tea. She said, "No, no"; but I made some anyhow, and then went upstairs for a quick bath. When I came downstairs and looked for her, I found her lying on the carpeted floor beside Mother's bed with her eyes closed. Kneeling beside her I said, "Darling Bibi Amma, won't you have some tea? Perhaps it will help."

She did not answer and a little frightened, I said, "Bibi Amma, you have always been a mother to all of us, and now we have only you. We need you desperately."

She opened her eyes and put her arms around me saying, " I have always loved you like a daughter, Beti, but you have only one mother. I can never take her place. I lived only for your mother and now my task is done. I, too, must go."

For a while I sat beside her stroking her hair until she seemed to fall asleep. Then I left the room, but kept going back, for I was uneasy. Each time Bibi Amma was still sleeping, but so deeply that finally I was frightened and, since Bhai had not yet returned I called Nan. She was worried, too, and we sent for the doctor. He said that Bibi Amma had suffered a stroke just as Mother had. Again we watched all through the night and at five o'clock the next morning, exactly twenty-four hours after Mother's death, Bibi Amma left us too.

After Mother's death, Bhai was more restless than ever. Nan was in Lucknow, I was with Raja and the children in Bombay, and Bhai hated to come home alone to Anand Bhawan. He said that he felt like a stranger, a guest in his own house. He wrote to me:

Nan, especially since she has become a minister, has also got more and more wrapped up in her work, although, of course, she is not quite as much of a political animal as I am. Political problems and difficulties fill my mind, and to a certain extent Nan's.... Perhaps this makes you feel that you are neglected and pains you. But surely you do not think that this makes any difference to our attachments and affections?

We are an abnormal family, or rather force of circumstance has forced us to lead abnormal lives, and the emphasis of these lives is more and more cherished, though it is hidden from the public gaze. You must remember that Anand Bhawan is your own home and those who live there love you dearly and would gladly do anything for you....

Then he invited me to go to Europe with him that summer (which I was unable to do to my great regret) and added:

Raja and I will go to Lucknow tomorrow night probably for three days, returning to Allahabad on or about the twenty-seventh [of April]. Then four or five days at Allahabad. After that we might go to Srinagar in Garhwal. This will take a week there and back. On the tenth night I leave Allahabad for the Working Committee meeting which might be held in Wardha [where Gandhiji's ashram was now located] or Bombay. Not settled yet.

Love

Your loving brother

JAWAHAR

As can be seen from this letter my husband had virtually given up his practice in Bombay to assist my brother in his work. Bhai was far from happy with the way things were going in the Congress and in India. Communal troubles were increasing with bloody rioting in many cities, including Allahabad, and the widening split between Muslims and Hindus caused him great distress. It was about this time that M. A. Jinnah, the coldly elegant leader of the Muslim

129

League, with his London clothes and his monocle, first began to speak of the Muslims as a separate nation within India, and tentatively mentioned the idea of a new Muslim state—Pakistan.

Within the Congress there were also increasing tensions. Subhas Bose was elected President. He was a dynamic advocate of violence who once said, "Give me blood and I will give you freedom"—the exact opposite of Gandhiji's beliefs. To dramatize his common origins he rode to the opening of the Congress in Haripura in a country cart with huge wooden wheels drawn by fifty-one oxen. The Conservatives, led by Vallabhbhai Patel and the Congress provincial ministers, swung as far in the other direction in co-operation with the British. "We are sinking to the level of ordinary politicians," Bhai wrote to Gandhiji. My brother, caught between the factions, made a wise move in going abroad "to freshen up my tired and puzzled mind."

In Europe, in 1938, there was little refreshment for an idealist like Bhai. Fascism and naziism were everywhere on the march, and the forces of freedom and democracy were falling apart for lack of dynamic leadership. After pausing in Egypt for talks with Wafdist leaders, Bhai went to Barcelona at the invitation of the Republican Spanish Government and witnessed their losing struggle against General Francisco Franco's Fascist rebellion. The Nazi government invited him to go to Germany, either officially or incognito, in the ridiculous hope of converting him; he declined with thanks. In England, at a party given for him by Lord Lothian, he talked with members of Prime Minister Neville Chamberlain's Cabinet as well as with Lady Astor and (aptly named) General Ironside, Chief of the Imperial General Staff, and found them tired and frightened, half-convinced that naziism was "the wave of the future."

Bhai met Indira in London and took her with him to Munich, where they were "oppressed by the Hitlerian atmosphere," and on to Czechoslovakia where Bhai watched the Allied statesmen playing "the difficult and intricate game of how to betray your friends . . . on the highest moral grounds"; and to Geneva where the marble palace of the League of Nations reminded him of "archeological remains with the dead bodies of hundreds of international organizations . . . lying about."

Bhai was in Geneva, Paris and London throughout the Czecho-slovakian crisis and Chamberlain's abject appeasement of Hitler at Munich. He described himself as "nauseated" by the weakness of the British and French statesmen and their fear of Hitler, which he shrewdly observed was combined with "a sneaking admiration for him."

Bhai, bringing Indira with him, returned to India in November 1938, thoroughly disillusioned and more convinced than ever that imperialism and fascism were but two sides of the same coin. However, he realized that complete victory for the totalitarian states would be the beginning of a new dark age for mankind, and so supported the cause of England and France, although unwillingly.

In this he came into direct conflict with his former ally Subhas Bose, who was running again for president of the Congress. Bose was strongly sympathetic to the totalitarian states and Japan, with which he had close contacts. He believed that if they were victorious in the war which everyone saw was inevitable, India would gain her independence. Bhai, much more aware of the situation in Europe, realized that it would only lead to a new and worse enslavement. He and Gandhiji opposed Bose in the bitterly contested Congress election early in 1939. In spite of this, Bose was re-elected president of the Congress. However, Gandhiji had not lost his enormous influence over the people of India; and his opposition to Bose's policies, together with that of my brother and a majority of the Working Committee, forced Bose to resign the presidency in April, 1939. Bitter and violent, Bose formed a new radical party called "the Forward Block" —which, however, soon petered out.

In July 1939, Bhai again invited me to go on a trip with him, this time to Ceylon. I was delighted that I was able to get away from domesticity and the children long enough to go—I had always wanted to visit Ceylon. In a tiny chartered plane we took off from the airport at Poona into a sullen misty sky that made me wonder if the pilot could find his way. However, we landed at Hyderabad in full sunshine and had a gay luncheon with Sarojini Naidu. Then we flew on via Madras and Trichinopoly, where we spent the night. The next morning we flew over the Gulf of Bengal whose waste of waters made our little plane seem small as a gnat. The green peaks of Ceylon coming up out of the sea were a welcome sight to me.

As we looked down on Mount Lavinia Airfield at Colombo we saw a great crowd, whose multicolored clothes made patterns like a kaleidoscope. Our pilot swooped and banked over the field in joyful abandon. When we landed the crowd rushed up, almost engulfing us in their eagerness to greet Bhai. The warmth of their welcome was a revelation to me, and a source of great satisfaction to Bhai who had come on a semiofficial mission to try to ease tensions that had arisen between the Singhalese and the Indians residing in Ceylon.

I loved Ceylon, from its tropical coastal jungles to the cool heights of Kandy with its superb Botanical Gardens; and my pleasure was intensified because once again, as in Europe long ago, Bhai was my fascinating companion and guide. No matter how busy his schedule he always found time for a little sightseeing. Going through the lovely old temples with him was a delight because of his appreciation of their beauty and his knowledge, kept somewhere in the vast store-house of his mind, of their history.

Naturally, we had all too little opportunity for such excursions. Much of the time was spent driving through the steaming heat and the swift, violent storms of the monsoon so that Bhai could address the workers on the rubber and tea plantations, who turned out in thousands to hear him. They were mostly Tamil laborers, men and women, who you would not suppose had heard much about Jawaharlal Nehru. But they had, for they lined all the roads along which we passed waiting patiently for hours in the heat for a glimpse of him. Sometimes, seeing Bhai so worn out at the end of the day and pretty exhausted myself, I wondered if it was all worth-while; but when I saw the glow in their faces and the hope in their eyes as they looked at the man who was leading their country to freedom, I knew it was.

Our weariness was not helped by the lavish hospitality of our island hosts. Singhalese and Indians vied with each other in friendly rivalry to entertain us, and nearly killed us in the process. At the parties I noticed that after the first greeting the men would all get together with Bhai leaving the women alone with each other. I did not like this for it implied that women were not worth talking to, and, in India, since our fight for freedom beside our men, this was not done. Yet the Singhalese must have got bravely over it for the only woman prime minister before Indira was Madame Bandaranaike of Ceylon.

At one of the parties I had the fun of encountering Bernhard Aluvihari, who had paid my fine the first time I was arrested in Allahabad. In fact, I had so much fun in Ceylon that I stayed on for a week after Bhai left.

The Singhalese were so kind and polite to my brother, and apparently were so friendly to the Indians while he was there, that he left feeling that his mission was truly accomplished. But he had not counted on the courtesy and sweetness of the Singhalese which makes them say what you want to hear when you are with them, and the moment you leave, turn around and do just the opposite. That is what happened. A few weeks later the government of Ceylon abruptly dismissed eight hundred Indian employees leaving them on their uppers, and, with that, relations between the Singhalese and the Indian laborers became even worse than before.

In spite of this, my brother always loved Ceylon and its charming people, and believed that India and Ceylon should develop the closest ties. His hope for the future was a great Asian federation which would consist of India, China, Ceylon, Burma, Afghanistan, and possibly other countries. This dream was finally shattered by Red China's unprovoked attack on India in 1962.

No sooner was he home again in Anand Bhawan than Bhai set off for China at the invitation of Chiang Kai-shek. I took Raja and the children to Allahabad to see him off on what was, after all, a rather perilous journey. Japan had conquered the greater part of China and Chiang was holding out in Chungking against greatly superior forces, with little help from the great democracies.

My brother spent two weeks in that beseiged capital. It suffered daily air raids, against which the Chinese had only the most primitive defenses. Thus he met Chiang and the beautiful, courageous, and extremely difficult Madame Chiang during their most heroic hour. He was filled with admiration for them and the Chinese people who could take Japanese bombs as a matter of routine, simply scurrying into their caves in the hillside as the sirens shrilly sounded and cheerfully coming out again to resume their daily tasks at the all-clear. He referred to Chiang Kai-shek as "that great man who has become the symbol of China's unity and her determination to be free."

Thus, another disillusionment awaited Bhai as the very qualities of pride, courage, arrogance and inflexible determination which had made Chiang a great wartime leader, turned him in peacetime into a Right-Wing dictator.

Bhai had planned to spend at least a month in China; but two weeks after he reached Chungking, the fragile tissue of European peace was torn apart as Hitler's panzer armies crashed across the Polish frontier and World War II began.

The Viceroy of India, Lord Linlithgow, who had succeeded Lord Willingdon, was a more liberal and imaginative man than his predecessor, but he was the servant of Chamberlain's ultraconservative government. Without so much as a courtesy consultation with any Indian statesmen, he declared war against Germany on behalf of India on the same day England did. It was an exceedingly stupid thing to do, for a majority of Indian leaders, including my brother, understood the danger of a totalitarian victory, and, had they been consulted, would almost undoubtedly have agreed to support the Allied cause. As it was they viewed the Viceroy's action as one more evidence of British imperialism. To make matters worse, an amendment to the Government of India Act of 1935, giving the Viceroy dictatorial powers, was rushed through the British Parliament in eleven minutes.

Bhai, hurrying home from China, was confronted by this situation. Still he had no sympathy for those who, like Subhas Bose, hoped for a Nazi victory, or even for those who wanted to use England's necessity as an opportunity to force concessions. He expressed his philosophy in his first statement on the war: "Freedom is too precious to be bargained for, but it is too precious also to be ignored or put aside because the world has gone awry. . . . If we participate in the joint effort of freedom, that effort must be really joint, based on consent as between free equals. . . ."

Gandhiji also expressed his "sympathy for France and England" and said, "My whole heart is with the Poles in the unequal struggle in which they are engaged for the sake of freedom." However, he could not forsake his principle of non-violence, and, realizing that it was not shared by the majority of the Congress leaders who wanted actively to support the Allied war effort, he withdrew from any part in their deliberations. Trusting my brother's humanitarian ideals, Gandhiji wanted him to lead the Congress in formulating its policy toward the war; but Bhai was not president of the Congress. To get around this constitutional difficulty Gandhiji and the Working Committee created a War Committee of which Bhai was made president and given the power to name his colleagues. Meanwhile my brother had written the "Resolution on War," in which the Working Committee condemned the aggressors but demanded of the British government a full statement of their intentions in regard to independence for India and of their war aims, before the Congress could decide whether or not to co-operate in the war effort.

But India was not united behind the Congress. Many of the princes and the Muslim League gave their unqualified allegiance to England. Strengthened by this, the British government, through the Viceroy, gave Congress an evasive answer, promising only discussion on Dominion status for India after the war, and making no satisfactory declaration of their war aims. The Working Committee rejected this reply in a statement written by my brother, and announced that the Congress "cannot possibly give any support to Great Britain, for it would amount to an endorsement of the imperialist policy which the Congress has always sought to end." As a first step the Committee called upon the Congress ministries of the Provincial governments to tender their resignations. They all did.

However, the same statement warned all members of the Congress against violence or taking any action such as civil disobedience against the British government of India for the time being.

In July 1940, after the fall of France and the Nazi conquest of Norway, Denmark, Holland and Belgium, Congress made a fresh effort to reach an accord with the British by passing a resolution proposed by Rajagopalachari and concurred in by my brother. It proposed that if Great Britain gave India independence and a central Indian government, they would wage war as an ally of England. Gandhiji objected to this on the ground that India should not do any fighting and also on the ground that whatever support was given to England should be given unconditionally.

Winston Churchill, who had now become the great wartime Prime Minister of Britain, had no intention of granting India complete independence, then or ever. On his instructions, the Viceroy turned the Congress offer down in a long flowery statement which boiled down to a flat "No."

So my brother and the Congress came back to Gandhiji, who in a speech to the September 1940 meeting of the Congress in Bombay said, "I do not want England to be defeated or humiliated. It hurts me to find St. Paul's Cathedral damaged. . . ."* And he announced that he would go to see the Viceroy and say to him, "We do not want to embarrass you . . . in regard to the war effort. We go our way, you go yours. . . . But Congress must have the freedom to preach against helping in the war. . . ."

In that second meeting with Lord Linlithgow the Viceroy again said "No."

Under these circumstances Gandhiji felt that he must register a protest. At first he proposed another fast, but Mahadev Desai, horrified at this prospect, convinced him it would do no good. So Gandhiji; in order not to embarrass England's war effort by calling for complete civil disobedience, instituted Individual *Satyagraha*. He designated Vinoba Bhave as the first to go. Bhave made some antiwar speeches and was arrested. Then Gandhiji wrote to my brother, "If you are ready, you may now ceremonially declare your civil disobedience."

Bhai formally announced that he would begin *Satyagraha* on November 7, 1940. The government did not wait. On October 31 he was arrested, and on November 3, in Gorakhpur Prison, he was tried and condemned to four years' rigorous imprisonment. In December he wrote to me that he was back in Dehra Dun, quite literally cultivating his garden.

* Gandhiji burst into tears when he heard of the destruction of the House of Commons.

13
Indira

At Badminton School in 1936, a lonely young girl who had just lost her beautiful, adored young mother began the final stages of her checkered formal education. As I have indicated, the upbringing and education of the girl who was to become India's first woman prime minister violated every canon laid down by the experts on the education and rearing of children. First among their requirements is that a child must have a sense of love and security. Love Indu had, but no security. Her earliest memories were of policemen arriving in the middle of the night to take her beloved father and grandfather to prison, coming again to cart off cherished possessions from her home. Then she visited her loved ones in their prison cells—that is quite a shock even for an adult. One visitor to our home at this time remembers a grave-faced little girl saying politely to him, "I'm sorry, but my grandfather, father and Mummy are all in prison."

Even when the whole family was at Anand Bhawan the constant stream of visitors, the unending conferences in which there were usually disagreements and raised voices among the conferees, the constant sense of impending trouble, often realized in rioting with the vast screaming crowds and the *lathi* charges just beyond the gates of the compound, the frequent journeys to other cities for political conferences or tremendously emotional ceremonies like the openings of the Congress over which her grandfather or father presided: all these things were, to understate it, extremely unsettling for Indu.

In addition, Kamala's precarious health, her long absences in sanitariums—or in prison—piled anxiety on fear. Then there was the long stay in Switzerland in 1926–27, when Kamala was so ill, and Indira at nine years old had to face the strain of adjusting to completely foreign scenes and customs, and to a foreign school where she had to cope with an entirely different system of education carried on in an unfamiliar language. No wonder Indira was a strangely intense child—if child she ever was. The wonder is that she did cope successfully.

Early in 1928, on their return from Europe, Bhai and Kamala sent Indu to a convent school, but she had already seen too much of living to be content with a cloistered life; she hated it. Then her parents put her in The Pupils' Own School in Poona, a more modern establishment, run by a couple who made it more like a family home than a school. It was co-educational at a time when such a thing was almost unheard of in India. Indu got some formal education there, and it was one of the few places where she ever knew any serenity, although she did not seem to appreciate it. Perhaps she was bored by serenity after all the excitement she had lived through by the time she was ten.

When she came home for vacations, Bhai and Kamala were usually either out in the village exhorting peasants, or in jail or in a hospital, so I tried to take their place as best I could. Indu and I would sit in the lovely garden full of the scent of flowers and the song of birds, and I would read the classics with her as Nan had read with me.

Indira took her Senior Cambridge examination at the age of fifteen. We do not stick to grades and years in India as closely as they do in the States and England; when we are ready, we take the examination and go on. Bhai then sent Indu to the Tagore School at Santiniketan in Bengal. It was started by our famous poet, Rabindranath Tagore, who was a great friend of my father and brother, and who was a sort of poet-in-residence at the school, which was run by his son. It was a center for the study of Indian arts and culture rather than academic subjects. The girls and boys, who came from all parts of India, were supposed to be very arty and learn to paint or sculpt or dance or make music, or do *batik* work. They also had regular academic studies, but took them pretty casually in those days. This did not matter to Indu for, as I said, she had already passed her secondary-school examinations at Poona. On the other hand, the school was not particularly fascinating to her, as her talents lie in other fields than art. Bhai only sent her there because he thought the atmosphere would be good for her, and in any case she had to be alone because her father and mother again were either in prison or traveling the villages. It was just a way station on her road to education. However, she was popular in the school as is shown by this letter written by Tagore when she left to go with her mother to Badenweiler:

My dear Jawaharlal

It is with a heavy heart that we bade farewell to Indira, for she was such an asset in our place. I watched her very closely and have felt admiration for the way you brought her up. Her teachers all in one voice praise her and I know she is extremely popular with the students. I only hope things will turn for the better and she will soon return here. . . .

With my affectionate blessings

Yours

RABINDRANATH TAGORE

Badminton School put an English classical finish to Indira's education. She took her college examination—the London Metric—there. During her years in England, she naturally saw a good deal of Krishna Menon, and became quite fond of him. In spite of his waspish ways with many people, I think he was very kind to her. However, the vital element in Indira's early education was none of the schools she went to or even her later studies at Oxford University. It was the brilliant series of letters which her father wrote to her from various prisons giving in a simple but eloquent language a history of the whole world, as seen through his own idealistic philosophy. They were at once so wise and so comprehensive that they were later somewhat expanded and published as a book under the title of *Glimpses of World History*.* Every Indian schoolchild today reads that book as an introduction to the story of mankind.

In addition, when my brother was in Europe in 1938, he took Indu with him to Czechoslovakia, Munich, Geneva and Paris. This trip, made at the height of the Czechoslovakian crisis, and the opportunity it gave her to meet and talk with the statesmen who were so feebly trying to cope with it, was most educational, though surely not edifying. My brother's intimate talks with her and his explanation of the moves and countermoves in that sordid game of power politics

* (Allahabad, 1934–35; New York: The John Day Company, 1942.)

139

clarified her mind which otherwise must have been completely confused.

Indira came home with Bhai in November 1938, and stayed in India for five months. Because of her rather delicate health, my brother took a cottage for her at Almora high in the hills; and I took my two small sons, aged four and three, up there to keep her company. We were there from January until April, entirely cut off from the world by the deep snow that made it clean, silent and remote, in delightful contrast to the noisy, dusty cities we were accustomed to. It was a wonderful experience for my little sons, who had never seen snow before; and for me. Indira and I had time to read and think and talk of great books and the great men of our own country and all the world, and discuss their philosophies and their contributions to mankind. It was, I believe, as important a part of Indira's education as any of the schools and universities she attended, for it gave her perspective, and time to think things out for herself.

In April 1939, she went back to England to attend Oxford University. She was there only a year because she became quite ill with pleurisy. Knowing her mother's medical history, the British doctors were afraid to let her brave another English winter, and sent her to Switzerland. Although she had not really enjoyed going to her various schools, she found Oxford stimulating and liked it very much. It was a pity she had to leave so soon.

Meanwhile World War II had broken out and India was in a fresh turmoil. Indira, isolated in neutral Switzerland, did not succeed in returning home until late in 1941. She followed a circuitous route because by then Germany had most of Europe in its grip. She went by train to Antibes, in Occupied France; thence by air to Barcelona, in neutral Spain; across the Iberian Peninsula to Lisbon, which was then the international spy capital of the world, and on to England by air. There she had to wait for months before obtaining passage on a returning troop ship which sailed in convoy around the Cape of Good Hope—the short Suez Canal route was completely interdicted to Allied shipping by German command of the sky above the Mediterranean. I was quite worried about her making the journey through all the perils of war—German planes patrolling the skies, their submarines lurking in the Atlantic and Indian Oceans—and I am afraid I conveyed my anxiety to Bhai, who was once again in prison. His reply was characteristic: "I am glad Indu has decided to return. There are all manner of risks and dangers, of course, but it is better to face them than to feel isolated and miserable. If she wants to return, she must do so and face the consequences."

Indu came home to find her father once again in Dehra Dun Prison, her grandmother and Bibi Amma dead, the family scattered, and Anand Bhawan virtually deserted.

On June 6, 1941, soon after Indira's return from Europe, I received a letter from Bhai in Dehra Dun Prison:

Darling Betty:
Indu has rather suddenly gone to Calcutta. I have been dissatisfied with her health. Madan Atal [A doctor cousin of Kamala's], going to Calcutta, consulted Bidhan Roy [our family doctor], who, as was expected, said, "Bring her here and we shall overhaul her." So Madan wrote to Indu to go to Calcutta for a week or so; and, in the middle of this heat, she has departed. It all seems crazy but I hope she will be back soon. . . .

You know, I suppose, that a small cottage—St. Clair Cottage—has been engaged for Indu in Mussoorie. I do not know how long Indu is likely to stay there but the cottage is for the season. It is a tiny affair—2 bedrooms and 2 other rooms. If at any time you would care to come up there with the children I am sure Indu would be glad. You need not come because of Indu. I think a month or so of full quiet and rest will be good for her. But later if the children require a change or you feel like it yourself, you can think this over . . .

Love to Raja and the children and yourself.

Your loving brother
JAWAHAR

It was evident to me that Bhai was terribly worried about Indu, as well he might be after his tragic experience with Kamala. So, early in August, I brought Harsha and Ajit to Mussoorie to be with Indu. It was indeed a tiny cottage but we fitted in somehow. We had a cook and two servants and a nursemaid for my two sons, so we were very comfortable. I stayed nearly three months with Indira, getting to know her all over again and seeing how she had grown and developed during her final years in Europe. We had a very quiet time, living more or less cut off from the world, which was just what Indu needed. As September gave way to October and the chilly winds of the Himalayas' eternal winter blew down the valley her health improved and her dark eyes sparkled with vitality.

Our only excitement was going to see Bhai once every fifteen days when he was allowed to receive visitors. Of course I took my sons along, although Harsha was only seven and Ajit six. I was afraid it would upset them, and at first it did, but children are more resilient than one thinks and they soon came to regard it as a matter of course.

In October, I went back to Bombay while Indu remained in Mussoorie where she could visit her father. On one of those visits she gave him a piece of news which she had kept secret from me and which upset him greatly. She told him she wanted to marry Feroze Gandhi.

Feroze, whose family lived in Allahabad, was no relation to Mahatma Gandhi; in fact he was of a different caste, a Parsee. The Parsees are descended from Persians who came to India about A.D. 700 to escape religious persecution from the Muslims who had conquered their country. They are followers of Zoroaster and revere fire and sun as emblems of the glory of Ormazd. The sacred fire brought down from heaven by Zoroaster is kept burning in their temples tended by hymn-chanting priests. Theirs is the ancient religion of Persia and they treasure their Persian heritage.

We had all known Feroze well for ten years or more. As a young man he had admired Kamala in a romantic, Dante-and-Beatrice way, content if he could just be near her. Because of her, he had given up his college education to join the Movement; but all he did was to follow her on her journeys to the villages carrying a little box with her tea or coffee and some sandwiches in it, because she was unwell and not allowed to eat everything. I can see him now, a stocky, fair young man, walking just behind her carrying the little box.

When Kamala was sent to Badenweiler, Feroze persuaded a rich aunt to send him to England to study at the School of Journalism. But as soon as he heard how seriously ill Kamala was he went to Lausanne, where she had been taken, and was with my brother and Indira at her bedside when she died.

In England afterward, the two bereft young people naturally saw a great deal of each other, and also in India when they came home. At eighteen and nineteen Indira had thought she would never marry; she still had the Joan of Arc ideal of leading her people to freedom. But she gradually came to rely on Feroze's genuine affection and protective kindness.

Bhai was upset by Indu's desire to marry Feroze, not because he was of a different caste and religion, that was not his way of thought; but he felt that, because Indira had been away from home so much and had very few chances of meeting young Indian men, she should have an opportunity to do so before deciding whom she would marry. Though my brother was so modern in his ideas, in his distress he fell back on ancient tradition. He told Indira that since he was in prison and her mother was dead she must ask permission to marry from her aunts, Nan and me.

Indu went first to Nan, and, of course, got exactly the same answer her father had given her; she must meet more young men before she made up her mind. Then she came to stay with me in Bombay.

She and Raja and I talked for a long time that evening. She told us that she truly loved Feroze and earnestly enumerated his good points, his fine character and kindness. My first answer was like the other two she had received: "Meet some more boys first."

With a flash of Nehru temper and considerable logic Indu said, "Why? It took you only ten days to make up your mind to marry Raja Bhai; and I have known Feroze for years. So why should I have to wait, and why should I have to meet other young men?"

I had no answer to that, for I was happy with Raja; so smiling I said, "Darling, if you think he is the right person go ahead and marry him."

That, I think, was why Feroze was always very fond of Raja and me, because we had given our consent so much more quickly and willingly than either Bhai or Nan.

As far as my brother was concerned, when he found his daughter was adamant, he said, "Well, as soon as I get out of prison you can get married."

That may have seemed to him a fairly safe delaying tactic because he had been condemned to four years' rigorous imprisonment, but soon afterward, in December 1941, the British abruptly released six or seven thousand political prisoners, including my brother.

The objections to Indira's marriage by her father and Nan were minor compared to those of other members of the family and also the orthodox Hindu community. The fact that she had known few young men had not prevented her receiving many offers of marriage in the old-fashioned Hindu manner. These came from the families of eligible young men, many of whom later rose to high places in our political, military and diplomatic services. There were also offers from princelings, though if she had accepted one of these it would have upset her father a good deal more. Many of her relations were furious at her "throwing herself away" on a young Parsee who was not even rich, when she could have made a match that would have reflected credit on the family.

In addition, as soon as the engagement was announced, Indira began to get hundreds of letters from perfect strangers, mostly orthodox Hindus, begging her not to marry a Parsee, or abusing and threatening her for setting such a bad example. As Indira once said, "The whole Nation seemed to be against my marriage" (though there were a few letters that said, "Good for you!").

Even then, the Nehrus had become so much a part of our national history that the Indian people seemed to feel that we belonged to them, which in a sense we did—but not to the extent of letting them rule our private lives. This public outburst might have upset a conventional bride, but Indira took it calmly. She was neither embittered nor disturbed, but simply unmoved by what she called "the fanatical fringe." However it did change her wedding plans.

She and Feroze had wanted to have a very quiet wedding, but in view of the clamor, they and my brother consulted Gandhiji; we always turned to Bapu in moments of doubt. Gandhiji said to Indira, "Under any other circumstances I would agree with your wishes, but with a wedding as controversial as this people would think that your father was unwilling to do anything for you; and that would not be fair to your father or to you."

So Indira gave in and planned a more elaborate affair, though nothing nearly as spectacular as the weddings of her father and Nan. In order that they might have the Vedic ceremony, Feroze went through the rite of becoming a Hindu.

I arrived in Allahabad from Bombay with my two sons a night or two before the appointed day; Raja came a little later. As we drove through the stately gates I saw Anand Bhawan all lit up and bustling with activity, people pouring in and out, servants rushing around, and laughter echoing in every room. It was like going backward in time; happy memories magically made real again. Bhai came out of his familiar room to hug me and my sons, and then we were engulfed in the joyful excitement. With all the family who were still living present, it was a golden moment in those dark years.

The wedding day was quite perfect, with the clear and brilliant light of a March morning in India. Indira had never looked more lovely as she waited in her shell-pink wedding sari, embroidered with silver and made of the finest khadi, which had been spun by her father in prison. She was tall and rather frail, ethereal-looking, with very black hair that fell to her shoulders. She had large dark eyes in an aquiline face, and a complexion the golden color of ripe wheat. In profile Indu looked like the head on a Greek coin.

She sat in her room surrounded by crowds of cousins and friends, who had come from all over India, teasing her and laughing together. When the "auspicious" hour approached everyone gathered in front of Anand Bhawan. It did not have a courtyard like the old Anand Bhawan, but Father had built a marble platform on the lawn, designed for such ceremonies, with removable marble slabs where a fire could be built, to please my orthodox mother. The traditional canopy of brocade supported by tall poles had been set upon it, and the sacred fire burned, tended by the priests. Bhai escorted his daughter to the platform where she sat beside Feroze, while he took his place on the other side of the fire. Beside Bhai was an empty seat that would have been for Kamala.

So Indira and Feroze were married in the same ancient Vedic rite as her father and mother and all the generations before them. They exchanged the vows, and took the seven steps while the fire blazed up as the priests threw ghee on it and chanted the blessing: "May you be blessed and may you live as the god Shiva and his wife Parvati, and like the Lord Krishna and his wife Radha. . . ."

Feroze and Indira went away for a short honeymoon and when they returned to Allahabad they took a small house near our own.

Feroze designed all the furniture for their new home, and he was constantly working in his garden. He enjoyed that most of all, and had the magic touch that is called a "green thumb," but which is really a combination of experience, hard work and love of growing things. He was extremely proud of his beautiful flowers.

For a few months Indu and he were idyllically happy in their little home. Then politics caught up with them and Indira's whole world fell apart again.

14
"quit India"

On December 3, 1941, the government of India had another of its sudden changes of heart. Perhaps it was due to the gathering storm in the Pacific, as it became evident that Japan was about to launch a great attack on Southeast Asia. Whatever their reasoning the government expressed its confidence that the Indian people would support the war effort, and suddenly announced that some 7,000 civil-disobedience prisoners whose offenses had been "symbolic or formal in character" would be released. This, of course, included Bhai, who was freed on December 4.

Just three days later on December 7, the Japanese launched their campaign with the sudden attack on Pearl Harbor. The United States immediately declared war on Japan, Germany and Italy. When he heard the news Winston Churchill danced with glee—he knew then that, however long it might take, the war would be won.

At first it seemed that his joy was premature. Japanese armies and warships swept through the Pacific taking the Philippines, the Dutch East Indies, the great British naval base at Singapore and all of Southeast Asia. Rangoon, the capital of Burma, fell on March 2, 1942, and by May Japanese troops had conquered Burma and stood on the eastern borders of India.

From the moment of the Japanese attack on Pearl Harbor my brother committed himself to the Allied cause. That same day (it was December 8 in India), he said, "There is no doubt that the progressive forces of the world are aligned with the group represented by Russia, China, America and Britain. . . ." As the Japanese approached the borders of India, Bhai officially broke away from Gandhian principles saying, "When we face the enemy, as in the case of Assam, which may be bombed, it would be preposterous indeed to advise the people to offer passive resistance against the war." But he still demanded independence for India as the *sine qua non* of co-operation. To Louis Fischer, Gandhiji's biographer, he said, "I would fight Japan sword in hand, but I can only do so as a free man."

With the fall of Rangoon the British became desperate. Two days later, on March 4, 1942, Churchill sent an extraordinary envoy to India with a new offer. He chose Sir Stafford Cripps, a brilliant lawyer and Left-Wing Labour member of Parliament, who had been brought up on the Fabian socialism of Beatrice Webb, his aunt. Sir Stafford, a thin, ascetic vegetarian, whose sympathies were for Indian independence, had a long-standing friendship with my brother. He was the last man Churchill would have sent had he not been terribly anxious about the fate of India.

Cripps arrived in New Delhi on March 22. A few days later he asked Gandhiji to come to see him. Always ready to meet anyone who might be helpful, he went. In a long conversation with Sir Stafford, Gandhiji learned that nothing short of active Indian participation in the war would satisfy Britain. True to his principle of non-violence, but unwilling to impose it on his colleagues, Gandhiji withdrew to his Sevagram Ashram near Wardha and took no further part in the negotiations, leaving them in the hands of my brother, who was quite ready to fight Japan if agreement could be reached.

Sir Stafford was empowered by Churchill and his coalition government (which included the Labour Party leader, Clement Attlee, as deputy prime minister) to make Britain's best offer yet. It provided for full-fledged Dominion status for Indians after the war. An Indian constitution would be framed by India, and they could even vote themselves complete independence if they wanted to. That looked at first glance like the Constituent Assembly and everything else Bhai had fought for. But on second sight there were several traps. One-third of the Constituent Assembly was to consist of representatives of the princes, and two-thirds were to be elected according to the communal voting laws then in effect. Bhai saw at once that the British could probably manipulate the maharajas and thus control their vote which, when added to the Muslim vote, might deprive the Congress of control of the Constituent Assembly. In addition, there was a provision that any state which did not wish to accede to the Indian Union could refuse and negotiate its own arrangement with

Great Britain. This, my brother believed, might result in the breakup or balkanization of India.

The Cripps offer would not do; most of the Congress leaders agreed on that. So did Jinnah and the Muslim League—though for exactly opposite reasons. But Bhai and the other Congress leaders continued to negotiate with Sir Stafford, and Cripps, without consulting the Viceroy, actually made a much more favorable offer which afforded a possibility of agreement. When Lord Linlithgow heard of it he angrily cabled Churchill, who ordered Cripps home immediately. Though it might lose India temporarily to Japan, Winston Churchill was confident that England would win the war. Thus he threw my brother and the Congress back into the arms of Gandhiji.

All through May, June and July, Bhai with Rajagopalachari, and the Muslim President of the Congress, Maulana Abul Kalam Azad, made constant trips to the tiny village of Sevagram to consult with Gandhiji in his ashram. Together they worked out the principles of a new *Satyagraha*. They agreed upon a formula of neither putting any obstacles in the way of the British forces, nor co-operating with them. If the Japanese came, Gandhiji said, "Neither food nor shelter is to be given, nor any dealings established with them. They should be made to feel they are not wanted. . . . If the people cannot resist fierce attack and are afraid of death they must evacuate the infested place in order to deny compulsory service to the enemy."

My brother did not for one moment believe this would work. Gandhiji himself, in a letter to the Viceroy, described how Bhai argued against such a step for days at a time fearing that it would speed the impending ruin of China and Russia. "He fought against my position with a passion I have no words to describe," Gandhiji wrote. "He yielded only when he saw clearly that without the freedom of India that of the other two [countries] was in great jeopardy."

In July, my brother reluctantly agreed with Gandhiji and the Working Committee that the British might be too weak to hold India unless they got wholehearted co-operation from the Indian people; so they came up with the famous "Quit India Resolution." This is not the real wording of the document; an American journalist first used it as a catch phrase and it caught on. The resolution demanded "the immediate withdrawal of British Power in India." But it was

149

careful to explain that this did not mean the withdrawal of British armies or civilians. It was expressly stated that "It was never intended to mean the physical withdrawal" of the British, and furthermore, upon the withdrawal of British *political* power the Congress promised to form a provisional government which would become an ally of the United Nations in resisting Japanese aggression. It said: "The Congress is anxious to avoid the experience of Malaya, Singapore and Burma and desires to build up resistance to any aggression on or invasion of India by the Japanese or any foreign power." But it maintained that only in a free India could this be done, as ill will against Britain was building up in the Indian masses, who would soon be ready to accept Japanese conquest without a struggle. At the end of the resolution came the threat that "Should, however, this appeal fail, the Congress . . . will then be reluctantly compelled to utilize all the non-violent strength it might have gathered since 1930."

In the final version, the Congress added that they had resolved "to sanction, for the vindication of India's inalienable right to freedom and independence, the starting of a mass struggle on non-violent lines on the widest possible scale . . . such a struggle must inevitably be under the leadership of Gandhiji, and the Committee requests him to take the lead and guide the nation in the steps to be taken. . . ."

However, the Working Committee was not prepared to take such a vital and far-reaching decision on its own authority, and a full meeting of the All India Congress Committee was called to assemble in Bombay on August 7, 1942.

Early in August the leaders of the Congress began to gather in Bombay. Gandhiji stayed at Birla House, the magnificent residence of the great Indian industrialist G. D. Birla, who financed his ashram.

As always when he came to Bombay, Bhai stayed with Raja and me. After living in three smaller apartments we had moved to a large flat in Sakina Mansion, an old-fashioned Indian apartment house on Carmichael Road. It had a big semicircular verandah and a dining room, sitting rooms, kitchen and servants' quarters—we had three houseboys. There were also three bedrooms all in a row off a broad corridor looking over a lovely garden, and three bathrooms. The rooms were very large with high ceilings which made them cool. It had Western-style furniture which Raja designed himself and had built to order; but it was decorated with Indian bronzes and both

Indian and Western paintings, and there were Kashmiri carved coffee tables. The dining-room furniture was also designed by Raja in a rather modern style.

When Bhai came to stay with us the flat always erupted into chaos. This time he brought Indira and Feroze with him, so Raja and I gave them our room; Bhai had his usual room, which was the guest room, and the children had theirs. Raja and I slept in the apartment of a neighbor, Chinni Sundaram, across the court; but we spent the rest of the time at home.

Bhai and his family were with us for nearly a week while the Congress leaders gathered and confusion was compounded by the intense excitement over the momentous decision before them. There were constant visitors, telephones and doorbells ringing all day and half the night, and crowds of people I hardly knew sitting and talking or moving about in a haze of tobacco smoke. A great many stayed on for every meal possible. It was nerve-wracking at times because I never knew how many people would be there for each meal; but I had servants who were the children and grandchildren of my father's servants, and they were used to odd hours and to many guests in the house. They were also used to arrests in the house at any moment of the day or night.

Though many of those who came to the interminable meetings were strangers to me, I knew most of the great leaders well—Sardar Vallabhbhai Patel with his jowled face and sad, heavy-lidded eyes; Rajagopalachari, whom we called Rajaji, who had a thin face, untidy white hair and a neatly trimmed white mustache and Vandyke beard. These two were Liberals or Moderates, who had opposed my brother's uncompromising policy. On the other side there was the Socialist leader Jayaprakash Narayan, young, dynamic and even more radical than Bhai. My brother, with his quiet voice, logical arguments, sudden flashes of humor and a gentle manner that cloaked his steely determination, kept the balance between them all. Not that this was so difficult now, for all of them, except Rajaji, were in accord on what must be done; they were dedicated and prepared for whatever rigor the action they were about to take might bring upon them and those they loved. Nevertheless, as the hour of decision approached, tension tightened to almost unbearable stress.

The Congress met on August 7, 1942, and Bhai moved the "Quit India Resolution" in a rousing speech in which he said:

We are accused by some newspapers [in America] that we are blackmailing. It is a curious charge for a people to make who themselves had for generations carried on a struggle for freedom. If by demanding freedom we are called blackmailers then surely our understanding of the English language has been wrong. Whatever happens in Whitehall it is not going to stop us from working for independence. We live for it and will die for it. I do not want to say anything . . . which might add to the feeling of bitterness that exists everywhere. . . . But . . . the fact is patent to me that the British Government, and for certain, the Government of India, think the Indian National Congress to be Enemy Number One. If the Government of India treats us like this, then we know how to treat them. We have seen in the last few months an unparalleled example of the inefficiency and incompetency of this Government. The system is a rotten one. I do not want to associate myself with the creaking, shaking machinery that the Government of India is. As for the so-called National War Front, there is neither the nation nor the war nor any front in it.

The next day, August 8, my brother spoke again, this time more quietly, saying:

This resolution is not a threat. It is an invitation. It is an explanation. It is an offer of co-operation. On any other terms there will be no co-operation. On any other terms our resolution promises only struggle and conflict. . . . We are going to face great difficulties in the days ahead. All I can say to those Englishmen and Americans who consider that it is not right for the Indian people to decide for themselves, is that they do not know what it is to be under subjection. . . . After all, it is the Indians who will have to undergo the enormous sufferings and privations if there is a Japanese invasion.

At about six o'clock that afternoon, August 8, 1942, the Indian National Congress approved the "Quit India Resolution" by a huge majority.

Many people came back to our apartment, some of whom I had asked to meet my brother; among them were American and English

Mother and Bhai.

*This was taken
when I was a few months old.*

*Nan and me,
when we were children.*

*Our governess,
Miss Hooper.*

*This is the last picture
of Father, taken in 1930 during his
last illness, just before he died.*

*My mother, in 1930.
This picture was taken at the same
time as Father's last picture.*

Bhai, when he was a young man.

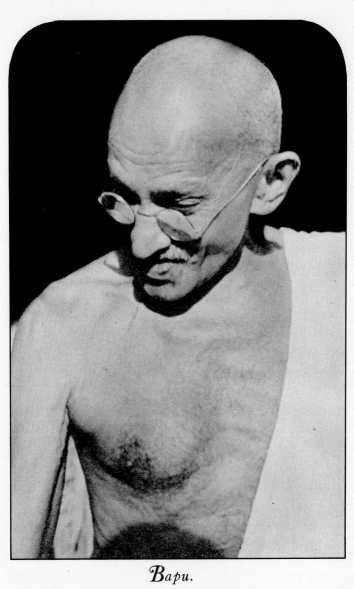

Bapu.

Father, as a lawyer. This picture was taken about the time I was born and is the way I remember him.

*Father, soon after he joined Gandhi
and the Congress.*

Nan and her husband, Ranjit Pandit, sometime in the late twenties or early thirties.

Raja and I in October 1933, at our wedding.

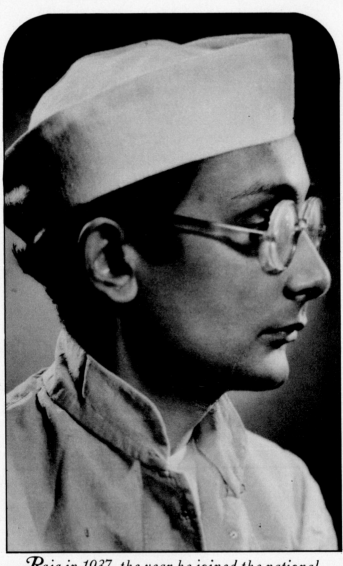

Raja in 1937, the year he joined the national movement and acted as my brother's secretary.

Raja in 1933, when I first knew him.
This picture was taken at Oxford.

Nan, Bhai, and I at Bhai's house in Delhi.

My brother and I in August 1942, just before the time of the Quit India Movement.

Anand Bhawan, our new home, built in 1929.

*This was taken in 1963
after my brother had recovered
from his illness of the previous year.*

*In 1948, at the airport. I am at the far left. Then,
Sheikh Abdullah, Bhai, the Yuraraj of
Kashmir, and Indira.*

Immersing the ashes of my brother in the Ganges.

Bhai placing flowers on Gandhiji's "samabhi" at Raj Ghat, on the third day after Bapu's cremation. His ashes had not been collected yet.

Bhai and Lord Mountbatten.

President Radha Krishnan greeting Bhai on his last birthday, November 14, 1963.

Bhai, at a prayer meeting after Bapu's death. Sardan Pard is behind him.

reporters and, of course, some of the Congress leaders. They were half-elated, half-appalled by what they had done. The talk swirled around our heads like smoke. They ate a great deal, but they still talked with their mouths full; they were too wrought up to stop even though the die was cast and it was too late for talk.

Raja, who had been working very hard for the Congress, had a dreadful cold, but he could not tear himself away. The talking went on until after midnight. Then my brother retired and the others drifted off. As our close friend Phillips Talbot was leaving, Raja put his arm around him and said, "Phil, if and when I get arrested look after my wife."

Phil laughed and said, "You are not important enough to get arrested."

But Raja had been in complete charge of functions and arrangements for the Congress.

Raja and I finally got to bed in Chinni's apartment; we were very tired and fell asleep immediately. At about five o'clock in the morning I was awakened by the doorbell ringing. With a strong premonition of trouble I jumped out of bed just as Chinni knocked on the door. One look at his gloomy face confirmed my fears. Without saying a word I looked across the court at our apartment. Every room around was ablaze with lights, and this was a time when we had blackouts. Then I knew that this was an arrest, and that they had come for Bhai.

Throwing on some clothes, I rushed outside to get to our apartment. As I came out I found the street filled with police cars and jeeps, and the halls full of policemen. When I tried to enter my building they stopped me and said, "No one can enter."

I tried to explain that I was going to my own apartment, but they looked incredulous, nor do I blame them; it was an odd hour to be going home. However, an English sergeant let me go through, and Raja soon followed. We found our apartment full of policemen, and an English inspector pacing up and down saying crossly, "How much longer is it going to take for Pandit Nehru to get ready?"

I looked up at him and said, "You'll have to wait until he *is* ready, and he's not going without having his breakfast for I don't know what he'll get for the next few months."

Then Indira came into the room looking quite calm though very grave. I passed her as I was going to my brother's room, but I heard later that she went to my husband and said, "Raja Bhai, why aren't you getting ready?"

Raja was stunned. "You mean they are arresting me, too?" he asked.

"Yes," Indira said. "You had better pack."

Meanwhile I was in my brother's room, where I found him sitting on the bed, his eyes red from lack of sleep. I put my arms around him and said, "Bhai, darling, the inspector out there is getting difficult and wants you to hurry up and get ready."

My brother was very cross. "Tell him to go to hell," he said.

I promptly did just as he said. I went out and said, "Go to hell!"

"If you carry on like that we'll arrest you, too," the inspector said.

"I couldn't care less," I answered. "And I am not going to hurry my brother, for he is very tired."

Raja came up and said, "Indu tells me I am also under arrest, but I don't believe it." Then he turned to the inspector and said, "Am I supposed to be under arrest?"

The inspector, who was getting more irritable all the time, said, "Yes. You go and get ready quickly!"

With his legal training, Raja said, "I must see the warrant for my arrest first."

The inspector took it out of his breast pocket. Raja and I read it together. It said he was charged with attending the Congress Committee meeting and being a member of the Congress party; and that he was to be taken to "an unknown destination."

I was hard hit by that, harder than about my brother, who after all was accustomed to prison and had the inner strength to withstand it. But gentle, soft-hearted Raja, how would he bear it? I did not know whether to help my brother get ready or to help my husband.

Raja settled it. "Go and look after Bhai," he said. "I'll pack for myself."

My two little sons had slept all through the noise and confusion; now I told their Nanny to wake them up so they could say good-by. They came out rubbing their eyes and rather cross at being waked up just to see their uncle off on what they considered one of his usual trips to jail. They stood there looking curiously at the police officers and admiring their uniforms. After a while I said, "Your father has also been arrested and he is going to prison."

With that they set up an awful howl and flew at the police like little furies. I was quite annoyed and asked, "Why this sudden frenzy? Don't you love your uncle, too?"

"Oh we do," Harsha said, "but he is used to it, and Father isn't." Just what I had thought.

My cook and the other servants went into the usual arrest routine; without asking, they laid the breakfast table and hurriedly made eggs, bacon, toast and coffee. There was a bowl of cornflakes for Bhai who was especially fond of them. Once again the inspector said there was no time for breakfast. My brother glared at him and said, "Shut up! I intend having breakfast before I go."

He and Raja had a good breakfast, but none of the rest of us could eat. When they finished breakfast one inspector took Bhai and another took Raja—Indira and Feroze were not arrested at that time. We went with them down to the street where they were put in separate cars. I saw Chinni, who had come to say good-by, and said, "Drive us after the police cars. We don't know where they're taking them."

His car was parked at the curb: Indira, Feroze and I piled in and we followed the motorcade of police cars and jeeps to the railway station. When we got there we found two lines of policemen guarding the gates, letting nobody through but the police cars. Indu and I jumped out, ran down the street a bit and tried to scale the walls, but when we were halfway up and could look over we saw policemen inside the walls as well, so we jumped down again.

There was nothing more we could do but wait and watch. As we stood outside the iron gates of the railway station, police car after police car drove through filled with leaders of the Congress party; we knew them all and each time a car went by our hearts sank lower. Many young Socialist leaders, friends of ours, some of whom had been to Oxford with Raja, were also taken in groups to the station. Suddenly a car came by with Gandhiji in it, and when we saw that we thought, "This is the end!"

Now there was no use waiting so we three decided to go home, but on our way we were blocked by rioting crowds, and police throwing tear-gas bombs; for word of Gandhiji's arrest had spread and the city was rising against the British. We were undecided whether to join the angry crowds or beat a discreet retreat until such a time as

155

we could meet without police interference. We decided to go to Birla House where Mrs. Gandhi might still be—we did not know whether she had been arrested or not.

As we expected, many people who were in the Movement, mostly the younger ones, were there, shrilling like an alarmed flock of parakeets and milling about in uncertainty and confusion, staggered by losing so many of their leaders in one massive sweep. Kasturba Gandhi was still there, calm though sad. We had hardly been in Birla House fifteen minutes when one of the younger Birla men came fluttering in and said, "Please quit my house. I don't want it confiscated."

We looked at him angrily, saying, "You did not ask Gandhiji to leave your house and you want us to leave, even though his wife is still here."

"You don't understand," he shouted. "We are not in politics, we are business people. We don't want anything to do with any of you, so please leave immediately." The elder Birla would not have acted thus.

We refused to go, and sat there for forty-five minutes longer, during which time we decided that it was best not to defy the government openly, but to start an underground movement. Then we left Birla House and went to our own homes.

Wholesale arrests of Congress leaders continued throughout the month. Early in the morning of August 12, my sister, who was in Allahabad with her daughters, was awakened by the servants, who told her the police had arrived. She was terribly worried about the children. Luckily Indu and Feroze were there to see her off and to make temporary arrangements for the children.

Nan was taken to our old stand in Naini Prison. On August 20, my sister was awakened by the clanking of iron doors and saw her eldest daughter Lekha walk in following a matron. Lekha told her that she had taken part in a procession of protest that was considered subversive and, as usual, early the next morning the police had come for her. Nan was terribly distressed, for Lekha was only eighteen and my sister had been trying hard to give the girls a normal life, to get them to America—anything to keep them from dabbling in politics with all the stress and misery and soul damage that taking part in Indian politics meant at that time.

Less than a month later, on September 11, Indira walked into the same prison. There had been a women's meeting at Anand Bhawan. Before it even got started, the police arrived to arrest Indira and some of the other women. A crowd, who had gathered to see the women arrive, attacked the police and there was a wild melee, with *lathis* and clubs swinging, heads cracking and the police dragging women through the screaming crowd. Indira was pulled and shoved between police and rescuers, and her sari half torn off. Finally the police got her into the house, and gave her a bare ten minutes to pack, before they formed around her and charged through the growing crowd to a police car.

That same evening poor Feroze was arrested, for no particular reason except that he had married a Nehru, and condemned to a year's imprisonment. On September 19, Nan's husband, Ranjit Pandit, who had returned to Allahabad after lying low in Bombay for a month, was also arrested and held as a détenue without trial, at the government's pleasure—not knowing for how long.

Whatever comfort Nan might have got from the presence of her beloved daughter and niece was destroyed by her worry about little Tara and Rita left alone at Anand Bhawan with only a new Chinese governess, recommended by a friend, who turned out to be incompetent.

Now I was the only member of our immediate family still free, and I was quite frantic, not even knowing where Raja and my brother were. For months I did not know. I did get a letter from Bhai in September headed:

SOMEWHERE IN INDIA
BUT NOT AT ANAND BHAWAN ALLAHABAD

In it he said he had received a letter from me and one from Indu, and then, typically, began to worry about our faithful servants at Anand Bhawan:

. . . There is one matter I would like you to deal with. I am anxious that our servants in Allahabad should not suffer from rising prices. Recently some additional allowance was made them but I doubt if this helps much. . . . I presume prices are going up,

157

and I should like all our people including Hari . . . to be treated well and generously. . . . So will you please write to Ladli Bhai [Our first cousin who took care of Anand Bhawan when we were away] about this and give him my message?

Do not worry about me if you do not hear from me frequently. You ought to know by this time that I can look after myself and flourish like the proverbial green bay tree even in restricted surroundings. Prison always serves as a tonic to me, a change from the horrible dullness of normal life. . . . I am having a dip into Urdu poetry with the Maulana's [Abul Azad, who was still President of the Congress] help.

All my love,
Your loving brother
JAWAHAR

This was some comfort but I was desperate to know where Raja was. There were all sorts of rumors; some that he had been taken to the Andaman Islands and some that he had been shot. Others said he had been taken to some foreign place. I went to the Secretariat and said to the Home Secretary that if he would tell me where my husband was I would promise not to reveal it to anyone. He was adamant and said he had no knowledge at all of where either my brother or Raja were, because, he said, the military had taken good care not to let any Indian civil servant know. This was not true; I found out later that he did know. Again I went to him and got the same answer.

One evening I got a long-distance call from an unknown person who said, "This is to tell you to leave tomorrow morning and go to Poona by the morning train and be at the gates of Yeravda Prison at five P.M." Then the phone clicked off.

Almost distracted between hope and fear I called Chinni Sundaram and told him I had got this message and was going. "You must not go. It's crazy," he said. "You don't know who sent it or anything."

"Whatever or whoever sent it, I'm going," I said, "for it means Raja is there and maybe he is being transferred somewhere. This may be my only chance to see him."

"No. I promised Raja not to let you out of my sight," he said. And then he said, "Well, if you insist, I'll go with you."

We got to the station early in such a rush that I forgot to take any baggage, not even a toothbrush. All these three months since Gandhiji had been imprisoned, there had been terrible riots; train service had been disrupted and, as our old locomotive puffed and grunted through the Western Ghats, we could see why. All along the line we saw dead cattle, overturned railway carriages, and the wreckage of war—civil war. The train was constantly held up and instead of three hours it took us ten to cover the hundred and fifty miles to Poona.

When we got there I saw to my horror that it was eight o'clock. There was a curfew throughout the city and the police would not let us leave the station. I came close to panicking. Then I had a brain wave. "Look," I said to the officer in charge, "I have to go to the house of the Inspector General of Prisons; and if you won't let me go, get in touch with him and find out."

I don't know whether they believed me or not, but they were *Indian* police and inclined to be sympathetic. They let me go. We took a taxi to the Inspector General's house where his little daughter said, "Father is not home; he's at the club playing bridge."

So I rang up the club, and he came to the phone. When he heard who it was, he was all in a lather; of course he knew me and my whole family. He was an Indian, a most unpleasant man, who was rude and mean to his prisoners to please his British masters. "Why have you come here? What have you come for?" he asked in a frantic voice. "I don't know anything about your husband! I don't know where he is."

"I know he is here," I said, "and I'm not going back to Bombay. I'm going to stay right here in your house, and that will look bad for you."

"Please don't do that," he begged. "If you have nowhere to stay, please go to Prem's house."

His son-in-law, Prem Bhagal, was a true friend of ours and a fine man, whose family lived close to Anand Bhawan in Allahabad. He was the first Indian to win the Victoria Cross in World War II, and although he was in the British Army he was, of course, more politically courageous than his father-in-law. I telephoned him and told him the situation. He immediately said, "Yes, do come along."

While he fed us delicious food which we badly needed, he told us that his father-in-law was the wrong person to go to, considering how nervous he was about these things. I suspect I had completely ruined his bridge game. Prem was a darling. He told me that Raja was, indeed, in Yeravda, but that it was impossible for the Inspector General or anyone else to arrange a meeting because of strict orders from above to keep the prisoners incommunicado. Though I had forgotten to bring any luggage of my own I had brought a suitcase of clothes and books for Raja. Prem promised to try to get it to him, he did not know how. He also said he would get a message to Raja that I had come.

I had to be satisfied with that. At least I knew that my husband was alive; and where he was. I did not see him for six months.*

Meanwhile I learned that Bhai was confined in Ahmednagar Fort, which was not a regular prison but an old stone Mogul fortress which the British used only for political prisoners because it afforded maximum security. Presently the extreme rigor of his confinement was relaxed, and he could write regularly and receive gift packages. At various times young hotheads in the Movement made plans that were anything but non-violent to rescue prisoners like my brother, but they were never successful. In fact, I doubt if Bhai would have willingly co-operated, for he could not picture himself skulking through India, a nameless, faceless fugitive. On the contrary, if he had escaped, the first thing he would have done would have been to make a big public speech, probably notifying the government in advance. That is the kind of man he was.

* Much later I learned that the mysterious phone call had come from an Indian employed in the prison who hoped to be able to slip me in at the lax time around five o'clock.

15
underground

The British made a terrible mistake when they arrested Gandhiji; for the moment his voice was silenced, all India erupted into a violence that only he could check. I had seen it from the train and in Bombay; and heard of acts of terrorism, sabotage of planes, tearing up rail lines and telephone wires, burning police stations and killing Englishmen throughout India. In many country places the British lost all control and government collapsed in chaos. Our Movement had become a civil war, with an organized underground of which I was a member. It was led by young Congress and Socialist party people like Narayan, Mrs. Aruna Asaf Ali and Achyut Patwandhan and many others who risked their lives for freedom, moving secretly across India, organizing bands of guerrillas for acts of violence. As Gandhiji had once said, "Non-violence is a matter of principle with me; with the Congress it is only a matter of policy." Without him the principle practically disappeared.

Not only that but, just as my brother and Gandhiji had feared, many Indians were hoping for a Japanese victory to set them free. Subhas Bose was the leading extremist in this direction. He had escaped to Axis territory; and we heard his voice on the radio from Tokyo and from Berlin spouting Axis propaganda. Furthermore, he organized a force called the Indian National Army, mainly consisting of Indians who had been serving in the British Army and were taken prisoners by the Japanese when Singapore and Burma fell. They were fighting alongside the Japanese.

My brother was terribly disturbed by all this, for he still believed that victory for the Allied nations was vital for world freedom; and even in prison he tried to counter Bose's activities by writing to people of influence. Luckily Bose's movement amounted to very little; the Indian National Army played no significant role in the war. Bose was killed in an aircraft smash in 1944.

Meanwhile Gandhiji was confined at Yeravda; not in the prison with Raja, but in a mouldering palace owned by the Aga Khan. A very select group was imprisoned with him including the faithful Mahadev Desai, and Sarojini Naidu. The day after his arrest, his wife, Kasturba, got herself arrested by announcing that she would address a meeting in Bombay at which he had been scheduled to speak. She and her personal physician, Doctor Sushila Nayyar, were sent to join her husband in the Aga Khan's palace.

Gandhiji's first act on arriving at the prison was to write to Sir Roger Lumley, the Governor of Bombay, protesting the fact that he had been taken to jail in a private automobile while the others had been forced to ride in a lorry. He wanted no extra privilege, said Gandhiji, other than his special food. Indeed he kept up a running fire of correspondence with the Viceroy and other British officials, who kept trying to induce him to stop the acts of violence. Gandhiji announced again and again that he was helpless to do so, and blamed them on the government of India; but he was so deeply distressed that he went on another twenty-one day fast which almost killed him. During the fast, the government of India was so upset and anxious to calm Indian fury that they actually allowed crowds of his well-wishers to enter the palace grounds and file through the room where Gandhiji lay.

The Mahatma's distress was deepened by two personal tragedies. Six days after he was imprisoned Mahadev Desai suffered a fatal heart attack. As he lay unconscious, Gandhiji sat beside his cot calling out "Mahadev! Mahadev!" Conscious of his own inner power the Mahatma said: "If he would only open his eyes and look at me he would not die." And Kasturba Gandhi said in Desai's ear, "Mahadev, Bapu is calling you!" But Mahadev did not hear.

The second tragedy occurred after fourteen months of imprisonment when Kasturba came down with bronchitis. Frail from years of strain, she could not throw it off, though the British sent their best doctor to supplement Doctor Nayyar; and also an Indian-medicine practitioner whom Kasturba, who believed in the old ways, asked for. They also offered the rare, newly discovered drug, penicillin, but when Gandhiji heard that it was given by injection he refused to permit it.

So Kasturba died with her head resting in her husband's lap. She had been a faithful, obedient wife in the oldest Hindu tradition. She had little education—she never learned to speak English or even to know the geography of her own country though Gandhiji tried to teach her. She was content to serve him and, without understanding them, to abide by his decisions about everything. When he abjured all material things in his quest for spiritual enlightenment, he also gave up the physical side of marriage, and for the last thirty years they lived together, but apart.

At Kasturba's funeral within the palace grounds Gandhiji recited Hindu, Muslim, Parsee and Christian prayers and his son, Devadas, lit the funeral pyre. When he returned to his room Gandhiji said a curious thing that only he could conceive. "I cannot imagine life without Ba. Her passing has left a vacuum that can never be filled. . . . And she passed away in my lap. Could it be better? I am happy beyond measure."

Quite soon after Kasturba's death Gandhiji became ill; first it was malaria and then anemia. On May 8, 1944, he was released from prison.

My own part in the underground was modest though at times somewhat risky. Soon after the mass arrests of August 9, 1942, the group that had gathered at Birla House met again to organize. We were all given specific tasks; mine was to help run the secret Congress radio with a group of young boys and girls. I pretended that I was just having a good time and went out a lot in so-called society circles, but I used to gather news about the rioting and shooting which was taking place in Bombay and all over India. I would write a report of what had happened and take it to where we had the transmitter set up in someone's apartment near our own. There, one of the boys or girls would broadcast it and so we kept the people informed of what was going on. In spite of their frantic efforts, it was months before the British found where the Congress radio was located. However, I was very cautious, for with all my immediate family in jail, I knew of no one who would care for my young sons if I, too, were arrested.

Another of my jobs was collecting money from business people who wanted to help without becoming personally involved. They sometimes gave me very large sums in cash which I had to take to different parts of the country. On the first such journey I did a very stupid thing. I had about 100,000 rupees in a suitcase. When I went to bed in my compartment I left both the room and the suitcase unlocked. Very early in the morning, before daylight, I was awakened by people shouting outside. The train was standing in a station and there was an excited crowd swirling around on the platform. I stuck my head out the window and asked what had happened. A man yelled back that someone on the train had been robbed. My heart stopped dead and I dove for the suitcase. Thank God! The money was still there.

Acting as a courier, carrying the money that financed the rebellion, was a more risky job than I should have undertaken in my circumstances; people who were caught got sentences of from five to seven years.

As the Movement strengthened, tensions and tempers rose. The demonstrations against the British became ever larger and more violent, and the troops reacted by shooting instead of just *lathi* charges. With a group of women friends, I began taking first-aid lessons so that we could help the wounded. On the very day we were to go to get our badges, which would admit us through the police lines, I got a telephone message from a doctor friend who said, "There is a big riot in Shivaji Park, people are dead and dying and no ambulances are there. Will you go down and see what you can do?"

First thing, I rang up several private ambulances whose owners refused to go because they said the shooting was still going on and people were throwing rocks. So I gathered two or three women friends, one of whom was Mr. Jinnah's daughter. We went first to the woman doctor who had given us lessons in first aid and asked her to go with us. Though she was Irish, she was *Anglo*-Irish for she said, "I certainly will not help the rebels of any country."

"But you told us that the first rule of first aid was to help *anyone* who was sick or hurt, and one has to give up everything to help them," I protested.

She replied, "I don't care. If I come with you I will be the first casualty, and for people I disapprove of."

We argued heatedly, saying nasty things to each other, but the upshot was that on no account would she help people who were rebelling against the British.

So we went home to get our cars, and went on our own to Shivaji

Park. It was a shambles, with dead, dying and wounded lying on the lovely green lawns under the trees. We got the cars as close as we could, and volunteers went in to drag the wounded out to us. Fortunately we had rather big cars; mine was a Buick and there was another Buick and a Cadillac. We took the wounded and dying and piled them in, one on top of another, four or five people to a car. Then we drove them to hospitals and came back for more. When the British saw women in saris running out to pick up the wounded they ordered the troops to stop shooting, and allowed us to take the wounded away.

As the British-American Front held on the Burma-India border, it began to look as though the Japanese might be stopped; but another enemy came to add to the confusion and misery of India—the great Bengal famine of 1943. The monsoon failed and the country, already dry from the usual rainless winter, simply burned up. In addition, cattle sickened and died of a mysterious disease, so the landless peasants, who always lived on the verge of starvation, began to die in thousands. Many of the desperate villagers abandoned their homes and trekked with their families along the dusty roads to Calcutta in the hope of finding food there. The city was already bulging with people, half of them sleeping in the streets. Some brought their cows and sheep with them to sell in the markets in order to buy food for themselves. But there was famine also in Calcutta, not as bad as in the villages, but serious nevertheless. Both the government of India and the Congress set up canteens where a little food—milk and a sort of porridge—was given to the starving crowds daily as long as it lasted.

I wrote to the Indian National Congress Committee and asked if I could go to Calcutta and help; I was alone in our apartment now, with my husband and brother still in jail and my children in a boarding school where I had sent them to be safe. The Committee answered that anybody who could help was welcome. So I went to Calcutta.

During my first few days in the city I was sent from one canteen to another as shortages of volunteers developed. Eventually I came to one of the largest canteens, which happened to be near Firpo's famous restaurant. At lunch time the restaurant was crowded with officers of the different armies and their women—British, Indians, Americans and various other nationalities.

The canteen was crowded, too, with long lines of ragged villagers in tattered loincloths or saris, desperate teen-agers on their own, and naked children with the swollen bellies of hunger. The first day I worked there I saw several people lying under a tree, too weak to get up and stand in line for food. When I went to them with some other volunteers and tried to get them up, they just collapsed; some of them died in our arms.

And right across the way I could see this restaurant flourishing, people in uniform and mufti, laughing and joking; waiters staggering under big trays loaded with food. It infuriated me so that I wanted to round up a group of people, break through and take some of that food and distribute it. But I thought that with the hundreds of people we had to feed, perhaps it would not go far; and I knew I should not do it. So that day I just looked my disgust and went on working.

The second day was too much. Across the road I could see lots of officers drinking and eating and laughing, heedless of the fact that a little distance across the street they could see, if they looked, people dying of hunger; and it did not seem to bother them in the least. That temper of mine flared. I had been trying to feed people for a week now and their misery had worn my resistance thin. So I lost control, dropped the civilized veneer, and burst out to some volunteers, saying loudly, "Why are our people so resigned to fate? Why don't they do something? Why don't they get up and throw a stone through those windows, then barge in and grab any food they can?"

Like a flash, the large Indian lady who ran the canteen was beside me. She was a great admirer of Gandhiji and *very* non-violent. In a shocked voice she said, "You must not talk like that. Whatever fate has in store for us, we must bear patiently. Don't incite these people."

Rather stridently I said, "Well, why not? Can you bear to go home and eat a full meal?"

"No, I cannot," she answered. "I get sick."

"I can't either," I said. "Why don't you get sick when you see those other people eating?"

She did not answer, but gently made me sit down with my back to Firpo's so that I could not see.

I worked in Calcutta for a month, but from then on the volunteers were careful to send me to canteens in poorer quarters, where there were no fine resturants to fire my rage. However, there was enough else. I never saw so many people die, hopelessly, uncomplainingly, just lie down in the street and die. And not only people, but animals as well; dogs that would stagger about looking for a bone and just collapse—dead like that. Or when a person died the dogs would be on him, voraciously gnawing his flesh, before they could be driven off. And the children, little dead children in the street. After a month I could stand no more and went back to Bombay.*

Meanwhile, our family began to come out of prison. The first was Nan, who in March 1943, was allowed out for thirty days on parole due to illness. I went to Allahabad to be with her, arriving late at night. Tara met me at the station, which looked very shabby, and we rode in a horse-drawn *tonga* to Anand Bhawan. The tall gates stood open, but the house seemed dim and cheerless. Nan was subdued, her face drawn and thin with wrinkles I had never seen before. One happy thing was that Lekha was released a little later. While Nan was out, we made plans to send the two oldest girls to college in America. Lekha did not want to leave India during the time of trouble but agreed to go because it might lessen her mother's worries.

Nan went back to prison in April, got out again briefly, and was in and then out again in June; after that she did not go back. Meanwhile all three of the girls stayed with me in Bombay, while I worked on the arrangements to get the two older ones to America, which was not easy in wartime and involved a great deal of correspondence. I was also very anxious about them because of the dangers involved in crossing the ocean on a returning troop ship; and our friends thought we were crazy to send them. But their father, Ranjit, was for it; and a typically courageous letter from my brother settled the matter. From Ahmednagar Fort he wrote:

Darling Betty:
    The first news of Chand [his name for Lekha] and Tara going to America for their studies reached me through your letters. . . . My immediate reaction was in its favor and the more I have

* The famine cost approximately 3,000,000 Indian lives. My brother always maintained that many could have been saved had an *Indian* government been in power.

167

thought of it the more I have liked it. The alternative to joining college in America is to carry on with the university here. At any time this is not a particularly attractive proposition; just at present it is less attractive than ever.

As for risk or possible danger involved in the journey, that surely cannot be a reason against the proposal. To my mind it is an inducement in favor of it. We have never made "safety first" our motto and I hope we never will. In this world full of risk and danger we must take our share of them and not shirk them. It would be bad training indeed for the girls to be made to feel that they must avoid all risks and dangers at all costs. They are old enough to learn to look after themselves and to face the world with, of course, all the help we can give them. But without that help, also, if necessary....

So I am quite clear in my mind that it is right and proper for Chand and Tara to go to the U.S. for their studies and the sooner the better. They can and should only go by air. The possibility of their being stranded in Cairo or elsewhere does not worry me in the least. Some such adventure would be good for them.

It was impossible to arrange for the girls to go by air; so Lekha and Tara sailed on the fifteenth of May, 1943, in a returning American transport in a large convoy. Their ship, which carried some fifty regular passengers and seven hundred Polish refugees, went to America via Australia. The only place the girls got stranded was in Los Angeles, which was not very dangerous. Eventually they got to Wellesley College whose president had cabled to their mother: WELLESLEY COLLEGE PLEASED AND PROUD TO WELCOME YOUR DAUGHTERS.

Neither Lekha nor Tara ever saw their father again. Early in the summer of 1943, Ranjit was transferred to Izatnagar Central Prison in Bareilly—the worst of all the prisons where political prisoners were held. It was surrounded by a wall twenty-five feet high which cut off all sight and sound of the outside world, and a great deal of life-giving sunlight as well. In addition, the climate was atrocious, with summer temperatures going to 110 degrees and above; and that high wall cutting off the breeze made it an inferno. When Ranjit and my brother were there in 1932, Ranjit almost died and was months

168

recovering, and even my brother, strong and accustomed to prison life, became so ill in Bareilly that the government quickly transferred him to Dehra Dun.

In Bareilly, Ranjit continued to work on his beautiful translation of the *Ritusamhara*, the poetic description of the six seasons by Kalidasa, which was published soon after he died. But the asthma which had afflicted him ever since his first imprisonment, grew steadily worse. Night after suffocating night, he struggled for breath in that hell-hole. When the government finally released Ranjit on compassionate grounds in October 1943, it was too late. Asthma and pleurisy had worn down his resistance. In November he went to Lucknow to stay with Colonel G. R. Oberai of the Indian Medical Service, who kindly took him until my sister could be located. There his respiratory difficulties increased as pleurisy turned into pneumonia. Nan hurried to join him, and, of course, the best doctors were called in, but his wasted body would not respond. On January 14, 1944, he died.

Poor Ranjit never should have been involved in the Movement and only was by the accident of marriage. My sister saw this truly when, even before he died, she wrote of him: "Ranjit . . . is not meant for the rough and tumble of Indian politics. With his wealth and learning and fastidious scholarship, his love of art and of all those finer aspects of life which are understood by so few people. . . . [prison life] is breaking him down physically. It is a slow daily sacrifice which can be so much more deadly than some big heroic gesture made in a moment of emotional upheaval. . . ."

That was the tragic truth about the gay and gentle man whose fatal error was to love and marry a Nehru.

Ranjit's death left Nan at a loose end, despondent for the first time in her life. She conceived the idea of going to the United States to lecture and attend the Pacific Relations Conference. Gandhiji supported the project, feeling that she would be India's best spokesman to Americans. In order to have an official reason for the trip Nan got herself appointed Indian representative to the Pacific Relations Conference at Hot Springs, Virginia, her first semidiplomatic job. American General G. E. Stratemeyer found a place for her on a transport plane returning to the United States, and off she went in a bucket seat to conquer the new world. Rita, now fifteen, followed on a troopship.

Nan's lectures were a stunning success, both in bringing an understanding of Indian problems to Americans, and financially—everyone wanted to hear her. She was, of course, already a nationally known figure in India; her American tour gave her an international reputation. And at the San Francisco Conference where the United Nations was founded Nan, who had no official status, played a far more important role than the official Indian delegation which had been hand-picked by the Viceroy.

Indira was let out of prison about the same time as Nan. As early as November 1942 she had contracted pleurisy again—how that disease runs through these pages!—from the horrible damp and cold of those unprotected cells which I have described. At that time there was talk of her being released, but they kept her in until June 1943. Feroze was released soon afterward. He got a job in Lucknow, as manager of a newspaper my father had started long ago as *The Independent*; it was now called the *National Herald*. Indira and Feroze lived happily there for a few months in a little cottage they rented. Indira took a small role in the underground, but soon stopped for a very good reason.

In November 1943, Raja came home to me, released on parole because of illness. He was very thin and his large brown eyes looked enormous in his sunken face. In addition he also was suffering from asthma, and sometimes hardly slept all night, wheezing and gasping for breath. But at least he was alive. We tried various doctors, even some who practiced the Ayurvedic or Unani systems of Indian medicine that had come down the centuries. Bhai took a dim view of this treatment and wrote worried letters from Ahmednagar Fort. He was quite right, of course; the treatment did no good and we went back to Western medicine under Doctor P. Bharucha, a famous doctor in Bombay who looked after many members of our family. Raja slowly, very slowly improved.

In January 1944, Indira wrote that she was pregnant and coming to Bombay for a checkup; she and Feroze stayed with us. Bhai was both elated by the news that he was to be a grandfather and worried because of Indu's delicate health. In his prison cell he remembered that Kamala had never been well after her first child was born, and he urged Indu to stay on in Bombay where she could have more expert care than in Allahabad or Lucknow. So she stayed with me all through her first pregnancy while Feroze went back to his job in Lucknow. He rejoined us when Indu's time care near.

Her son was born on August 20, 1944. I sent a joyful telegram to Bhai telling him that he had a grandson, and later sent a list of about twenty names which Indu, Feroze and I had selected for the baby; as the head of our house, we were agreed that Bhai should have the last word. He chose the name Rajiv which means lotus; I think in memory of Kamala whose name also meant lotus.

Raja took a long time to recover from his asthma. In the spring of 1945, we took our sons to Srinagar in Kashmir in the hope of clearing it up for good. We rented a houseboat as Father had done long ago, and lived very quietly. Srinagar was greatly changed, full of Allied and Indian soldiers, and accessible by a new military road, but the lovely lake was still serene and the high escarpment of the Himalayas was a barrier shutting out the tumultuous world.

When Raja got stronger we did a little trekking into the mountains; and toward the end of our stay we took the children up to the Kolahai Glacier which rises to 17,000 feet. We pitched our base camp at the 13,000-foot level and went on from there over the snow bridges and up that vast sloping field of ice. Kolahai is to me the most beautiful glacier in the world, to which I have returned many times with my brother and Indira, who loved it as I did. Though Harsha and Ajit were only nine and eight years old they stood the rigor of the trip every well and thoroughly enjoyed it.

When we returned to our base camp I wanted to linger awhile enjoying the tingling cold of early May, but Raja was uneasy. We were completely cut off from news of the world—we had no radio— and he sensed that something terribly important was happening. It was a five-day trek over mountain roads back to Srinagar if you did it quickly. As we entered the city the streets and marketplace were thronged with people. Right across from our houseboat there was a service club and the street in front of it was full of English Tommies and American G.I.'s singing and dancing together. Raja ran across to ask why they were so full of joy; had the British and Americans won some great battle? They told him that they had won the last battle. Germany had surrendered, the war in Europe was over.

All we wanted to do now was to get home quickly. Rumor by radio said that the Congress leaders would soon be released. Bhai had been in prison for almost three years and in all that time I had not seen him. Never before or since have I been so anxious to leave Kashmir. So, it seemed, was everyone else; all rushing toward the centers of civilization. By using all the influence we could command, we got four seats in an automobile going down to Pathankote where the railway ended. The station was teeming with people, but with great difficulty we managed to get on an overcrowded train which took us to Delhi where we stayed with some cousins, waiting for news.

On June 14, 1945, we got a telegram from my brother saying that he had been released from prison and was passing through Bombay; could he use our flat? We tried to telephone him but the lines were jammed with official and unofficial business; everyone in India seemed to want to talk to everyone else. So we telegraphed him: OF COURSE USE THE FLAT WE ARE COMING TO BOMBAY. Then the telephone rang and it was Bhai's dear voice telling us he was coming to Delhi; to wait there for him.

So there was a great reunion in Delhi as Indira and Feroze also arrived. Bhai no sooner joined us than he decided to go immediately to Allahabad and we all went with him. It was wonderful to be all together in Anand Bhawan. Never had it seemed so beautiful, even though shabby from wartime neglect. Who cared about a little peeling paint? We were together and the gardens were bright and serene, and the old house warm with laughter. We hoped we would have a month of happiness. But in less than a week, Bhai got a telegram summoning him to New Delhi to meet with the Viceroy to discuss the future of India.

16
the
cabinet
mission

The Viceroy of India was now Lord Wavell who might be called the unluckiest soldier of World War II; everything went wrong for him through no fault of his own. He had beaten the Italians in the Libyan Desert only to have half his army taken from him to reinforce Greece. When the redoubtable General Erwin Rommel then defeated him, he was relieved and made Commander in Chief, India. In October 1943, with the Japanese on the borders of Assam, Churchill decided that new blood was needed. Dashing, dynamic Lord Louis Mountbatten was made Supreme Commander, Southeast Asia; Sir Claude Auchinleck, another casualty of Rommel's Desert War, became Commander in Chief, India, and Wavell was kicked upstairs to the thankless role of viceroy.

Big and stocky with dense black hair turning iron gray, and a weatherbeaten face in which one glass eye was hardly more lively than the real one, he looked the perfect picture of a stolid British general. But he was not stupid. A brilliant soldier, his battles were lost from lack of manpower and matériel, not lack of ability. In private he liked to talk philosophy and quote Kant and Matthew Arnold. Completely untrained for the office of viceroy, he was, in spite of this, a good one: conscientious, understanding, and humane. Where Linlithgow had not bothered to go to Bengal during the famine, it was the first place Wavell went; and when Kasturba

Gandhi died in prison, the new viceroy was among the first to send Gandhiji a warm letter of sympathy.

Granted that Lord Wavell lacked Mountbatten's quick perceptions, charm and imagination, he might have, indeed he almost did, pull off the impossible task of negotiating a formula for Indian independence satisfactory to all concerned. With a little luck he would have; but Wavell never had luck.

When my brother was sent for to confer with the Viceroy, Raja and I thought of going home to Bombay. But then we thought better of it; for we did not know whether or not the talks would end with all our people back in jail again, as they so often had before; and I wanted to be with Bhai as much as possible. We went with him to New Delhi.

When we got there, we found the city was a furnace in the dry heat of late June and the meeting had been transferred to Simla in the hills. So we all trooped up to Simla except Indira who had a small baby and was not very strong. Raja and I stayed at a hotel, while Bhai and Maulana Abul Azad stayed in a house the Viceroy had rented and staffed with servants for them.

The whole Congress Working Committee was in Simla, as was Jinnah with Liaquat Ali Khan, and Gandhiji (as an observer). The latter had come from his ashram in a special train composed of *third class* railway carriages containing his ashramites and two goats, which led Sarojini Naidu to make her classic comment: "If only Gandhiji knew how much it costs to keep him living in poverty!"*

The discussions were held in the Viceregal Lodge, an enormous pile of gray stone that the fantasy of some victorian architect had raised on a Himalayan foothill. Since my brother never breathed a word of what went on at the time, I will tell now what I learned only much later.

On June 14, Lord Wavell, just returned from England, had announced a new and genuinely liberal plan for the future government of India; and simultaneously ordered the release from prison of all members of the Working Committee. The purpose of the Simla meet-

* According to G. D. Birla, who partly financed the Mahatma, it cost about 50,000 Rs. a year. Mr. Birla, being a leading industrialist, liked to have a foot in both camps.

ing was to discuss the new British proposal. The conference opened with high hopes, which were dashed by the intransigence of one man —M. A. Jinnah. This aloof, cynical gentleman could also be very charming and witty when he wanted to; but one never felt any warmth. He always seemed icy beneath the dazzling surface. His warped, introverted nature may have been due to a personal tragedy. In his forties Mr. Jinnah married a very beautiful Parsee girl of eighteen whose name was Rati Pettit. He was deeply in love with her at first and, because she was not of his faith, allowed her many liberties rare for the wife of a Muslim. She wore lipstick and elaborate makeup, and gossamer-thin saris that hardly concealed her lovely body. She was a very glamorous, witty person, a great favorite of my father's and of many other people who enjoyed her sparkling conversation. Soon after the birth of their daughter she left her husband —a terrible blow to Jinnah's inordinate pride. He tried desperately to effect a reconciliation. Just as he hoped he was making progress, she died on her twenty-ninth birthday. Though the cause of death was given out as peritonitis, I have reason to believe that she planned it that way.

Mr. Jinnah's soul seemed permanently scarred; and the final blow came years later when his daughter, whom he had raised very strictly, married a Parsee-turned-Christian against his wishes. All her other relations approved the match, as her husband was a fine young man and very rich to boot, but Jinnah disowned her.

After that Jinnah's sister, Fatima, moved in. She was an evil influence; a diamond-hard spinster who dedicated her life to the protection of her brother and to furthering his egotistic ambition— and her own.

The thing I remember most about Jinnah was that he was always very elegantly dressed, often in superbly tailored English clothes; and, whatever he wore, there was always the monocle dangling on its cord or screwed into his eye making him look like an English dandy. His ardent Mohammedanism was, I am convinced, put on.* We Nehrus had known him all our lives, for he had once been my father's junior in the law office, and Bhai had been his junior for a short time. So I know that until it became politically expedient, he had never

* Gandhiji believed Jinnah's religion was sincere; but then Bapu always believed the best of every man.

cared a fig for religion. In fact, his family were recent converts to Islam; and Jinnah could not even say the Mohammedan prayers properly, let alone speak Urdu. Indeed he was not fluent in *any* Indian language.

This intensely ambitious man knew that he could never hold first place in India as long as my brother lived; for that reason, he was determined to found a state in which he would be first. This, I firmly believe, was what made him so adamant for the partition of India and the creation of Pakistan. He gloried in the title which he assumed of *Quaid-i-Azam* ("Great Leader").

The means Jinnah used to wreck the Simla Conference was to insist that he must name *all* the Muslims on the Viceroy's new Council. This, my brother and Gandhiji could not allow, because it would be a betrayal of all the good Muslims who had been loyal to the Congress party, including Maulana Abul Azad, who was still its president. Though everyone, including Gandhiji and the Viceroy, tried hard to bring Jinnah to some compromise, he was as inflexible as an iceberg. After two weary weeks the conference broke up having accomplished exactly nothing.

In its latter stages, an incident occurred showing how superstition may inform prophecy. At a big reception I was chatting with one of our political leaders who remarked, "Whatever happens here, victory is sure to be ours; and Lord Wavell will have to go."

Dying of curiosity I asked sharply, "How do you know? Has my brother been talking to you?"

"No," he said. "Jawahar is a perfect sphinx. I haven't a clue as to what is going on, but this I know: In India whenever a man with one eye has held power as king or prince or warrior, that one has always lost his kingdom or his life in battle. Now that the head of the British Raj is a one-eyed man, he will fall and it will rule us no more."

Of course, I thought my friend was talking nonsense, but that is what happened.

What a summer that was! No sooner had the Simla Conference broken up than Churchill's government was unexpectedly defeated in the British general election that he had called to assure his power for another five years. The new Labour Prime Minister, Clement

176

Attlee, had campaigned on the basis of independence for Inda, but my brother was very wary. Other Labour governments had disappointed him and he expected the same old evasions.

Hardly had Attlee moved into 10 Downing Street than the Japanese war ended in the terrible atomic pyrotechnics over Hiroshima. Though my brother had never ceased to hope for Japan's defeat, the manner of it shook his soul, as indeed it shattered that of every thinking person of every country in the world. But, because Gandhiji's principle of non-violence had so deeply impregnated Indian thinking and the Indian ethic, this ultimate violence had a greater impact in our country.

The surrender of all the Japanese forces in Southeast Asia to Lord Louis Mountbatten on September 12, 1945 produced new problems as victory always does. One of these was what to do about the members of the ill-fated Indian National Army that Subhas Bose had raised. The British, and many Indian Army officers as well, regarded them as traitors, to be treated as such. On the other hand, there was great popular sympathy for them, because they had been fighting for India's freedom, so they truly believed, however misguidedly. My brother shared this point of view. "Whatever their failings and mistakes," he said, "they are a fine body of young men . . . and their dominating motive was love for India's freedom."

While most of the Indian National Army were held prisoners in Malaya, the government of India brought three high officers to India to stand trial for treason. The Congress, following my brother's lead, raised a defense fund for them; and the best lawyers defended them. So my brother, for the first time in thirty years and the last time in his life, put on the black gown and curled white wig of a British barrister (which I may say were vastly becoming to him) and at the head of counsel for the defense entered the Red Fort at New Delhi where the trials were held.

Needless to say, Bhai was not successful in getting them off scot-free, but none of them was shot. They were sentenced to life imprisonment, which meant a little over a year, for Bhai freed them as soon as he had the power to do so.

That summer my brother was elected president of the Congress for the fourth time, in the first election since that of 1940. And on

September 19, 1945, Prime Minister Attlee announced that the British Labour Government sought "an early realization of self-government for India." The first step was to be elections to the central and provincial legislatures, after which the Viceroy would again try to form an all-India Executive Council, representing the main Indian political parties, and to restore democratic government in the provinces. Then, guided by the results of the elections, Lord Wavell would convene a Constituent Assembly to draw up a constitution for India.

Bhai, still leery of British promises, considered the proposals "vague, inadequate and unsatisfactory," but when the British government showed further signs of good will such as releasing other political prisoners, my brother, at the urging of Gandhiji, agreed that Congress candidates should contest the election in good faith. All the other political parties including the Muslim League did so as well.

Again Bhai traveled the length and breadth of India campaigning for the Congress slate, but this time he, too, was a candidate. It was conceded by all that when independence came he would be the first Indian prime minister. Again the Congress candidates won overwhelming victories in a majority of the provinces; only in the heavily Muslim districts did the Muslim League candidates win. Congress ministries were formed in eight provincial legislatures. But still, due to the obduracy of Mr. Jinnah, there was no agreement on the form of a central government. In a statement in Bombay Jinnah said: "We could settle the 'Indian problem' in ten minutes if Mr. Gandhi would say, 'I agree that there should be Pakistan; I agree that one-fourth of India composed of six provinces—Sind, Baluchistan, the Punjab, the Northwest Frontier Province, Bengal and Assam, with their present boundaries, should constitute the Pakistan state.' "

Gandhiji characterized this proposal in one word: "Blasphemy!"

Meanwhile, India was growing more chaotic. Food and clothing were terribly short; famine conditions prevailed in some places. This and communal tensions, whipped up by hotheads, provoked violent riots and looting in the great cities. Poor Wavell's good intentions could not cope. Finally, an alarming occurrence prodded the British government into further action.

On the morning of February 18, 1946, I drove my car into downtown Bombay to do some shopping. As I came out on the famous park facing the bay and the Apollo Bunder, known as "the Gateway of India," where the viceroys used to land, I heard the sound of shots. I immediately parked the car and went into a shop from which I rang up my husband whose office was nearby. "There seems to be a lot of shooting," I said. "Do you know what is happening?"

"I don't know," he said, "but there are crowds surging around. They are breaking windows. We have been asked to close our offices."

Crowds were gathering where I was, too, so I went out and found a vantage point from which I could see what was happening. Looking toward the sea I saw that all the little gray ships of the Royal Indian Navy—which were normally swinging at anchor or moored alongside the naval docks—were formed up in line of battle with their black guns pointing at the city. Instead of the Union Jack, orange, white and green Indian national flags were streaming out from their mastheads.

Not knowing whether to cheer or tremble I started for my car, but before I could reach it hordes of mounted police and soldiers came dashing past and cut me off. By now I realized that the fleet had mutinied. The sailors on the ships were shooting off the cannons, sometimes in the air and sometimes at the shore where large crowds had gathered. The soldiers were shooting back. I could see the Indian boys who had mutinied throwing their officers into the sea—not only British officers, but also Indian officers who had refused to join them. There were lots of heads bobbing up and down in the water; some of the officers swam toward shore and others climbed into lifeboats which were lowered from the ships and cut adrift for their benefit. Some of them even managed to clamber back onto the ships. For three days and three nights the shooting and the rioting went on as the city rose in sympathy with the sailors. Surprisingly few people were killed, and whether this was because of very poor or very good shooting no one knew.

My brother, who was due in Bombay, sent messages to the mutineers begging them to surrender the ships peacefully. The ringleaders must have known he was coming to stay with us, for one night the doorbell rang and we found four of them outside our flat. They looked terribly young, very earnest and rather frightened. Raja was sympathetic to them as were most of the people of Bombay, in spite of their shooting cannons at us. He took them to see Sardar Vallabhbhai Patel, who later became deputy prime minister in my brother's cabinet. It was Patel and Raja who finally persuaded these young lads to give up the ships and surrender, by telling them that it was a disgrace for Indians to behave like that. They must have discipline, for their behavior would only make our final goal of independence more difficult to achieve.

Patel also promised them that they would not be harshly dealt with, a promise he was unfortunately unable to keep. To the British, a naval mutiny is the worst crime that can be committed; and they acted accordingly. Some of the boys were flogged and they were given long prison sentences—which were not so long in the end because my brother came into power.

Bhai certainly did not approve of the mutiny, which had definite political overtones: Muslim League flags were flown from the ships, as well as our national flag. There were also Communist implications, as Left-Wing parties shouted, "Hindus and Muslims to the barricades," and the sailors formed what they called the "Central Strike Committee," while the Bombay mobs roared Communist slogans.

My brother's first reaction was the sorrowful remark that "What has happened in Bombay clearly demonstrates how antisocial elements... can exploit a situation.... [After tremendous sacrifices] our freedom is near at hand today. We have all the virtues for winning our freedom, but I confess we lack the discipline which is essential for a free country."

At the same time my brother sympathized with the sailors who had genuine grievances in addition to the usual postwar unease which often appears in military bodies, victorious or otherwise. At a press conference on March 1, 1946, Bhai said, "I understand in official army parlance there is no such thing as a strike. Everything is a mutiny. If two persons sign a letter of protest together it is a mutiny. ... It is obvious that the rules are so rigid that even a respectful joint protest is a mutiny.

"I understand that instructions have been issued which can only be interpreted to mean a great deal of victimization, not only [that] but terrorization. . . . Such a course of action is bound to have repercussions....

"Obviously there was tremendous sympathy in the city of Bombay for the naval ratings. . . . A great deal of excitement has been caused by gunfire which was more or less harmless. . . . There are all manner of groups in the city who immediately rush in to exploit such a situation . . groups which call themselves revolutionary. The Communists consider themselves very revolutionary but I consider them counterrevolutionary. Far from being revolutionary they are conservative." (Bhai might be enthralled by Russian Communists, but not Indians.) Then my brother demanded a fair and open trial for the naval ratings.

One result of the naval mutiny, and other minor mutinies that took place in the Royal Air Force in Calcutta and also in the Royal Indian Air Force, was that the government of India lost face in the nation and in all of Asia. Another result may have been a coincidence. On March 19, the day after the naval mutiny began, the British government announced that it was sending what was called "the Cabinet Mission" to India to make a grand final effort to reach a satisfactory agreement for the independence of India.

Before the Cabinet Mission arrived Bhai received an extraordinary request from the Viceroy. Lord Wavell called him to New Delhi to suggest that he go to Malaya, where there was a big railway strike and great unrest among the large Indian population as well as the Indian National Army prisoners, and try to get the situation calmed down. Bhai accepted and took Raja along as his secretary. Before he left, my brother requested permission to land at Rangoon, the capital of Burma, en route. Permission was denied by the British military authorities. Unfortunately, Bhai's plane had a "forced landing" in Rangoon, and by a remarkable coincidence all the high Burmese officials happened to be at the airport.

My brother's mission to Malaya might have been a disaster but for the intervention of Lord Louis Mountbatten. Two days before Jawahar was expected, Lord Louis returned from India to his headquarters in Singapore to find the local military administration in an uproar. They were terrified that my brother's presence might cause the Indian National Army prisoners and the local Indian population to rise in revolt. Their prescription for avoiding trouble was to "ignore Nehru" except for lining the streets with soldiers with fixed bayonets.

Mountbatten was furious. He called a meeting at Government House and said, in effect, "Pandit Nehru is our invited guest and a distinguished statesman who one day soon may rule India. He must be treated as such. I hear you haven't even offered him a car. If you don't, I'll give him my car. Furthermore you will send lorries out to bring Indians in from the suburbs who want to see him. We will have no armed soldiers lining the streets. Passes are to be issued to distinguished Indian residents to meet him at the airport. I shall give a luncheon for Pandit Nehru at Government House."

So when my brother came to Singapore he found himself treated as though he were already Prime Minister of India instead of a newly released jailbird. At Government House, Mountbatten put on all the panoply of state, with troops in dress uniform presenting arms, bagpipes skirling, and all the top brass assembled to meet him.

After the luncheon my brother was to drive through the streets of Singapore to show himself to the crowds. Mountbatten proposed to drive with him in an open car. When they heard this his aides were horrified. With affectionate concern they said, "There is no way to protect you from assassination"; and when Mountbatten shrugged that off, they said, "You'll only enhance Nehru's prestige."

"Don't be silly," Lord Louis said. "He'll increase mine."

So it turned out. My brother rode beside Mountbatten through streets lined with wildly cheering Indians, and mingled with the acclaim for Nehru were shrill shouts of "Mountbatten *Ki Jai.*"

They ended the drive at the St. John Ambulance Canteen which Lady Mountbatten had opened in a Nissen hut near the center of the city. A tremendous crowd had collected there. Raja, who was in the car behind Bhai and Mountbatten, stepped out and was standing behind Lady Mountbatten when the crowd suddenly surged forward, knocking him down. He lay flat on his back looking up at the face of the lady who was to be Vicereine of India. Then she went down too. Bhai sprang forward and lifted her to her feet, and with Mountbatten carried her safely into the hut.

The informality of that meeting was a happy augury for my brother's relations with the Mountbattens. That night, Bhai and Raja dined with them, and in a long, intimate conversation Bhai recognized that they were people of great good will. A friendship was formed that endured as long as they lived, and had a tremendous effect on the future of India.

Mountbatten asked Bhai to address the Indian National Army prisoners and the strikers, and try to make them have sense and reach some understanding with the British; and above all not to do anything that would upset the negotiations about to begin on Indian independence. This Bhai did, and then hurried back to India leaving my husband as his representative.

Raja remained in Malaya for a whole month. He conciliated the strikers and got them back to work, and apparently did a good job with the I.N.A. prisoners as well, for when he came home and reported to the Working Committee in New Delhi, he was given the highest praise by Gandhiji and my brother; and the Committee voted him a sort of certificate of merit for having handled a difficult situation well.

When the makeup of the Cabinet Mission was announced even my brother felt hopeful that the Attlee government meant business. It was headed by Sir Stafford Cripps and included the Secretary of State for India, Lord Pethick-Lawrence, a true friend of India; and the First Lord of the Admiralty, Mr. A. V. Alexander. They arrived in New Delhi in the last week of March 1946. Virtually all the Indian leaders were there to meet with them including, of course, Gandhiji, who this time, instead of stopping at Birla House, stayed in the Bhangi Colony in the Untouchable Quarter of Old Delhi. This had a useful dramatic effect as the world saw the great men of England and India going down to the slums to confer with the humble spiritual leader of India. It also cost Mr. Birla a pretty penny because part of the Colony had to be cleaned up, new huts built to replace the filthy chawls in which a man could not even stand upright, and Khus grass hung in the doorways and windows to provide our home-grown air-conditioning against the stupefying heat.

The talks with the Cabinet Mission were mostly held in the pea-green study of the Viceroy's House, its only air-conditioned room. Unfortunately they were little better than a repeat performance of the Simla talks of the year before. The British were ready to accept any solution the Indians could agree on, but Mr. Jinnah blocked every plan that did not include Pakistan. After six weeks of fruitless discussion in the blazing heat, Lord Wavell invited the Mission and four Hindu leaders and four Muslims to Simla in the hope of cooling heated minds and bodies; Gandhiji also went along, as no decisions could be reached without him.

In Simla my brother had two long conferences with Jinnah to no avail. Everyone else worked on the Muslim leader with equally poor results. At the end of ten days they all came back to New Delhi. Then Gandhiji told the Cabinet Mission that they should suggest their own plan, since the Indians could not agree on one.

On May 16, the Cabinet Mission published their plan. They stated that the idea of Pakistan was unworkable and would not solve the communal problem because so many Muslims would be left in India and so many Hindus in Pakistan. Then they proposed a federated Indian Union with only foreign affairs, defense, and communications reserved to the Central Government, in which the Muslim and Hindu provinces would have equal representation. At the next level the provinces could form groups according to their wishes. Finally, most domestic matters would be left to the provincial legislatures. A Constituent Assembly appointed by the legislatures would meet to draft a constitution for India on these lines. After studying the plan for four days Gandhiji announced that, "After searching examination my conviction abides that it is the best document the British government could have produced in the circumstances." In addition he quashed the old idea that communal differences were still the fault of the British, saying, "The Congress and the Muslim League did not, could not agree. We would grievously err if at this time we foolishly satisfy ourselves that the differences are a British creation."

My brother was not happy about the plan, nor were most of the Congress. Jinnah objected that "the plan was simply to please and placate the Congress." Nevertheless, on June 4, the Muslim League astonished everyone by accepting the plan. Whereupon the Working Committee and Gandhiji took to the hills in Mussoorie to deliberate on what to do. Gandhiji prevailed. He dared not risk another *Satyagraha* campaign in the violent state of the nation; the Constituent Assembly seemed the only road to freedom. My brother feared violence less than British guile; he hated the thought of accepting a British plan for India. The Working Committee took a long time about deciding. Finally, after Lord Wavell unilaterally announced that he would appoint an Interim Provisional Government of India, the Working Committee accepted the British plan. The Cabinet Mission left for home with high hopes for a united independent India. It might have worked.

On July 7, 1946, the All India Congress Committee met in Bombay to ratify the Working Committee's action. As usual, Bhai stayed with us. The meeting was a rather small one of only 255 voting delegates. They met in a hall with a stage at one end, and the floor was covered with coarse khadi on which everyone sat, leaning against fat bolsters. Bhai, wearing tight khadi trousers and a long *kurta* with a sleeveless fawn-colored jacket* over it, presided as president of the Congress, and made the opening address.

In assessing that speech which, together with my brother's press conference of July 10, is said to have given Jinnah the excuse for wrecking the Cabinet Mission plan, one must remember two things: first, that there was strong resistance among the delegates to ratifying the Working Committee's action; and, secondly, that my brother still distrusted the British and any plan they devised. In order to get a favorable vote he had to say that the Constituent Assembly would have freedom of action. He put it rather strongly:

> The Congress idea of independence is certainly different from what the Muslim League or the Viceroy thinks. Our idea of independence is that there must be absolutely no foreign domination in India and that India may even break her connection with the British. We want to establish the Republic of India. . . .
>
> There is a good deal of talk of the Cabinet Mission's long-term plan and short-term plan. So far as I can see, it is not a question of our accepting any plan—long or short. It is only a question of our agreeing to go into the Constituent Assembly. . . .
>
> We will remain in that Assembly so long as we think it is good for India, and we will come out when we think it is injuring our cause, and then offer battle. We are not bound by a single thing except that we have decided for the moment to go into the Con-

* This type of jacket is still called "the Jawahar jacket."

stituent Assembly, not, certainly, to deliver fine speeches, but to build something to overcome some of our problems.

On that basis the Congress Committee voted, far from unanimously, to go into the Constituent Assembly.

That speech of Bhai's was all that Jinnah needed to back out of a commitment he already regretted. Leonard Mosley in *The Last Days of British Raj** put it picturesquely: "Mr. Jinnah . . . dived for cover screaming treachery as he did so." The fact is that Jinnah not only dived for cover, he resolved to make sure of Pakistan and make an Indian Union impossible by fanning the flames of communal hatred to incandescence. In a rabble-rousing speech to the meeting of the Muslim League on July 27–29, 1946, Jinnah in effect declared a holy war, a jihad, against the Hindus. The League passed a resolution calling for "direct action," and setting August 16, 1946 as Direct Action Day. They set up a Council of Action to remind Muslims that "it was in the month of Ramzan [August] that the first battle between Islam and Heathenism took place." Leaflets were printed calling on Muslims to "take up your swords." Jinnah himself said, "Today we bid goodbye to constitutional methods. . . . We have forged a pistol and are in a position to use it!"

While the Muslims prepared for August 16, the Viceroy, on August 6, sent for my brother and invited him to form an Interim Government. Bhai conditionally accepted and on August 12, the arrangement was publicly announced. My brother immediately went to Mr. Jinnah and offered him five out of fifteen seats in his cabinet and any ministry he personally wanted. Jinnah, of course, refused.

In the dawn light of August 16, 1946, Muslim mobs poured out of the slums of Calcutta armed with broken bottles, old automobile cranks, chains, monkey wrenches and *lathis* to start their "holy war." Rampaging through the narrow streets they killed every Hindu they could find, from old gentlemen to baby girls. Taken by surprise the Hindus fled, then rallied. Hindu mobs charged into the Muslim slums slavering for revenge. It must be admitted that they behaved as savagely as the Muslims. For four days "the Great Calcutta Killing,"

* (London: Weidenfeld & Nicholson, 1962.)

as it was called, continued. No one knows how many died: 5,000 dead and 15,000 injured is a low estimate.

Nor did it end when the troops finally restored order in Calcutta. The communal fighting ran up the sacred Ganges Valley, and city after city exploded in violence like a string of firecrackers. It spread through Bengal and Assam, even to the villages of distant Bihar.

At the height of the rioting Bhai went to Calcutta, fearlessly touring the worst districts in the hope of stopping the killing. Both sides allowed him to speak to them, and he sternly condemned Hindus and Moslems alike for their atrocities. With the help of the government of India he opened first-aid camps and canteens for the injured and dispossessed. I, too, went to Calcutta for about a month and worked in one of those camps. It was a dreadful sight. In both camps, whether Muslim or Hindu, there were hundreds of wounded—men, women and children, many with hands or feet hacked off or still more horrible mutilations. Even worse, perhaps, was the psychic damage, the soul-destroying effect of rape and degradation, of terror and hatred combined. Many of these people who came to us seemed utterly bewildered; even those who had taken part in the killings seemed not to know why. Often they said to Bhai, "We don't know. It's you politicians who have done this, because we have lived in peace for years.'"

They, Muslims and Hindus, were in truth one people, speaking a common language, Bengali; and they could not even talk with the Muslims or Hindus from Bombay, where Gujarati is spoken, or New Delhi, where the people speak Hindustani. They had every right to say the politicians had triggered it. Mr. Jinnah's speech had triggered it, although fear and hatred and bigotry must have been there underneath the surface all the time.

As the rioting and killing spread up into the Punjab and the Northwest Frontier Province, Bhai followed, and was sickened by the terrible sights he witnessed, the crazed resort to mass murder among normally placid peasants. "There appears to be a competition in murder and brutality," he reported to the Central Assembly.

To Bhai it was incredible that religion could turn men into such savages; he had perhaps discounted it too much. He was too civilized, too gentle to understand the power of hatred—of hatred unto death.

This was the condition of India when, on September 2, 1946, my brother became technically the vice president of the Viceroy's Executive Council; in fact, the prime minister of the Interim Government of India. His cabinet consisted of five Hindus and one Harijan, who were Congress members; a Christian, a Sikh, a Parsee, and two Muslims.

17
half a loaf

From the first, my brother had a frustrating and nerve-wracking experience as prime minister of the Interim Government. Jinnah proclaimed the day he took office as a day of mourning for Muslims, and black banners were flying. Not only Muslim intransigence and communal killings, but the balkiness of British members of the Indian Civil Service, who distrusted all Indians and were resigning as fast as they could and still collect their pensions, made things difficult. In addition, the Viceroy kept interfering. Though theoretically he was supposed to accept the advice of my brother's cabinet, he sometimes acted as though he were still the autocratic satrap of the British Raj. Many meetings between them and a somewhat acrimonious correspondence ensued over the next few months; for until a constitution could be agreed upon, the powers of each were ill-defined, and Lord Wavell was undoubtedly as unhappy and frustrated as Bhai.

However, Lord Wavell made one fortunate suggestion to my brother, that he appoint my sister as head of the Indian delegation to the first session of the United Nations General Assembly in New York. Bhai hesitated a bit, for fear she would have a difficult time, but finally decided to send her. Nan's brilliant performance established her as one of India's best diplomats.

Since he now had to be in New Delhi most of the time, my brother chose a rather pleasant house at 17 York Road as his headquarters during the whole period of the negotiations for independence, and for some time afterward. It was not a very large house; it did not look like the residence of a head of state, but it was fairly spacious. As one entered there were two rooms, used as offices by Bhai's secretary and staff. Then came a drawing room opening on a large verandah overlooking the lawn and gay flower gardens. There were also a large dining room and two nice guest rooms on the ground floor. My brother's suite was upstairs—I can see him now running lightly up those stairs like a graceful youth—and two more bedrooms that members of the family used.

The thing none of us could quite get used to at first was the guards outside the two gates; Indian Army soldiers in British-style khaki uniforms and green berets, or bearded Sikhs wearing turbans over their long hair. Two of them marched back and forth at each of the two gates—tramp, tramp, kick, stamp, turn—in Buckingham Palace form. Others waited to relieve them in a small guardhouse that Lord Wavell had built beside the gate. No one was allowed to come in until the guard had checked by telephone with my brother's secretary. This irritated Bhai because he was not used to being guarded, except as a prisoner, and he'd ask people to breakfast and forget to tell anybody, so there would be complications. He wanted to get rid of the guards, but the Viceroy was taking no chances and said they must remain. In this case he overruled my brother.

After Bhai had been in office about six weeks, on October 15 the Muslim League decided to join the Interim Government, not to co-operate but to make things difficult. In fact they openly said, "We are going into the Interim Government to get a foothold to fight for our cherished goal of Pakistan. . . . The Interim Government is one of the fronts of the Direct Action Campaign." Hardly an agreeable prospect for the Prime Minister.

Mr. Jinnah appointed five cabinet members—four Muslims and an Untouchable—to show he, too, was democratic, I presume. The Muslim contingent was headed by squat, heavy-faced Liaquat Ali Khan, who later became the first prime minister of Pakistan. There was quite a row because Jinnah wanted Liaquat Kahn to be Deputy Prime Minister. However, it was now too late, as my brother had given this post to Sardar Vallabhbhai Patel and refused to demote him. So Liaquat Khan became minister of finance, and leader of the house (lower chamber of the Assembly).

Gandhiji played no part in this intricate maneuvering because he was tramping through the villages of Noakhali. Communal rioting in the cities had horrified and sickened him, but when it spread to his beloved villages he almost despaired. At first he thought of another fast, and then he decided on a pilgrimage of peace. In that inaccessible part of Bengal, so swampy that even bullock carts bog down, and where the population was eighty per cent Muslim, Gandhiji, accompanied only by his Bengali interpreter, his secretary and Manu Gandhi, his cousin, walked on bare feet through mud and miasmas from village to village. When night overtook him he simply asked for shelter in some peasant's hut, preferably a Muslim. He was never refused. His pilgrimage not only calmed the communal troubles in Noakhali; it was a penance that soothed his troubled soul; and it was a rare triumph of spirit over the flesh, for Gandhiji was seventy-seven years old.

The Constituent Assembly was scheduled to meet in December, but Mr. Jinnah opposed this, knowing he would be outvoted. Prime Minister Attlee's government and Lord Wavell, frantically trying to save the Cabinet Mission Plan, invited—no, begged—the leaders of both camps to come to London for a final effort. With great reluctance, my brother agreed to go. The others who went to London were Lord Wavell, Jinnah, Liaquat Khan, and Sardar Balder Singh, who represented the Sikhs.

It was a wasted effort. Again, the best persuasions of Indians and Englishmen alike, even in the atmosphere of 10 Downing Street, failed to shake Jinnah's determination. To a considerable extent the British sympathized with his position. In all of India Hindus outnumbered Muslims by over three to one, roughly 300,000,000 to 92,000,000, and he played on British fears, as he had evoked Muslim fears, that they would become a persecuted minority. On the other hand, my brother's ideal had always been to found a secular state in which all religions—Muslims, Hindus, Sikhs, Jews, Christians, Parsees, everyone—would be treated exactly alike. The British may have believed in his good intentions, but doubted his ability to pull it off; the majority of Muslims doubted both his intentions *and* his ability. There was a total impasse.

In this situation Lord Wavell threw in the sponge. In answer to Prime Minister Attlee's demand for a new, workable plan for Indian independence all the Viceroy could suggest was a phased withdrawal of all British forces, leaving the Indians to fight it out among themselves. Personally I wish they had done so. However bloody the civil war and whoever won, the integrity of India would have been preserved.

191

But Attlee could not face this prospect. He said, "If we did it, Winston would surely call it a sordid scuttle; and he would be right." So Attlee began looking for a new viceroy.

One lighter moment brightened this dismal interim. Madame Chiang Kai-shek decided to visit India. She stayed with the Viceroy, but because of his new position and their old friendship, my brother had to entertain her. Bhai hastily sent for Nan and me to act as his hostesses and show Madame Chiang the sights—Indira's second son, Sanjay, had recently been born and she was busy in the nursery.

Naturally Madame Chiang wanted to see the Taj Mahal at Agra, so an expedition was arranged. Nan and I arrived at the Viceroy's House to find a big American limousine with the Viceroy's coat of arms on the doorpanel and the Union Jack flying from the staff, waiting for Madame Chiang. Four jeeps were also lined up; one contained Indian military police, the others were filled with Chinese of her entourage; they were all armed. Madame Chiang walked down the great steps until she saw the cars and stopped dead. "Where is the Chinese flag?" she asked. "I will not go in that car unless it also has the Chinese flag."

There was a great to-do with aides rushing around trying to find a Chinese flag and a suitable staff to mount it on. Only when this was done would Madame Chiang put foot in the car.

It is normally a three-hour drive to Agra, but our mixed motorcade took somewhat longer. By the time we arrived, our guest declared that she was exhausted and went straight to her suite. One is supposed to see the Taj three times—at sunset, by moonlight and at dawn. Although we reached Agra at lunchtime, Madame Chiang did not make the sunset, so arrangements were made to stay over a second night.

At dinner time Nan and I knocked on the door of her suite and were shown in. We found Madame Chiang lying on her bed. Beside the bed was a large wooden box, like a treasure chest, full of little jars with all sorts of greasy ointments in it. Three women were working over her, one massaging her legs, another her arms, while the third worked on her face. We found out later that she normally had two or three hours of massage to equip her for the rest of the day. Even during the war when Chungking was being bombed every day we were told she never missed; she had a little nook in an air-raid shelter where she took her massage.

We finally got her up in time to see the Taj by moonlight, and again the next day at sunset. She never saw it at sunrise—that was too early for her.

Madame Chiang is a very brave lady and a good friend of India, and of the Nehrus—Nan's daughter was the first to benefit by the scholarship she endowed at Wellesley where she went to college. But her luxurious tastes seemed a little incongruous in the austerity-minded India of the last days before independence. It is fortunate for her that she never had to go to jail.

Another bright moment of that year was the birth of Indira's second child. We were all staying at my brother's house on York Road that December, and Raja and I were due to leave for a lecture tour in the United States. Indira was very reluctant to have me go before the baby was born because I had been with her all through her first son's birth, and looked after her before and after he was born. On the night before we were supposed to leave, her family doctor, who was also a friend, came to examine Indu and told me that it would be another three weeks. But he said, "She is very upset at the idea of your leaving tomorrow."

"Well, this is her second baby," I said. "There shouldn't be any trouble."

"No, she's perfectly all right, but she is so keyed up that anything might happen."

He left about nine o'clock and we had dinner at nine-thirty as usual. My two sons were back from boarding school and we had a merry family meal. Indu was in good spirits and Bhai, despite his cares, was like his young self, joking and teasing all of us.

At about three o'clock the next morning a maid woke me up saying, "Mrs. Gandhi is not feeling well."

I went quickly to Indu's room and found her sitting up in bed. "I'm having the pains," she said. "They're not much yet, but they seem to be increasing."

After what the doctor had said I was skeptical, but he had also said that she did not want to have her baby after I left so, perhaps, in some mysterious subconscious way, that started things, for the pains got worse. Feroze and I decided to take her to the hospital without waking Bhai. We sneaked out of the house in the dead of night, and when we reached the hospital I telephoned her English obstetrician. He arrived an hour and a half later in a very bad temper and said to me, "Do you have to get me out of bed at this ungodly hour?"

"I can't help it," I said brusquely. "It's quite obvious she's in labor. So go ahead with it."

"You stay out!" he snapped.

Feroze and I walked up and down, up and down that cold hospital corridor; it was very different from the first time in Bombay when I had been with her in the labor room holding her hand. I was frantic with anxiety which boiled up in alternate fury against the doctor and fear for my little Indu.

Ages later—it was not so long but it seemed so to Feroze and me—the doctor came out in his white coat and exultantly said, "Well, I saved her."

"Saved her," I gasped, "what do you mean—what about the child?"

"Oh the kid's all right, but Mrs. Gandhi had a very terrible time and lost a lot of blood. She would have died if it hadn't been for me."

Feroze said nothing, but I disliked that doctor and his bragging. I said icily, "Thank you, Doctor. If she was supposed to be saved she would have been saved in any case; and it is not due to you anyhow."

He walked away in a fury. Feroze and I finally found out that Indu had a son. Then, though it was still early, I rang up Bhai to tell him he had another grandson; and also what a bad time Indu had had. He rushed straight over to the hospital and we were allowed in her room. I won't ever forget his face when he saw his daughter lying semiconscious and whiter than her pillow with all her blood drained away; to me she seemed not even to be alive. It was two hours more before she began to revive a little and all that time Bhai and Feroze and I stood around her bed.

Indira named her son Sanjay after the philosopher in the *Bhagavad Gita* who relates the epic story of Arjuna and his battle with his wicked cousins when the Lord Krishna acted as his charioteer.

Raja and I got off to America in January 1947. I shall tell about our trip later. I returned to New Delhi in May 1947, in time for the immensely stirring and tragic events of that spring and summer.

Our much-sought-for Constituent Assembly met briefly in December 1946, and again in January 1947, but its deliberations were an empty exercise because the Muslim League would not take part, and the British would not let go unless they did. Nevertheless, things were moving. In February 1947, Prime Minister Attlee announced that, come what may, the British would leave India by June 1948. He also announced the appointment of Lord Mountbatten of Burma as the Viceroy to undertake the transfer of power. By a curious oversight, Lord Wavell was not informed ahead of time; he heard it over the radio. Sadly he said to his private secretary, George Abell, "Well, George, I always seem to get the short end of the stick"; and, it is said, he did not speak again for three weeks.

The last Viceroy had more personal power than any of his predecessors. Attlee had a most difficult time persuading Mountbatten to take a job which his friend Lord Ismay characterized as, "Like taking command of an ammunition ship that is already afire." Mountbatten's heart was with the Royal Navy; his greatest ambition was to become First Sea Lord. Furthermore, he knew that the Viceroyalty was sure to bring obloquy upon him in England. At best he would be known as "the man who liquidated the British Empire"; at worst he might be blamed for civil war in India and the slaughter of millions of people.

Mountbatten was so firmly set against taking the job that Attlee had to get King George VI to persuade his cousin to do it. In these circumstances Mountbatten was able to make his own terms which were: his naval career must not be compromised; a definite date must be set for the transfer of power; and he must have a free hand to negotiate with the Indian leaders. No other Viceroy ever had that.

Though I was not in New Delhi when Lord and Lady Mountbatten arrived with their eighteen-year-old daughter Pamela, I went there as soon as I returned from America to act as hostess for my brother, while Raja acted as an assistant to him. And this I can say: never had two such beautiful and charming people occupied the great sandstone palace at the head of the King's Way. Perhaps the Mountbattens were too charming for India's good, because they persuaded our leaders to accept things of which many of us disapproved.

When Bhai first called on the new Viceroy their former friendship was instantly, effortlessly renewed. At the end of their talk Mountbatten said with complete sincerity, "Mr. Nehru, I want you to regard me not as the last viceroy winding up the affairs of the British Raj, but as the first to lead the way to the new India."

Bhai, always emotional beneath his public reserve, was tremendously moved. Then he pulled himself up and with a twinkle said, "Now I know what they mean when they speak of your charm being so dangerous."

Gandhiji, too, was completely won over by the Mountbattens, though not so far as ever to agree to the partition of India. He told Mountbatten that the British policy of divide and rule had brought about a situation in India in which there were only two alternatives: "Either a continuation of British rule or a bloodbath."

"What should I do then?" Mountbatten asked.

Realistically the mystic advocate of non-violence said, "You must face the bloodbath and accept it."

There is no question that Lord Mountbatten wanted to do the best he could for India, though his primary purpose was to get England out with honor and dignity. These two things, which sound compatible, actually were not. The easy way for England was to get my brother and the Congress to agree to partition, to Pakistan. And I shall never believe that was best for India, though Lord Mountbatten probably honestly thought it was, and also persuaded my brother of it.

The essence and danger of Mountbatten's persuasive power was that he not only sincerely loved India and her people, which we all instinctively felt; but also that he knew just how to handle us. He knew how we love pomp and a good show, for he loved that sort of thing himself; and he was determined that the British Raj should not end with a whimper, but with the grandeur and panache of the Empire maintained to the very last moment.

Never was there a more splendid ceremony than his installation as Viceroy. The great Durbar Hall was filled with all the leaders of India from my brother in his white, fitted sherwani with the red rosebud that became his symbol pinned on it, to the princes glittering in all their jewels. The silver trumpets blew and Lord and Lady Mountbatten walked slowly up the aisle opened for them by the scarlet-uniformed men of the Governor General's Bodyguard. Mountbatten wore the pale blue, ermine-trimmed robe of the Grand Master of the Star of India over the full dress uniform of a British admiral, crossed by the dark blue ribbon of the Garter and with such a blaze of orders on his breast as no other man in the world was entitled to wear. Edwina wore a diamond coronet and a long gown of ivory brocade crossed by the pink ribbon of the Crown of India which she had truly earned by her Red Cross work in the steaming, muddy jungles of the Burma Front. As they took their places on the gold-and-scarlet thrones on the dais at the end of the hall they looked so radiantly young and beautiful that my emotional countrymen were swept away.

Then came the oath-taking, following which Mountbatten broke precedent to make a short, touching speech to the assemblage in which he spoke of the urgency of the task which he and they had before them, and recalled the friendships he had made in India while he was Supreme Commander, Southeast Asia. He ended by saying, "I am under no illusion about the difficulty of my task. I shall need the greatest good will of the greatest possible number of people; and I am asking India for that good will."

Then he sat down beside Edwina. The trumpets blew again while the Viceroy's flag was hoisted on the staff atop the dome, and in the park, and simultaneously in every British garrison throughout India, cannon fired the thirty-one gun viceregal salute.

Though he could be so royal on ceremonial occasions Lord Mountbatten could also be completely simple and friendly when meeting privately with the Indian leaders. In a long series of talks with all of them he finally came to the conclusion, which even my brother and other Congress leaders were reluctantly beginning to accept, that a united India was impossible without an incredibly bloody civil war, perhaps chaos.

Though the Viceroy personally believed that a federated union on the lines of the Cabinet Mission plan was the best solution, bloody communal rioting in the Punjab and rising tension between Hindus and Muslims throughout the land reinforced this conclusion. However, Bhai admitted it was wrong when in a speech in New York on October 16, 1949, he said that, had he foreseen the terrible results of partition, he would have fought to the end against it.

A trip my brother made to the Punjab, just before Mountbatten's arrival, to try to stop the fighting, during which he "saw ghastly sights and . . . heard of behavior that would degrade a brute. . . ." undoubtedly weakened his resolve to hold out against Pakistan. Conditions were so bad that the civilian Prime Minister of the Punjab resigned and the British established martial law with my brother's tacit consent.

Gandhiji, who was staying in the enormous but tasteless Birla House, in the wing which Mr. G. D. Birla always kept for him, bleak and bare of furniture except for a cooking stove, mattresses and woven mats on the floor, did not accept partition, never accepted it. As a last desperate resort Gandhiji went to see Mountbatten again and advised him to pull the British troops out of India and "take the risk of leaving India in chaos and anarchy." He said, "We would still go through the fire without doubt, but the fire would purify us."

Mountbatten regarded this as the thing he most dreaded and continued to press for Pakistan. On April 18, the Congress conditionally accepted the principle of partition, and the Viceroy and his aides began preparing his plan based on a separate nation of Pakistan.

While these talks were in progress I saw a great deal of the Mountbattens, particularly Edwina who, with Pamela, was making a tremendous effort to establish friendly relations with Indian women. There was never a vicerein like her, for her compassion was matched by her courage, and her good will by her astounding energy. Besides those great qualities, which are often associated with deadly seriousness, she was great fun to be with. In those days of tension, and later when she came to stay with my brother after he became prime minister of the Republic of India, she was one of the few people left who could break his somber moods. When she was there, Bhai's laughter would ring through the house as it used to when we were young.

Their idyllic friendship was based on mutual admiration for the qualities each saw in the other, their idealism and their willingness to go flat out for the things they believed in. Lord Mountbatten won a place in the hearts of the Indian people which he holds to this day; it was in no small measure due to his wife's selfless efforts to help us solve our problems. As he often said in later years, "I never could have done it without Edwina."

The Mountbatten plan was presented to my brother on May 17. He turned it down flat because it did not contain the concept of India as a continuing unity. Bhai insisted that it must be established that the new Indian government was the successor to British India; and Pakistan was merely seceding from it. This was a legalistic point, but important in international law. So they all went up to Simla for another conference. Unlike the others this one succeeded. They got around the problem of constitutional continuity by getting Bhai to agree to temporary Dominion status. That he should do so seemed a complete reversal of his principles; but the point was that it was merely a legal device; and Bhai insisted that the terms "King-Emperor" and the oath of allegiance be eliminated.

The Mountbatten Plan envisioned the partition of the Punjab and Bengal if the Muslim majorities in those places voted for it. Jinnah objected to this with strong arguments as to the disadvantages of partition. Mountbatten said to him, "Every argument you have used applies equally to the parition of India. I quite agree with you, there should be no partition. But you can't have Pakistan unless the Hindu and Sikh majorities in those parts of the Punjab and Bengal can opt for India." Jinnah wanted Pakistan at any price. He agreed to the Mountbatten plan.

Gandhiji never agreed. He was heartbroken; but true to his principles of never coercing the Congress leaders, he withdrew completely from the negotiations and went on a pilgrimage to Bihar and Bengal to try to stop the killings there. On June 15, 1947, a full meeting of the All India Congress Committee, of which Professor J. B. Kripalani was president, accepted the plan by a vote of 153 to 29.

The Viceroy meanwhile had flown to England to get the British government to agree to the plan. No one but he could have done it. He not only convinced the Attlee government, but he talked the King into it; and he even got Winston Churchill to agree not to oppose it.

Because communal rioting was getting worse not better, the Viceroy advanced the date for Indian independence by ten months, setting August 15, 1947, as the time for the transfer of power. This left only two months for an infinitely complex operation, not like separating Siamese twins, but actually cutting one nation in two, with all its long-established, closely interwoven political, judicial, military and, above all, economic fabric. It was done, but the patient nearly died.

On August 14, 1947, Lord and Lady Mountbatten were in Karachi for the creation of Pakistan, Jinnah's misbegotten nation which consisted of two halves: West and East Pakistan separated by over a thousand miles of India—an obvious absurdity.* That afternoon they flew back to New Delhi.

An unprecedented action of my brother had testified to his confidence in Lord Mountbatten. With the concurrence of the Constituent Assembly he had asked the last Viceroy to become the first Governor General of the Dominion of India. Bhai did this not only because he believed that Mountbatten's knowledge of India's problems, his humanitarian, liberal thinking, and his sincere affection for the Indian people made him the best possible man for the job, but also because he hoped that Mr. Jinnah would do likewise in the new Dominion of Pakistan, thus making Mountbatten a sort of bridge between the bleeding fragments of India. But the *Quaid-i-Azam* was going to be just that. Jinnah made *himself* the first Governor General of Pakistan with almost dictatorial powers. When Mountbatten heard this he tried to withdraw as Governor General of India, but Bhai insisted that he must take it, because, though the Pakistanis had not fulfilled this last hope for some sort of unity, even Jinnah trusted Mountbatten and negotiations between the countries would thereby be eased. Jinnah himself told Mountbatten, "We want you to take it. We feel you will be a moderating influence."

I was not in New Delhi on Independence Day, because the Congress officials in Bombay wanted one member of our family in that city. I was distressed to go because I wanted to see the great ceremonies in New Delhi and, above all, to see Bhai become the first prime minister of India. He told me I had to go, so I went; but afterwards he described many of the things that happened.

Free India was born at one minute after midnight on August 15, 1947. My brother made perhaps the most moving speech of his life to the Constituent Assembly as they waited in the round Assembly

* Mr. Jinnah once said, "If I had not been a fanatic there would be no Pakistan."

Chamber for that moment in which they would be metamorphosed into the sovereign Indian Legislative Assembly. He said:

Long years ago we made a tryst with destiny, and now the time has come when we shall redeem our pledge, not wholly or in full measure, but very substantially. At the stroke of the midnight hour, when the world sleeps, India will awake to life and freedom. A moment comes, which comes but rarely in history, when we step out from the old to the new, when an age ends, and when the soul of a nation, long suppressed, finds utterance. It is fitting that at this solemn moment we take the pledge of dedication to the service of India and her people, and to the still larger cause of humanity. . . .

Freedom and power bring responsibility. . . . The future is not one of ease or resting but of incessant striving so that we may fulfill the pledges we have so often taken and the one we shall take today. The service of India means the service of millions who suffer. It means the ending of poverty and ignorance and disease and inequality of opportunity. The ambition of the greatest man of our generation has been to wipe every tear from every eye. That may be beyond us, but as long as there are tears and suffering, so long our work will not be over. . . . We have to build the noble mansion of free India where all her children may dwell.

I beg to move, Sir, that it be resolved that:

After the last stroke of midnight, all members of the Constituent Assembly present on this occasion, do take the following pledge: "At this solemn moment when the people of India through suffering and sacrifice have secured freedom I, ———, a member of the Constituent Assembly of India, do dedicate myself in all humility to the service of India and her people to the end that this ancient land attain her rightful place in the world and make her full and willing contribution to the promotion of world peace and the welfare of mankind."

From the Assembly my brother went straight to the Viceroy's house with the President of the Constituent Assembly, Doctor Rajendra Prasad. They found the Viceroy sitting alone in his study with his Public Relations Advisor, Alan Campbell Johnson. Reporters poured in behind Bhai and in a moment the quiet room became a scene of wild confusion with photographers leaping on sofas and polished tables, flashbulbs flickering like gigantic fireflies and everyone shouting orders and questions. Solemnity dissolved in confusion as laughingly the ex-Viceroy tried to restore order. Then Doctor Prasad began his little speech formally asking Lord Mountbatten to become governor general of the Dominion of India. He lost his notes and got stuck in the middle so Bhai similingly prompted him. Then Mountbatten, a deeply sentimental man for all his dashing ways, answered in a quietly intense voice, "I am proud of the honor and will do my best to carry out your advice in a constitutional manner."

The next morning Lord Mountbatten was sworn in as governor general in a ceremony slightly less splendid but even more enthusiastic than his installation as viceroy. After the ceremony the band played "God Save The King," and then, at a slight nod from Mountbatten our Indian National Anthem *"Jana Gana Mana."* Next Mountbatten drove in state through riotously enthusiastic crowds to the Assembly Chamber where he told the Legislative Assembly that as governor general he would be, ". . . one of yourselves, wholly devoted to the furtherance of India's interests."

The final ceremony of the day was the raising of our national flag on a tall flagpole in Princes' Park. Lord and Lady Mountbatten started down the renamed Raj Path in the state carriage with outriders and the mounted Governor General's Bodyguard clattering splendidly alongside. The program called for Bhai and the Governor General to make short speeches from the platform. The Mountbattens never reached it. Their carriage, postillions and Bodyguard were engulfed in a laughing, happy, wildly excited crowd of 300,000 people that no police lines could contain. Bhai on the platform could only see the lances of the Bodyguard tossing wildly above the people and Mountbatten standing slim and tall in his white uniform on the seat of the carriage signaling for him to go ahead. Bhai ordered the flag hoisted. As it crawled up the tall pole and the band played our national anthem a gentle shower of rain in the sunlight spread a rainbow in the sky that matched the colors of the flag we had fought under so long.

At that universal symbol of good fortune the crowd went insane.

Bhai plunged into it, fighting his way toward the state carriage. He just managed to get there. Mountbatten leaned out and lifted him bodily onto the back of the seat. As the postillions were trying to get the horses turned around, Mountbatten spotted a poor Indian family whose children seemed in danger of being trampled to death by the crowd, and hauled them into the overcrowded carriage.

Thus they rode back up the wide Raj Path, with the whole vast crowd running after them laughing and shouting in shrill acclaim, "*Hind Ki Jai!* Nehru *Ki Jai!* Mountbatten *Ki Jai!*"

So ended that great day as my brother never conceived it would, with the Indian crowd cheering the representative of the English King. But Bhai was far from triumphant; for his dream come true was darkened by forebodings; and the man whom he had truly called "the architect of Freedom" and "the Father of our Nation" was not there. Gandhiji could not bear to be present at the celebration of what to him was the defeat of all his principles and the bitter end of his hope of uniting Indians of all religions in love and peace. Instead he was in Calcutta desperately striving to check the rising tide of hatred between Muslims and Hindus.

18
the days after independence

On the day after Independence the Mountbattens came to Bombay. Raja and I were among those who met them at the airport and, of course, we took part in all the celebration ceremonies. Though I knew the Mountbattens were very popular I was amazed as we drove behind them in the motorcades through the enormously crowded streets to see Indians with our national flag in one hand and the Union Jack in the other shouting with equal fervor "Nehru *Ki Jai!*" and "Mountbatten *Ki Jai!*"

I had little heart for celebrating. From the first moment I heard that India was to be partitioned, I was bitterly against it. Even that late I had no idea there would be such hatred between our people, because we Nehrus had always been friendly with both Muslims and Hindus, and we could not care less what their religion was. Both Raja and I felt that partition was unnecessary. We would have liked to fight it out and if the Muslims won, well, they could rule us as they had before; and if the Hindus won I know my brother would have been fair to the Muslim minority.

In addition, I had many dear friends who were Muslims and I wondered if I would ever see them again—it was heartbreaking. My only comfort was that, at first, I thought partition would not last long; that the two parts of India would get together again. But I was wrong, for as the years have gone by we seem to be getting further apart.

As soon as we could, Raja and I went back to New Delhi where we lived in my brother's house, Raja assisting him in an honorary capacity, and I acting as his hostess. Indira at that time was too frail and too preoccupied with her children to do the job; and Bhai had sent Nan to be the first Indian Ambassador to Russia. So I was in New Delhi during all the agonizing days which followed that brief rejoicing.

On the day after Independence, the Boundary Commission published their report on the borders of the partitioned provinces of the Punjab and Bengal. It shocked the whole nation. Bhai and the other Congress leaders read it in deepening misery; the Muslims were livid with rage; and the warlike Sikhs, who had voted for partition, flew to arms to oppose it; for the rich lands of the western Punjab with its vital water supply and the great city of Lahore had been given to Pakistan.

The communal fighting had begun even before Independence Day, but the report touched off the most horrible massacres of all. The Punjab Boundary Force of 50,000 men, organized by Lord Mountbatten under the command of British General T. W. Reese, was helpless to combat it. Its efforts to restore order brought the hatred of both sides upon it, and it was disbanded late in August.

So shocking were the reports from the Punjab that my brother dropped everything else to fly there on August 17, two days after Independence. He was joined in the Punjab by the Prime Minister of Pakistan, Liaquat Ali Khan. Although they worked together trying to check the killings, they could not.

The slaughter and fear of worse to come started the greatest mass migration of peoples in the history of the world. Millions of panic-stricken Muslims fled across the Punjab plains toward Pakistan, encountering hordes of Hindus heading for India. These people had abandoned their houses and lands, on which some of them had lived for countless generations; and taking their portable possessions and their cattle, if they had any, started off in two-wheeled bullock carts or afoot, carrying their children, their sick and their ancients in their arms or on their backs, joining others in columns sixty miles long over which the choking dust of the dry roads rose like pillars of cloud.

Nor were they allowed to go in peace. In East Punjab, bands of armed Sikhs rose out of the wheat fields to attack the Muslim refugees, killing until their blood-stained swords became too heavy for weary arms to lift; while in West Punjab the hate-ridden Muslims slaughtered the Hindu columns. Even the special trains which my brother and the Pakistani Premier arranged to run between the two countries were hardly safer. As the trains, crammed with refugees even to the roofs of the cars, stopped briefly in Lahore, Muslim fanatics rushed them, killing, killing, killing. And in Amritsar, on the Indian side, Sikhs attacked each Muslim train; then squatted on the platforms wiping blood from their long curved swords until the next train came in.

In all this tale of horror there was only one bright spot. When Bengal was partitioned, Calcutta became part of India though twenty-three per cent of its inhabitants were Muslims. Yet Calcutta, where it all started with the great killing exactly to the day one year before, Calcutta, the most dangerous city, was peaceful, kept so by Gandhiji who day after day walked unguarded through its perilous streets preaching, praying, *commanding* the people, by his spiritual force, to respect each other.

There are no reliable statistics as to the great panic migrations or the numbers of people killed, but the most conservative estimate is that over 6,000,000 Muslims and 4,500,000 Hindus moved from one country to another, and of these from 200,000 to 700,000 were killed. One hundred thousand girls were stolen and sold to the highest bidder. Would the bath have been bloodier had my brother held out for a united India? He came to doubt it.

Over 400,000 of the Hindu refugees from Pakistan came to crowded Delhi. My brother set up camps for them outside the city as best he could, but we could not find even tents for 400,000 people, so many of them had to sleep on the bare ground. Thousands of others who got through the guards into the city slept in the doorways of buildings, in gutters and even on the streets where careless drivers sometimes ran over them. Camps were also set up for the Muslims who came from other parts of India trying to reach Pakistan in trains which got bogged down in Delhi. These camps had to be carefully guarded to protect the Muslims; our police and army units were strained to the limit and beyond.

We all did our best to feed and help these utterly destitute people in their wretched camps, where the appalling sanitation problems, which were impossible to solve, soon brought on epidemics of smallpox and cholera. Edwina Mountbatten did most of all. Her husband, on my brother's advice, appointed her head of the United Council for

Relief and Welfare, and her great organizational ability made it function more efficiently than anyone would have believed possible; while her advice to the Indian Red Cross services, based on her experience as head of the British St. John Ambulance, was invaluable.

In addition, she and Pamela Mountbatten flew thousands of miles to visit trouble spots in the Punjab and other refugee centers heedless of the dangers of disease or bodily harm from the half-crazed refugees. In New Delhi, Edwina often took me with her to visit the camps and temporary Red Cross hospitals. She would suddenly ring up and say, "I'm going to visit such and such a hospital, would you like to come with me?" and if it was at all possible I would go. It was amazing to see her in those terrible places, neither patronizing, nor oversympathetic, but just talking naturally to the inmates. This is the hardest thing of all to do when people are destitute, hopeless or dying.

But the most exciting times I had with her were during the riots.

Yes, we had communal riots in New Delhi, too; not as bad as those in other places, but terrifying nevertheless. The first one I got into was at the American Embassy shortly before Independence Day. Henry J. Grady, who was soon to be made American Ambassador, was then United States chargé d'affaires; and his wife was a friend of mine. They were very popular both in Indian and foreign circles. He was a large man, big-boned, broad and quiet; she was tiny, vivacious, talkative and always full of fun. She asked me to come to tea one day. I was driven over in one of my brother's cars and saw a huge angry crowd in front of the Embassy. I had the chauffeur park the car under a tree and got into the Embassy on foot through one of the side gates.

The Hindu crowd was howling angrily, and the guards had managed to close the main gates. They had sent for an aide-de-camp— Doctor Grady had left on a business trip by another door just as the crowd was gathering. As I walked across the courtyard toward the front door, I saw Lucretia Grady coming out with the A.D.C. Seemingly completely unruffled, she went up to the tall, wrought-iron gates and smiled at the crowd, and had an Indian secretary ask what they wanted. One Hindu who spoke English said, "We know you have some Mohammedan servants here; give them to us and we will go away."

Mrs. Grady said, "This is ridiculous. My staff is my staff, and this is American territory. You can't demand them of me because whoever is in the Embassy is on American soil."

The crowd started shouting and pushing, and it began to look dangerous; there were about four hundred people outside waving sticks and picking up brickbats to throw. Lucretia Grady smiled at them very sweetly and told the secretary to say to them that they should calm down and have a cup of tea.

Seeing this little woman standing there actually holding on to the closed gates did calm them down a bit. The man who spoke English said, "Madam, we do not wish to hurt you, but would you please let us have those servants of yours."

"I am very sorry," Lucretia replied, "but I have no intention of letting you have them—not one of them. If you want to do anything to me, well, you can, for I can't prevent it. But I can prevent you from breaking into the Embassy, and I am going to. If I were you I'd just think it over, and in the meantime have a cup of tea."

Then she saw me and waved to me. I went over to her, and she put her arm through mine; it did not tremble at all. Some of the crowd may have recognized me but I don't think that mattered.

By now Embassy servants—not the Muslim ones—were coming out with silver trays full of teacups. Of course there were not enough for everybody but the crowd caught the humor of it; besides, they thought Mrs. Grady was very brave. Some of them took cups of tea through a side door, as many as could. Others, the fanatical ones, shouted they would be back. But the whole temper of the crowd had changed and they soon went away after politely thanking Mrs. Grady for the tea.

Afterward I asked Lucretia if she had been very frightened underneath her calm. She said, "Well, I thought, if they are going to kill me I wish I had had time to kiss Henry good-by."

I doubt if there were any other women in the diplomatic corps who would have been as brave and resourceful as Lucretia Grady.

The riots I saw with Edwina Mountbatten were rather more dangerous, because that was after Independence and all the killings had raised tempers higher.

One night about eleven o'clock there was a telephone call from the Viceroy's House; Bhai was not home so I took the call. It was

Edwina, who did not behave like all the other vicereins, but phoned directly instead of having an A.D.C. ring up. I told her my brother was out and asked if she wanted to leave a message. "No," she said in an excited voice. "Haven't you heard that there is fighting between a Hindu and a Muslim camp? It looks serious. Have you heard anything?"

I told her we had not, and she said, "The rumor is that a Muslim from his camp shot a Hindu woman in their camp. So now the Hindus are up in arms throwing stones at the Muslims who are unable to protect themselves; and there aren't enough guards. So I am going down there and I called to see if your brother would like to come with me, but of course. . . ."

"Since he isn't here would you like me to come?" I asked.

"Certainly not," she said, "I can't have you hurt or dead on my hands."

"I'm not apt to be hurt," I said, "and I'd like to go; perhaps I could help. Will you pick me up?"

"Yes, you might help; yes, I'll take you."

Edwina came in a jeep escorted by another jeep in front and one behind. I presume the guards were armed but no arms could be seen by the people along the roadside as we drove to the camps, some distance outside the city.

A huge, angry mob had collected in front of the Muslim camp which they were trying to set on fire. Inciting them was a man who was screaming that his wife had been shot, and shouting "Nehru is protecting the Muslims and this is what they do!"

The mob was in a frenzy and the few guards were back to the wall. They had telephoned for reinforcements but we arrived before they did and pulled up in front of the Muslim camp, between it and the mob. Once again I was filled with admiration for Edwina's courage, the way she stepped out of the jeep and slipped past her own guards until she was standing facing that half-crazed crowd, who were throwing brickbats over our heads, as calmly as though she were at a garden party in the Moghul Gardens.

Edwina tried to talk to the crowd, but her Hindustani was not up to it so she asked me to speak to them. I stood on the jeep in my bright sari and harangued them at the top of my voice, begging them to be calm and telling them that my brother, the Prime Minister, was away, but that he would be back in the morning and would see to it that the man who fired the shot would be dealt with.

They listened to me, but the man whose wife was dead, and other agitators, began screaming and working them up again. "All right," Edwina said. "Now tell them that if they continue this way we will order the guards to shoot down the agitators, it doesn't matter which side they are on."

It was a dangerous gamble, we were so badly outnumbered, but I shouted out her message with all the force I could command. It worked. The agitators shut up and slunk into the crowd; they knew we'd get them even if afterward the mob overwhelmed us; and, at that, the frenzy and the shouting stopped.

Then we went over to talk to the Muslims. They said, "No, we have nothing to shoot with and have shot nobody. Please take our word for it. You have given us refuge, and if anybody among us has done this thing we will try to find out. But we have no guns."

Indeed, they had practically nothing; many of them were half-naked. We stayed there for about an hour to see if the riot would flare up again; but the Hindu crowd dispersed back to the building where they lived; and the Muslims lay down on the ground and in their tents.

When we reached the house on York Road my brother had just returned from his trip. Edwina came in and told him about the whole affair. Poor Bhai was so tired and distressed that he flew into one of his fine rages, angry at both sides. Oh, this was far from "the noble mansion of free India" he had planned to build!

He started an investigation the next morning, and, of course, nobody would admit to anything. Eventually, though, the investigators found that the woman who was shot had been ailing for a long time of tuberculosis. Her husband grew tired of her, and took what looked like an easy way out; he shot her and laid the blame on the Muslims. Eventually he was tried and convicted of murder.

After that there were other riots and, finding that I was useful in talking to our people and not afraid, Edwina often took me with her.

During that time, as is evident, our friendship with the Mountbattens grew deeper. They came to dine with my brother, and we frequently went to the Viceroy's House, now called Government House. When they came to dinner my brother, who had given up drinking long ago—and besides, abstinence was the Gandhian policy of the government—only served fruit juices before and with dinner; and the Mountbattens did likewise even when only Raja and I were there. Finally, when I felt I knew them very well, I said, "Edwina, don't you ever drink?"

"Certainly I do."

"Doesn't Dickie* drink?"

"Of course he does."

"Then," I asked, "why don't you give Raja and me whisky?"

"Your religion forbids it."

"It does not," I said, "and it wouldn't matter if it did."

Edwina's lovely laugh rang out and she said, "All right, but if you and Raja want a drink come early; for we don't like to serve it before other Indians."

The worst of all Bhai's troubles and anxieties, next to the communal killings, was the matter of Kashmir. The 565 princely states, of which the State of Jammu and Kashmir was one, had not been under the government of India. Their rulers simply acknowledged the paramountcy of the British Crown and they were governed by their maharajas, nawabs, and so forth, under the overall direction of the Viceroy, with a British agent in each state to oversee things. When the British pulled out, paramountcy lapsed, but, because it would be an impossible situation to have 565 independent nations, some of them only a few square miles in size, in the middle of India, the Mountbatten plan provided that the princely states could accede either to India or Pakistan as they chose. Lord Mountbatten himself talked the princes into accepting this arrangement; and Sardar Patel handled the negotiations with the vast majority of states which chose India.

Only three states refused to accede to either nation: Hyderabad Junagadh, and Travancore; they all eventually acceded to India. Kashmir hesitated. Though governed by a Hindu maharaja, it had a majority of Muslims; but they were not pro-Jinnah Muslims. The president of the All-Jammu and Kashmir Conference, the majority political party, was Sheikh Saheb Muhammed Abdullah,† known

* Mountbatten's nickname.
† Sheikh was his first name—not a title.

by the romantic sobriquet of "the Lion of Kashmir." He was a grand man, six feet five inches tall with a hawk face and twinkly eyes, who disliked Jinnah as much as he liked my brother. Sheikh Abdullah was extremely ambitious and so was the Maharaja, who fiddled and diddled about accession, hoping to make Kashmir an independent state.

Meanwhile the wild Pathan tribesmen of the North-west Frontier, fanatical Muslims, were being secretly armed by Pakistan which was also putting heavy economic pressure on Kashmir to accede to them. On October 12, 1947, the Pathans burst into Kashmir and started for Srinagar, looting, raping and murdering Hindus and Muslims alike, and burning their villages. When they were almost at the gates of Srinagar, the Maharajah of Kashmir, on the advice of Sheikh Abdullah, who was, of course, a Muslim, acceded to India and called for help. On October 27, my brother flew troops into Srinagar. They were only just in time to save the capital from massacre and arson. Even Gandhiji gave his approval to this resort to arms.

That was the beginning of the trouble over Kashmir which has embittered our relations with Pakistan more than any other thing. Pakistan sent help to the tribesmen and the fighting continued until the lines were stabilized in the western mountains of Jammu and Kashmir. My brother also took the matter up with the United Nations. Many people feel that this was a mistake and that he should have treated it as an internal Indian problem. As Bhai stated in the Indian Parliament, "Sheikh Abdullah . . . had undoubtedly the support of the large majority of the people of Kashmir, Muslims, Hindus, and Sikhs." On January 20, 1948, the Security Council of the United Nations appointed a commission to go to Kashmir to investigate the facts and try to mediate the dispute.

To get a little ahead chronologically, I went to Kashmir in 1948, to write an article for an American magazine. Because I wanted to get the truth about how the Kashmiris felt, I went secretly, without informing the Prime Minister, and I did not stay at a government rest house or in a houseboat but in the Nedous Hotel. Also I did not wear a sari for that, too, would have made it obvious; I wore a blouse and slacks with a scarf tied around my head. Very few people recognized me as Bhai's sister.

My room at the hotel was next to the suite of American Admiral Chester Nimitz of the United Nations Commission. We soon got to know each other, and I frequently had dinner or tea with Admiral and Mrs. Nimitz. Whether or not the Admiral knew who I was I do not know; he was very discreet and so, for a wonder, was I, and we never mentioned politics. The Admiral's greatest pleasure was playing bridge, a game I never had time for.

Every reporter needs a bit of luck. Mine was meeting Michael Peto, a Hungarian photographer on assignment for the *London Observer*. I had hired a car; he could not get one, so I made a deal with him. I would drive the car and he would take photographs; and he must give me any pictures I needed for my article. I also said to him, "Your only other job is to stay with me and in case we get a puncture, to fix it."

We drove to the little mountain villages outside of Srinagar; and not knowing who I was, I believe the people gave very true replies to my questions. In essence they said, "We cannot understand people of our own [Mohammedan] religion behaving as the raiders did to our womenfolk."

This annoyed me somewhat and I asked, "Why should your women be spared and not the Hindus who live here."

They would shrug and answer, "After all, Muslims dress a little differently so they knew us, and they should have spared our women and children, but they did not. They burned down our houses and spared nobody. They burned down convents; many nuns were burned; many Catholic fathers were burned, and many had to flee, though some stayed bravely on."

Thus, those Pathan raiders defeated themselves, for they might have won the sympathy of the people. Instead the peasants were embittered by all they had suffered—fields gone, houses burned, even houseboats—in Kashmir, unlike India, everything is made of wood from the great forests and it is easy to set them on fire. Nor were the people of that famous Vale of Kashmir very much interested in the struggle over their country. Time after time they said to me, "We do not care whether we belong to Pakistan or India, because all we want is to live a decent, normal life with our families, and to profit by the tourist trade which has been ruined by all this fighting."

Thus the simple peasants were not so simple as not to know which side of the bread their butter was on. I sympathized with them; for having been brought up in a house where people of all religions were regarded with respect, I could not ever understand the intense bitterness between members of different faiths.

If the people cared very little about what country they belonged to, my brother—and Mr. Jinnah—cared a great deal. As Bhai pointed out in his speech to our Central Legislature: "Kashmir, because of her geographical position with her frontiers with three countries, namely the Soviet Union, China and Afghanistan, is intimately connected with the security and international contacts of India. Economically also Kashmir is intimately related to India. The caravan trade routes from Central Asia pass through the Kashmir State.

"Nevertheless, we did not put the slightest pressure on the State to accede to the Indian Dominion, because we realized that Kashmir was in a very difficult position. We did not want a mere accession from the top but an association in accordance with the will of her people. . . ."

That is the only reason why my brother offered to hold a plebiscite in Kashmir, *after all the raiders had left.* He need not have done so for, by the standards of international law and also the Mountbatten Plan, Kashmir already belonged to India because the Maharaja, on the advice of his duly elected Prime Minister—and a Muslim at that —had exercised his option to accede to India. The plebiscite was never held simply because the raiders never left the state of Kashmir.

Quite often the question is raised as to whether my brother's intense desire to have Kashmir become part of India may not have been due to the fact that he was a Kashmiri. It is a question I cannot answer. It may never be answered, because who can plumb the innermost springs of a man's motivation? Certainly Bhai had strong logical reasons for his course of action, as he brilliantly demonstrated in his speeches, but how much they were reinforced by his love for the land of his forefathers is another matter.

In my own case, I admit that I am deeply involved emotionally. I have had the fortune to travel over most of the world and to see its finest scenery, but I still think that Kashmir is the most beautiful place on earth. Its clear lakes and rivers, its meadows and dark forests, its clean tingling air, and, beyond all, the incredible, ever snow-topped, ever changing, sky-piercing Himalayas make it so for me.

Whether this is a biased point of view I cannot say. But this I know: if we had to fight for Kashmir, even though I am far over the age when people are allowed to fight, I would still want to go and do my best, as I offered to do in the recent Indo-Pak War.

19
the ultimate violence

Throughout the autumn of 1947, while Calcutta remained calm, the communal riots in New Delhi increased in violence. Gandhiji came back to Birla House in New Delhi on September 7, and threw himself totally into trying to pacify the city. Daily he traveled to various trouble spots from the perilous narrow streets of the old city to the crowded, fetid camps of the refugees, exhorting them, pleading with them, praying with them. He refused any longer to obey his doctors' orders or even to let them take his blood pressure. On October 2, he was seventy-eight years old.

The old magic failed to work the wonders it had in Calcutta. Those 400,000 Hindu and Sikh refugees in the city, and in the great camps encircling it like a besieging army, formed a wall of misery and hatred he could not seem to touch; perhaps there were just too many of them and too much despair. Even the Congress no longer blindly followed his advice, nor did the new government of India. My brother did what he had to do, thinking Gandhiji too visionary to understand the hard realities of governing India.

Instead, this gentlest of men drew hatred upon himself. Louis Fischer states that at this time ninety-five per cent of Gandhiji's mail was invective—from Hindus accusing him of being pro-Muslim, and from Muslims just because he was a Hindu.

Gandhiji had one minor triumph. The small Muslim Jamia Millia Islami Academy at Okla outside the city on the plain amid the Mogul tombs was an island in an angry sea of Sikh and Hindu refugees. Each night from its walls its inmates watched the flames of burning

Muslim houses and wondered when their turn would come. One night, a taxi drew up at the gate and my brother stepped out of it. He had come alone to spend the night with Doctor Zakir Hussain, the great scholar who was its head and is now vice president of India. He thus put the Academy under the protection of the government. However, this was not enough; the refugees cared little for the government. So, on his first day in New Delhi, Gandhiji also went to call on Doctor Hussain. The fact that he had been there made the Academy hallowed ground which even hate-crazed Sikhs would not violate.

Elsewhere, Gandhiji's attempts to protect Muslims only further embittered the fanatic fringe of Hinduism. Its core was the *Mahasabha,* a rightist society dedicated to a return to the good old ways of Hinduism and the extirpation of everything Mohammedan. The *Mahasabha's* action arm was the R.S.S. (*Rashtriya Sevak Sangh* or National Service Society) an organization of young hotheads who drilled together (without guns) and wore green armbands with a black swastika. They whipped up religious passions and their special target was Gandhiji. As tensions increased they even picketed Birla House shouting, "Gandhi *murdabad!* [Death to Gandhi!]"

Once my brother, leaving after a visit with Gandhiji, heard them. Leaping out of his official car, wild with rage, eyes blazing in his sheet-white face, he confronted them shouting, "How dare you say such a thing! Kill me first!"

Shamefaced they slunk away.

In his despair, Gandhiji decided to start his sixteenth and final fast on January 13, 1948. He announced that he would fast until both the Hindu and Muslim communities gave proof that they would abandon their reigns of terror and live together in unity and brotherhood. It seemed like an impossible condition.

At the news of Gandhiji's fast, a tremor ran through India and Pakistan as well. One of the first messages he received was from Mrdulla Sarabhai in Lahore telling him that his Muslim friends in Pakistan, including officials of the Muslim League and the government, were anxious for his safety and asking what they could do.

That night Gandhiji walked as usual to his prayer meeting through the opulent garden of Birla House with its lawns and flowers and marble balustrades, for he said that the first day of a fast "weakens no one." He was able to go again the second evening. After that, though, he weakened rapidly; a seventy-eight-year-old man has slim reserves. He could not even drink water because it nauseated him. The doctors were very pessimistic.

On the third day, Gandhiji asked the government of India to pay Pakistan the $180,000,000 which they owed in the settlement after partition but which my brother had been withholding because of the Kashmir dispute. Bhai promptly ordered it paid.

That day also, the Governor General came to call upon Gandhiji, the first time he had ever done so. As Lord Mountbatten squatted down on the floor beside his cot Gandhiji smiled at him and said, "So it takes a fast to bring the mountain to Mohammed."

All the mountains came to the little man who was dying to bring peace to India, from maharajas in Rolls-Royces to long processions of workingmen. Of course Bhai went several times a day and most of the other members of the government went at least once a day including Sardar Patel with whom my brother was supposed to be at odds because Patel took a conservative line, and Bhai was pushing for a Socialist state. Sometimes thousands of people were allowed to walk through the gardens past the open porch, where Gandhiji lay sleeping, to get his *darshan,* the blessing which our people believe comes from the sight of a holy man.

The greatest crowd of all came on January 17, the fifth day of the fast. The lines of marchers, Hindus and Muslims, stretched out for blocks as they waited their turn. They carried forests of many-colored banners and signs identifying the organizations they represented— The Railway Workers Union, Post and Telegraph Workers, Delhi Women's League; students; professors. Five thousand cyclists came from a huge meeting in one of the parks, 5,000 pilgrims came on foot from outside Delhi. They were a noisy lot, as all Indian crowds are, shouting their slogans—"We shall die before Mahatma dies!" "Mahatmaji's life is more precious than ours"—and shouting pledges of religious unity.

In the morning of that day my brother had been to Birla House. Gandhiji seemed so close to death that as he left Bhai burst into tears; he went on a fast that day. But in the afternoon he received a letter written in Hindi in Gandhiji's own hand:

Dear Jawahar:

Give up your fast. . . .

May you live long and continue to be the Jewel of India.

Blessings from BAPU

In the evening Bhai came to Birla House again when that great tumultuous crowd was at its height, and he gathered them, as many as could get in, at the prayer place. In the pitch darkness the cyclists turned up their little lamps so they shone on Bhai, lighting his white clothes, his deep-lined face and luminous eyes, while he talked to them over the loudspeakers of what Gandhiji meant to India and of his own hopes: "I saw the freedom of India in a vision. I had charted the future in my heart. . . ." Then he told them how his hopes had been blasted in the very moment of freedom, by the mass killings; and he said, "But the sustaining thought is that there is something great and vital in a country that can produce a Gandhi, such a man comes once in a thousand years. Let us take our cue from the guidance which he gives us from his wisdom. . . . He will lead us to the true goal and not the false dawn of hope."

Meanwhile the leaders of all the religious communities and political factions were meeting at the house of Congress President Doctor Rajendra Prasad, to agree on a pledge that would satisfy Gandhiji and induce him to break his fast. Bhai was pushing them to hurry for he knew there was little time. By the morning of January 18, the pledge was ready and agreed upon. It read:

We take the pledge that we shall protect the life, property and faith of the Muslims and that the incidents which have taken place in Delhi will not happen again.

We want to assure Gandhiji that the annual fair at Kwaja Qutab-ud-Din Mazar [a Muslim shrine] will be held this year as in previous years.

Muslims will be able to move about Subzimandi, Karol Bagh and other [Muslim] localities just as they could in the past.

The Mosques . . . which are now in the possession of Hindus and Sikhs will be returned. . . .

219

Muslims who have fled will be able to return and conduct their businesses as before. . . .

These things will be done by our personal efforts and not with the help of the police or the military.

A great crowd of leaders were jammed into Doctor Prasad's house to sign the pledge and, also, to swear for themselves and for their people that they would honor it. They included Hindus, Sikhs, Muslims, Christians and Jews. The High Commissioner of Pakistan was there and Ganesha Dutt with other representatives of the *Mahasabha* and the R.S.S. Solemnly they all signed and swore by their different gods to fulfill the pledge. Then they went by whatever transport they could find to Birla House.

My brother and Maulana Abul Azad were already there, sitting on the floor beside Gandhiji's cot. Over a hundred people crowded into the big bare room where he lay. As they poured through the doorway Gandhiji managed to sit up in his familiar cross-legged position. Doctor Prasad read the pledge and explained it to him—Gandhiji had previously sent suggestions for some of the points—and begged him to end his fast. Another Hindu then described scenes of fraternization between Muslims and Hindus which were taking place in Delhi at that moment.

Gandhiji thought for a while, looking up at the faces of the people in the room. Then in his weak soft voice he told them he was moved by their words, but, he said, their promises were worth nothing and it would be a great blunder for him to give up his fast "if you only hold yourselves responsible for the communal peace in Delhi." Then, looking at the representatives of the *Mahasabha* and the R.S.S., he spoke directly to them saying, "Delhi is the head of the Indian Dominion and you are the cream of Delhi. If you cannot make the whole of India realize that the Hindus, Sikhs and Muslims are all brothers, it will bode ill for the future of both dominions. What will happen to India if they both quarrel?"

Weakness overcame Gandhiji at the thought and tears streamed from his eyes. Those standing close enough to see, the tough leaders of a successful revolution and a bloody peace, wept with him.

When Gandhiji tried to speak again his voice failed and Doctor Sushila Nayyar repeated aloud the words he whispered to her asking them if they were merely trying to save his life, and if they would guarantee peace in India so he could go to Pakistan and work for peace there. Did Muslims still regard Hindus as idol-worshipping infidels who should be exterminated?

Maulana Azad and other Muslims denied this. Jareb Zahid Hussain-Saheb, High Commissioner of Pakistan, bent down to add his reassurance; and Ganesha Dutt renewed his pledge on behalf of the *Mahasabha* and the R.S.S. A tall, blue-turbaned Sikh knelt to add his promise.

For a long time, or what seemed long, Gandhi sat in deep thought while the crowded room was absolutely silent except for the heavy breathing of a hundred people whose emotions were stretched to the breaking point. Then Gandhiji smiled his funny little impish smile and nodded. He would break his fast.

Instantly the room was noisy with joy; people laughing and crying with relief. Then and there the ashramites began a typical religious service, with readings from the scriptures of all religions. It ended with the ashram girls singing Gandhiji's favorite Christian hymn, "When I Survey The Wondrous Cross." Maulana Azad ceremonially handed him a glass of orange juice and, as Gandhiji slowly drank it, Bhai and the Maulana sitting beside him took turns holding it and passing it to him.

So Gandhiji worked his final miracle, for it was nothing less, that the spiritual influence of one man could soften the hearts and dissolve the hatreds of those passionate men and women. But the wonder of it was not that they signed the pledge. It was that they kept it. From that time forward, though there were sporadic oubreaks, there were no more great mass killings.

During Gandhiji's last fast I was not in New Delhi but in Bombay with my children. There, I became quite ill. My brother asked me to come to him to recuperate. It is always hot in Bombay, but the winter in Delhi is cold and he thought it would do me good. I arrived on January 25, feeling very weak, and for a day or two I did not go out at all. As soon as I felt stronger, I rang up Gandhiji's secretary and asked when he would be free to see Indira and me. Like all good secretaries protecting their employers, he tried to discourage us saying that Gandhiji was very weak after his long fast, and that delegations of Hindus and Muslims came to talk to him every day, and he did not think we should bother him.

However, something made me insist, which I would not normally have done. Indu and I decided to go at noon on January 29 because that was Gandhiji's lunch hour, when no one was allowed to see him; and since we were so close to him we had special privileges. Padmaja Naidu,* the daughter of Sarojini Naidu, came with us, and Indu brought her four-year-old son, Rajiv, along.

We found Gandhiji sitting cross-legged on a chaise longue on the terrace outside his room wearing a large straw hat to protect him from the hot January sun. He was eating his usual meal of mashed-up fruit and goats' milk and was surrounded by two or three of his secretaries and Doctor Nayyar who almost never left his side. He looked exceedingly well that day; his bare brown body was absolutely glowing. This was because, even during his fasts, he took very good care of himself; for he had high blood pressure, and used to have mud packs on his head and an oil massage to keep his strength up. In fact Gandhiji looked so well that Padmaja laughingly said to him, "Bapu, I wish I could look as well as you do after a fast. Tell me your secret and I will go on a fast, too."

Then we sat in the sunshine talking. He teased me about my lecture tour, but said seriously that he had heard glowing reports of what Raja and I had done in America. Then he asked about Raja and the children, and we gossiped about members of the family—nothing serious, just gay idle chatter. Little Rajiv began playing with some flowers that people had brought Gandhiji and was wrapping them around the Mahatma's feet. Gandhiji called him to come closer and pulling his ear, just as he had pulled mine forty years before, said, "You must not do that. One only puts flowers around dead people's feet."

After that, Doctor Nayyar whispered that we must not stay too long, so we prepared to leave. I went up to Gandhiji and said, "Bapu, I want to see you again and I want to see you alone."

"Why?" he asked. "Have you anything special to ask?"

"No, nothing special," I replied. "It's just that I don't like crowds, and, oh well, I would so much like to see you when there is nobody else, not even your secretary and doctors."

* Miss Naidu became governor of West Bengai.

Then he pulled me down so that I sat on the edge of the chaise longue, and he put his arms around me saying, "Don't you know that you cannot see me unless you see me among large crowds—at least not in the near future, because I don't think I shall be alone."

I don't know if he had any premonition or not; or whether my compulsion to insist could be called a premonition. But I did; I said I just wanted to come and talk to him without everybody listening, and I said, "Please, Bapu, can't I see you tomorrow?"

Very seriously he said, "My dear, I think the next time you see me it will have to be among a large crowd, because after this fast I have had to meet many people and I am never left alone. So you will have to wait a long time...."

That was all. We said good-by and went home.

The next day, January 30, 1948, I went to tea with an old friend Kay Stimson, whose husband, Robert Stimson was editor of *The Times of India*. She was living in a hotel in Old Delhi about twenty minutes' drive from my brother's house. Kay and I were having tea and chatting gaily about old times and old friends when the woman who ran the hotel burst into the room. Completely distraught she said, "It's happened. It's happened to him!"

I leaped up shaking, thinking of Bhai, because a few days before in Amritsar someone had thrown a small bomb at him, which had missed and hurt no one. "What's happened?" I demanded.

"I don't know," the woman wailed. "They've shot him. They've shot him! Turn on the radio, you'll get the news."

We rushed into Kay's room and turned on the radio. A voice was saying over and over again like a record with the needle stuck, "Mahatma Gandhi has been shot. We do not know how he is. Five minutes has passed and his condition is not yet known. We don't know. He has been taken inside the house. He was shot at his prayer meeting. We don't know his condition. Mahatma Gandhi has been shot...."

Afterward I learned that Gandhiji had walked through the late afternoon sunshine past the pergolas and flowers to the prayer meeting place. Just as he stood up to speak, bowing to the crowd with joined hands, a young Hindu in the front row stood up and shot him dead. But then I knew nothing.

"I must go to him," I said; and Kay said she would go with me. But then she thought of the great crowds and the terror and hatred of them, and she said, "No, I cannot go."

I rushed to where the car was parked and woke up the sleeping chauffeur; he was a Muslim who had been brought up in our house. "Bapu has been shot," I said. "Take me home."

The man began trembling so he could hardly start the car. "My God, I hope it wasn't a Muslim," he said.

Then he drove very fast toward York Road, constantly wiping his eyes, because he was crying so hard he could hardly see. I was so stunned I could not cry, I could not think. I just sat there while the car careened through the streets. I did not know Bapu was dead.

We got to my brother's house. It was winter and dark by six o'clock; the house, which was always lit from to top bottom, was in darkness but for a light or two. There did not seem to be a soul in it, no servants, not a person. I looked around not knowing what to do, and called out. Bhai's secretary came rushing out and said, "We've been searching the town for you but we didn't know where you had gone. We've been trying to get you."

With that he jumped into the car and said to the chauffeur, "Birla House!"

"How is he? How is he?" I asked frantically.

"He isn't any more," the secretary said.

My mind refused to understand that Bapu was dead, how it could have happened so suddenly, or how anybody could have wanted to shoot him; it remained blank and numb. I did not begin to realize it until we reached Birla House.

It was only a short distance from York Road but already the news had spread and a vast crowd had gathered; hundreds of cyclists had left their cycles piled up; automobiles bogged down hopelessly among thousands of people. Although hundreds of policemen were trying to control the crowds they were simply engulfed, struggling against a tidal wave of people, some of whom were climbing over the walls that surrounded Birla House, some breaking through the gates. People were being beaten back by the police but more got past them. It was a frantic, dangerous crowd whose emotion, rising to a pitch of intensity, needed only a spark to turn it into a raging conflagration of hate.

We jumped out of our stalled car. My brother's secretary took my hand and dragged me through the pressing, shoving people to a gate where they knew us and let us through. All the windows of the great house were shut; the curtains were drawn except for the one room where Gandhiji lay so the people in the compound could look in and see him. We went inside and suddenly it was very quiet but for muted roaring of the crowd outside. There were hundreds of people inside, too, people of all castes and creeds, men and women, standing in taut silence on either side of the long corridors down which we hurried. Only one person was weeping, Vincent Sheean, standing in a corner sobbing loudly. Everyone else was clutching, twisting their hands trying to hold back their sobs, trying not to make a noise.

So I came to the door of Gandhiji's room. Beside it was a great pile of shoes and sandals, for we do not wear shoes in the presence of the dead. I kicked off my slippers and entered the big bare room. It was crowded with people sitting on the stone floor in absolute silence except for an occasional sob. Gandhiji lay on a mattress in one corner of the room, his body covered by a cloth; his head resting in the lap of his disciple Brij Krishan while around him knelt his granddaughters and grandnieces. I went up to him and folding my hands, bowed to touch his feet.

I straightened up and saw my brother's face. He was standing in a corner, not sitting like the others. His face was drawn and tortured as it had not been even when our father died. I was quite controlled, or stunned, until then, but the agony which showed so clearly on Bhai's face made me break down. For a little while he did not move or seem to see me. Then he came to me and wiped my tears away with a large clean handkerchief; and for the first time wiped his own.

I sat on the floor with the others while the girls around Gandhiji chanted the last verses of the *Gita,* and afterward "*Ram, Ram, Ram,*" calling to God. Then Lord Mountbatten came walking softly on stocking feet to pay his homage. Afterward he went to another room to talk with my brother and Sardar Patel and other members of the Cabinet while the rest of us sat in silence that was presently broken by the crash of glass: windows broken by the enormous pressure of the crowd outside; we could hear them yelling and shouting. Doctor Jivraj Mehta, one of Gandhiji's physicians who is now our High Commissioner in London, went out to speak to them, and he told them to be quiet. Indian crowds are very unruly, but some reason, perhaps their deep sense of loss and solemnity, made them obey him. He told the foreign correspondents and photographers that they could not come in, but that Gandhiji's body would lie in state outside the house and then they could take pictures.

There was one unpleasant incident. Someone took pity on Margaret Bourke-White, who was being jostled and crushed in the crowd, and let her in. Doctor Mehta was surprised to see her, but when she promised not to take pictures, he let her come into the room. She did not have the knowledge or sensitivity to take off her shoes but came tick-tocking across the room in her high heels and bent over Gandhiji's body. The room was so silent that everyone heard the sharp click of the camera she wore around her neck. Instantly Feroze Gandhi jumped up from where he was sitting beside Indu, and snatched the camera from her neck. He took out the film and handed the camera back to her; then he led her from the room.

Outside, the crowds were still growing and the shouting got louder. Bhai went out to speak and calm them. Standing on the wall by the gate he said some things that he repeated in the famous broadcast he made later that evening:

"The light has gone out of our lives and there is darkness everywhere. I do not know what to tell you or how to say it. Our beloved leader, Bapu as we called him, the Father of the Nation, is no more. We will not run to him for advice and seek solace from him, and that is a terrible blow, not to me only but to millions and millions in this country. . . .

"The light has gone out, I said, and yet I was wrong. For the light that shone in this country was no ordinary light. The light that has illumined this country for these many years will illumine it for many more years, and a thousand years later that light will still be seen in this country and the world. . . .

"A madman has put an end to his life, for I can only call him mad who did it, and yet there has been enough of poison spread during the past years and months, and this poison has had an effect on people's minds. We must face this poison; we must root out this poison, and we must face all the perils that encompass us; and face them not madly or badly, but rather in the way that our beloved teacher taught us to face them. The first thing to remember now is that none of us dare misbehave because he is angry. . . ."

Then my brother told the people that Gandhiji had forbidden that his body be embalmed and lie in state for days; instead he would lie on a catafalque for a short time and the cremation would take place in ". . . Delhi City by the side of the Jumna River . . . and at the appointed time for the cremation, that is at 4 P.M. on Saturday, people all over India should go to the river or to the sea and offer prayers there. And while we pray, the greatest prayer that we can offer is to take a pledge to dedicate ourselves to the truth, and to the cause for which this great countryman of ours lived and for which he has died. That is the best prayer that we can offer him and his memory. That is the best prayer we can offer to India and ourselves."

We went home from Birla House at midnight, because my brother had to plan the funeral procession with his generals. He would have liked to have stayed there all night because he wanted to be with Gandhiji.

The next morning, Gandhiji lay in state outside of Birla House while enormous crowds inched by. Except for his face, he was all covered with flowers and with our national flag. The crowds were dangerous no longer for, by now, everyone knew that he had been shot by Nathuram Vinayak Goodse, a Hindu of the extreme Right; rather, they were sorrowful and ashamed.

Bhai and Indira and I stood with Gandhiji's family beside the bier until it was time to start for the burning ghats by the river. Then, they lifted him onto a gun carriage covered with flowers, like the caisson in front of it. Sailors from the Indian Navy pulled it by long ropes and mounted soldiers rode ahead trying to clear a way through the great multitude—a million people wailing and shouting their grief. To them, Gandhiji seemed not a man but a reincarnation of the Godhead.

I walked immediately behind the gun carriage with Indira and Padmaja Naidu. Even in January, the noonday sun of India is very hot and we moved terribly slowly, sometimes jostled by the crowds that broke the lines and followed after. It was nine miles to the river and, halfway there, we knew we would never last. I was drenched with perspiration, Padmaja almost fainting; and Indu was swaying as she walked. Seeing our distress some soldiers following in a jeep made us climb in saying, "It will do him no good if you fall in the road."

So we came at last to the bare mound by the river, on which stood a small brick platform piled with logs of sandalwood. From that slight elevation you could see a vast quivering white ocean of people, seven hundred and fifty thousand around that one place. As Gandhiji's tiny body was placed on the pyre everyone within reach, people of every class and faith—statesmen, Harijans, ambassadors and old peasant women, Muslims, Christians, Parsees—all India attempted one last act of devotion, putting a flower or some remembrance on the beloved tiny body.

Then more logs were piled upon it, so that only the dear face could be seen; and the priests chanted while they poured ghee upon the logs. It was full night, the black-purple night of India, when they finished. A priest gave a lighted torch to Devadas, Gandhiji's youngest son. In the act of supreme devotion that is the most harrowing an Indian son can perform. Devadas plunged it into the pile of sandalwood. The ghee crackled and caught in an instant. A column of red-gold flame and smoke shot upward and an incredible groan was wrung from three-quarters of a million throats as the heart of India broke.

20
the
republic
of India

So ended the heroic phase of India's struggle for independence. What was left now for my brother and his Cabinet, and for all of us, was the unspectacular, difficult business of trying to rebuild a nation out of the broken pieces of an alien empire. In the process, many hopes were dashed and ideals tarnished. Even Bhai gradually changed, becoming more careworn and more pragmatic, as the abrasive necessities of governing forced him to compromise with his beliefs and ground down his fiery spirit.

In those first years, Bhai was the government of India, though not in the Sun King's sense of "L'État c'est moi." His ambition was to make India the greatest democracy in Asia; so, rather than give orders he persuaded if he could. His tactics during the debates in the *Lok Sabha** were as brilliant as Disraeli's in his prime, and his leverage was reinforced by his hold on the imagination of the Indian people. The Nehrus had, and still have, an aura of saintliness because they gave up their wealth and great position, and an easy life, for the sake of India. To Indians this is a holy thing to do, following the tradition of Buddha himself. My brother, and my father, too, did not rise step by step to the position of leaders of the people, but sprang into it the moment they made the renunciation.

* The People's House or lower house of the Central Legislature.

So, though he governed democratically, my brother wielded tremendous power. He was Prime Minister, Foreign Minister, Chairman of the Planning Commission (which regulated the national economy), head of the Atomic Energy Commission and, part of the time, Minister of Defense as well. He worked from five-thirty or six in the morning until midnight or later, ever trying to alleviate the terrible impoverishment of our Indian people, always frustrated by lack of means. There was never even enough food for them, let alone the material graces of civilization.

When Gandhiji died Bhai completely abandoned the theory of a village economy,* which he knew would not work in the modern world. Instead, he tried to raise India by its industrial bootstraps with a series of five-year plans designed to increase our capacity for the production of all the things which have become necessities in a modern nation. To do this, he was obliged to appeal for help from richer nations such as the United States and Russia; and they gave generously, many billions of dollars in loans, outright grants, and food.

In spite of this necessity, my brother managed to keep India from becoming aligned with either of the great power blocs which divided most of the world between them. His foreign policy was truly Gandhian, for it sought to make India an influence for peace through moral suasion rather than by force of arms—which in any event our country was too poor to afford. Indeed, he may have trusted too idealistically in the promises of other nations and neglected our military establishment too much, as he began to see during the Chinese aggressions in the early 1960's. Nevertheless, India did achieve a unique position of moral influence in the world under his leadership.

My sister Nan was helpful to my brother in building Indian prestige in world diplomacy. Because of her success in the United Nations, Bhai asked her to continue her diplomatic career and, I believe, offered her a choice of three great ambassadorships: to the United States, England and Russia. Eventually she served in all three countries. This was not nepotism on my brother's part, but necessity.

* However, he did not forget his peasants. He inaugurated radical programs of land reform and instituted an effective system of village self-government.

Because India had lived so long under foreign rule, she had no trained diplomats; anyone who had any experience in diplomacy or showed an aptitude for it was a treasure beyond price.

Nan chose Russia because she thought it the most challenging post. She served there from 1947 until 1949, and I am afraid she was disappointed. It was certainly the least pleasant and also, as it turned out, the least interesting of the three. Those were the years of Stalin's iron rule. Foreign diplomats were regarded with intense suspicion and their contacts with Russian officials, indeed with all Russians, were strictly official. Their social life, except for a few big official functions, was confined to seeing other members of the diplomatic corps. Though Indo-Russian relations were friendly, Nan found that there was very little to do—so little that she also kept her post as leader of the Indian delegation to the United Nations General Assembly. In fact, she never even met Stalin, though she was on fairly friendly terms with Molotov, Mikoyan and Khrushchev.

The mere details of living were very difficult in Moscow at that time. At first, the Indian Embassy was a small two-story house on a side street.* Nan had to buy many of the furnishings for it in Sweden as they were not to be had in Russia. She took an Indian cook, one of our faithful family servants, along with her. The maids were Russian girls found for her by the Soviet government. They were frequently changed, as the Russians did not want them to become too friendly with foreigners.

Nan hated the bitterly cold Russian winters but they did not bother her daughters. Like me they all love cold weather. Nan wore saris, which can be very warm if they are made of heavy silk or cotton, for they come right down to the ground and keep your legs warm, as Western skirts do not. The girls mostly wore Western clothes with knee-high, soft-leather Russian boots. For skating, which they learned to love, they wore Russian-style outfits. Of course, it is perfectly possible to skate in a sari or even play tennis; it is so loose that it doesn't hamper your movements. I won many tennis tournaments playing in a white sari with tennis shoes.

When Nan came home from Russia she was too good a diplomat to say what she really thought of it. She would mention just that it

* Later my sister acquired a handsome residence for the Indian Embassy which it still occupies.

had been very interesting and so forth. This reticence was not the case with the other posts she held, so we drew our own conclusions. However, her service in Russia was useful to India because, being a woman, she was able to show the Russians that we were as advanced in the equality of the sexes as they were—perhaps even more so. Who ever saw a Russian woman ambassador to a great power? And her being a Nehru emphasized the importance India attached to friendship with Russia.

Nan's great diplomatic triumphs were in the United Nations and in Washington. While she was still Ambassador to Russia she went to New York twice, and led the fight in the General Assembly to condemn South Africa for its policy of apartheid.

In Washington Nan's objectives were threefold. She hoped to achieve a combination of India's non-violent policy with America's enormous material strength. In this she signally failed. Americans continued to regard my brother's policy of nonalignment with intense suspicion. In their minds, "Those who ain't with us are agin' us." Secondly, she hoped to bring to Americans a better understanding of Indian thinking and idealism. Finally, she desired to promote American aid for and capital investments in India. Her charm, her friendliness, and her wit enabled her to achieve a brilliant success in these objectives.

Soon after Nan arrived in Washington, Bhai and Indira went to the United States, in October 1949, on what he called "a voyage of discovery." It was the first trip to America for both of them, and they did make discoveries; they discovered the American people, with their warmth and hospitality and their directness—all rather different from their sometimes bellicose diplomacy. It was a good thing for my brother and Indu to know, especially since Bhai, despite his admiration for the founders of the United States, had a rather prejudiced view of modern America, because in his mind it was the great defender of the capitalistic system which he had distrusted ever since his Fabian Socialist days.

Raja and I were also there on our second lecture tour. The first one, in 1947, was a great success, mostly owing to Raja. For, at first, I was very bad at lecturing, so nervous and unsure of myself that our agent suggested that we lecture together. This worked very well. I spoke on the social and cultural aspects of India and how India had developed in recent years, while Raja talked about economic and political matters, which he knew so much better than I.

All of us, including Bhai and Indu, liked America and the Americans, many of whom told me that, with my forthright way of saying what I thought, I seemed more like an American than an Indian. Of course they meant it as a compliment, but I was not enthusiastic—I am proud to be *Indian*.

One thing that troubled all of us when we talked our experiences over together was that Americans knew so much less about India than we knew about their country—the same thing applies in England, though to a lesser extent. We had been taught in school about their history and geography, and it was a bit of a shock at the end of a serious lecture on our culture and economics to have silly questions thrown at us like "What about the sacred cows?"

Those infernal cows were not really sacred in the beginning. They were simply cherished as the givers of milk so vital to people on a mostly vegetarian diet. The priests made them sacred for their own purposes. I regard them as a great nuisance and when one of them gets in my way I have no compunction about nudging it off the street with my car.

While Nan was Ambassador to the United States, she also became our first Ambassador to Mexico—we did not yet have enough diplomats to go around—but she did give up her job at the United Nations. However, in October 1952, after she had returned to India, she again headed our delegation to the United Nations, with Krishna Menon as her second in command. It was an odd arrangement for my brother to make. He knew that Nan disliked Mr. Menon and disapproved of his extreme Left-Wing policies. Nevertheless, they worked well together; and together produced the seventeen-point Indian Plan which became the guidelines for the settlement of the Korean War. Getting the General Assembly—and particularly the American delegation—to approve it required a nice combination of Krishna Menon's subtle machinations and Nan's professed idealism, feminine charm (never underrate the leverage of that) and her underlying steely determination.

Her fellow delegates were so impressed that in September 1953 Vijaya Lakshmi Pandit was elected president of the General Assembly, the first and, so far, the only woman ever to have held that position.

Writing about my sister brings to mind her daughters who, though they have such a high-powered mother, are very much people in their own right. The eldest, Lekha, is plump and rather pretty with high cheekbones that give her an oriental look—we used to tease her about looking Chinese. She was always a good child, rather subdued, perhaps because she was growing up during our most difficult time and there was little encouragement for high spirits. When the time came, my sister introduced her to a nice young man. She liked him and they were betrothed—an arranged marriage if you like, but a happy one.

Tara, who looks very much like her father, was even quieter than Lekha, a true introvert, which is quite unusual in our family. She fell in love at a most inconvenient time—though I suppose any time would have been inconvenient. One day late in 1947, while my sister was in Moscow and Bhai, struggling to make India a nation, was beset by the communal rioting and the trouble over Kashmir, Tara came to me and asked me to meet a boy named Gautam Sahgal whom she wished to marry.

"Whoever he is or whatever he is, don't bring this up with your uncle right now," I said. "He is in no state of mind to look at things calmly. Wait until your mother comes home."

It was good advice, but Tara, like all young people in love, would not wait. She went to Bhai, and he told her off harshly. He did not know the young man, but he did know his family and did not like them. Furthermore, he was walking so many razors' edges that one more decision to make was one too many. He forbade Tara to see Gautam. She came crying to my room and asked me to help her, but there was nothing I could do. Gandhiji had just ended his fast and everything was in a turmoil. Then came the assassination and Tara had sense enough to know that there was no question of her going to Bhai again.

Meanwhile, Nan had heard of the business and asked that Tara be sent to her in Moscow. Sadly Tara went. But Gautam was a stubborn fellow and as much in love as Tara. He tried to get a visa for Russia, but the Russian Embassy refused to grant it. They were probably aware of the situation. However, he did get a visa for Sweden. The moment Tara got to Russia she dragged her mother off to Sweden to meet Gautam. Nan can be very determined with everyone except her own children. There was nothing really wrong with Gautam, so she gave her consent. They were married as soon as they got back to India.

Tara has made quite a career for herself in writing. She is undoubtedly very talented and can be very charming at a party; but she remains withdrawn, observing the crowd but never committing herself wholly, with many acquaintances but few close friends.

My youngest niece, Rita, is entirely different. A complete extrovert, nothing ever bothers her. She was lucky to have missed the worst days and, at least in her teens, could know the youthful gaiety and joy the others lost. Like Lekha she accepted an arranged marriage with Avtar Dar of our Foreign Service, willingly and happily. He is a Kashmiri. Lekha's husband is a good Gujarati, and Tara's husband a Punjabi.

Lekha and Tara each have two girls and a boy. Rita has a boy and a girl. I must admit her son, Gopal, is my favorite of them all. Nan calls him "my Japanese grandson" because he was born while his father was serving in our Embassy in Tokyo. When Avtar and Rita came home Gopal stayed with Raja and me in Bombay for six weeks while his parents waited to find out where their next post would be. We were delighted by him, the only difficulty being that we could not communicate. He spoke only Japanese. Every morning he would come to our room dressed in a little Japanese kimono and bow solemnly to Raja and to me saying, "Good morning honorable Grandfather. Good morning honorable Grandmother."

Rita's husband was later sent to Washington and when I saw Gopal there in 1965, he was a completely American little boy. Her daughter is also an enchanting child, named Jyoti. She, too, is completely American. When Nan was staying at the Carlyle Hotel in New York in the summer of 1963, Jyoti, aged six, came into the drawing room one day and pointing at a photograph in a big silver frame asked, "Who is that?"

"That is our President," Nan said.

"Grandmother, what do you mean 'our President?'"

"That is the President of India."

235

Jyoti rummaged in her little handbag and brought out a Kennedy campaign button. "I don't care who your President is," she said. "This is my President."

One thing about Nan's family is interesting, though of course it proves nothing. The two arranged marriages are reasonably happy. The love match did not work out, and Tara and her husband have recently parted.

Perhaps the most important of my brother's activities between 1947 and 1949 was the matter of framing the Constitution of India. The Mountbattens returned to England in June 1948, and C. R. Rajagopalachari became the first Indian governor general. Bhai had accepted Dominion status as a temporary legal expedient on the understanding that it was a transient phase. Though he was very meticulous to avoid putting pressure on the Constituent Assembly, at least openly, it was inevitable that his opinions, however they might be conveyed, should carry great weight. Bhai was determined that the result of their deliberations should be the sovereign Republic of India, with a responsible parliamentary government in the British tradition, with an upper and lower house to which the prime minister would be responsible. Almost all the members of the Assembly were equally in favor of a republic—there was simply no argument about it.

In addition, the Constitution specifically included a bill of rights more or less like that of the American Constitution, with a special injunction against Untouchableness. It provided for a federal form of government with the former provinces as separate states with their own provincial legislatures. The former princely states were amalgamated into much larger units which also became states.

If there was general agreement about most of these things there were hot arguments about other questions—for example, the matter of a national language. Bhai fully recognized the advantages of a national Indian language from the point of view of culture and national pride, and expressed his embarrassment in having to address the Constituent Assembly in the language of their former conquerors; but he knew that there would be an awful row about which of India's many languages should become official. If Hindi or Hindustani were chosen the people of southern India would be at a disadvantage; and the same would be true of the northern provinces if, for example, Tamil became the official tongue.

With his new pragmatism Bhai urged the Assembly to bypass the question of a national language for the present by referring it to a committee of scholars, and in the meanwhile get along with Hindi as the official language of the Central Legislature with English as the associate official language. This has not been changed; nor is it apt to be.

The most extraordinary *volte-face* my brother made was in the matter of India remaining within the Commonwealth. In September 1948 he went to England to take part in the annual meeting of the Commonwealth Prime Ministers, the first one he had attended. In talking with the other Prime Ministers, Bhai was deeply impressed by the advantages of being in the Commonwealth. There was no official discussion then about India remaining in, but my brother had long private talks with Prime Minister Attlee on the subject.

After sounding out the opinion of his colleagues in the Congress party, Bhai returned to London for the Prime Minister's meeting in April 1949, with the proposal that India remain in the Commonwealth provided she could do so as a sovereign independent republic, with no strings attached and no oath of allegiance to the Crown. Prime Minister Attlee was in favor of it and, oddly enough, King George VI thought it was an excellent idea; but the lawyers in the British Foreign Office were thrown into a flap. How could you have a republic in an organization that owed allegiance to the King? To them, it just did not make sense.

However, under pressure from the Prime Minister and the King himself, they finally worked out a formula. The Declaration of London stated that while the other members of the Commonwealth remained united by their common *allegiance* to the Crown, India became a full member simply by ". . . her acceptance of the King, as the symbol of the free association of its independent member nations and as such the Head of the Commonwealth." Thus the British actually altered the principle of membership in the Commonwealth in order to admit India.

Naturally my brother's proposal started a hot debate in the Constituent Assembly. The whole Left Wing, including the Communist and Socialist parties, screamed treason; they called it "the

237

Great Blunder" and "the Great Betrayal." Four years before, Bhai would probably have joined the outcry.

But the responsibilities of power temper the radicalism of sensible revolutionaries—though not of fanatics like a Robespierre, a Stalin or a Hitler. Bhai was never a fanatic; rather, an ardent fighter for freedom. Freedom won, he could therefore weigh the advantages and disadvantages of remaining in the Commonwealth. First and foremost in his mind was that in a world of terrible tensions India should not be isolated; that she could work more effectively for peace within the Commonwealth than outside of it.

Secondly, India's whole economic system, her trade and finance, was inevitably still tied to the pound sterling and her business associations to Great Britain. Bhai also felt that India could do more for the large Indian colonies in such countries as South Africa and Ceylon as a member of the Commonwealth than as an outsider.

Finally there was an intangible—Bhai's love of England and the English people, which had persisted underneath all the bitterness of our long fight for freedom; and to this must be added the pull of his strong friendship with the Mountbattens.

In return for all the advantages of Commonwealth membership, he felt that the only thing India was giving up was an emotional idea of complete separation from Britain. He said in his speech to the Constituent Assembly:

> We took a pledge long ago to achieve *Purna Swaraj* [complete independence]. We have achieved it. Does a nation lose its independence by an alliance with another country? . . . The free association of Commonwealth nations does not involve commitments. Its very strength lies in its flexibility and complete freedom. . . .
>
> It must be remembered that the Commonwealth is not a super state . . . we have agreed to consider the King as the symbolic head of the free Association. But . . . as far as the Constitution of India is concerned, the King has no place and we shall owe no allegiance to him.
>
> I have naturally looked to the interests of India, for that is my first duty. I have always conceived that duty in terms of the larger good of the world. That is the lesson the Master taught us. . . . The world is full of strife today and disaster looms on the horizon.

. . . Every step, therefore, which leads to a lessening of tension in the world should be a welcome step. I think it is a good augury for the future that the old conflict between India and England should be resolved in a friendly way which is honorable to both countries.

It has been India's privilege in the past to be a meeting place for many cultures. It may be her privilege in the present and future to be a bridge to join warring factions and to help in maintaining that most urgent thing of today and the future—the peace of the world. It is in the belief that India could more effectively pursue this policy of encouraging peace and freedom and of lessening bitter hatreds and tensions that I willingly agreed to the London Agreement. . . . I trust that the Indian people will also view [these decisions] in that light and accept them in a manner worthy of the stature and culture of India and with full faith in our future. Let us not waste our energy at this critical moment in the world's history over empty debates, but rather let us concentrate on the urgent tasks of today, so that India may be great and strong and in a position to play a beneficent part in Asia and the world.

Since the Congress party, which controlled the Constituent Assembly, had already authorized my brother to accept membership in the Commonwealth by a large majority, in which Sardar Patel enthusiastically joined, the debate, though violent, was merely a matter of giving the minorities their right to be heard. The proposal was easily carried.

On January 26, 1950, exactly twenty years after my brother had led all India in taking the pledge to work for complete independence, the Republic of India was born. Rajendra Prasad became its first president, a ceremonial post roughly equivalent to a constitutional monarch, though with some additional emergency powers. My brother, of course, remained as prime minister.

In 1952, the first general elections were held. Over 150,000,000 votes were cast, the largest number ever recorded in a free election anywhere up to that time. It remained a record until surpassed by our elections of 1957, and again in 1962, when 210,000,000 Indians went to the polls. The Congress party won a large majority in the Central Legislature, which they have held ever since.

However, though the opposition was in a small minority, my

brother never permitted India to become a one-party country. The leaders of the other parties were always free to speak their minds, to vilify him if they chose, and to win as many votes as they could. Perhaps his proudest achievement was that, in a huge, multiracial country with no less than fourteen official languages (in the different states), and which had been ruled from above for 3,000 years, he made parliamentary democracy work.

21
Feroze

After my brother and his daughter returned from their trip to America in 1959, Indira began to play a larger part in Indian politics. Her health became much better and, as the strain of Bhai's tremendous activities in the government increased, he needed more help than I could give him. For I was also concerned with Raja and my two sons; and our home, after all, was in Bombay. Nor am I as politically adept as Indu soon became. She began traveling a great deal throughout India, going into the villages to get close to the people. She did not do it for her own sake, because at that time she did not have high political ambitions, but to take some of the burden of having to go so many places off her father. She also made a total of twenty-four trips abroad with him.

Little by little, Indira became more and more involved in politics, working on some of the Congress party committees, though not in the Parliament, of which she did not become a member until after her father's death. In 1959 she was elected president of the Congress party and served for one term, after which she refused to run again because she felt she could be more useful helping Bhai.

About 1950, Indira went to live in the Prime Minister's House and act as Bhai's official hostess. She had to choose between helping him and having a home of her own. I think it was a difficult choice for her to make, because it meant giving up her privacy, sacrificing her companionship with her children and devoting herself to public service without any official recognition. Furthermore, Feroze did not enjoy that sort of life. I do not know what I would have done in her place, but Indira felt that her father's welfare meant more to her and to India than anything else. Feroze agreed to the arrangement, so they all moved into the Prime Minister's House.

However, Feroze, as a member of Parliament—he was elected by a huge majority—was entitled to a house of his own. It was a little two- or three-bedroom house, with a rather small drawing room and a tiny garden, of the kind allotted to every M.P. Although he lived with my brother he used to go daily to his own house into which he put all the furniture that he had designed when he brought his bride back to their first home.

As I have said, Feroze was passionately fond of gardening, and he worked for hours in the small garden of his house. He was always winning prizes at flower shows for the best gladioli, the best chrysanthemums, or the best roses. When I was staying with my brother in New Delhi, Feroze would often come straight to my room and sit there, waiting until I returned from wherever I had been, with a gorgeous bouquet of whatever flowers were in season—he was very fond of me.

I think Feroze had a great deal of influence with his sons. He often took them out on exciting expeditions and they adored him. He was great fun at a children's party, but he was not at ease at formal receptions or dinners, and he always evaded them unless they were at the Prime Minister's House, when he had to go. He wanted the boys to be engineers and, although he died before they were old enough to choose, they both are headed in that direction.

Though he was so closely involved with my brother's household Feroze remained his own man. At one point, he rose in Parliament and informed the people that he did not approve of certain actions of the Finance Minister. As a result an inquiry was ordered to be held before a one-man commission in Bombay. Feroze was the chief witness. He had always stayed with us when he came to Bombay, but this time, with his delicate sense of propriety, he did not even tell us he was there. Of course we knew that the Commission was being held in the Council Hall, with loudspeakers hooked up so that the crowd outside could hear what was going on. Feroze had all the facts and figures and presented an excellent case. I do not think my brother was very happy about his doing this thing, but I personally think he was in the right; that if he found out certain things that seemed wrong to him he had a duty to inform the public about them, even though it embarrassed his father-in-law's government. Actually, it made him quite a hero.

The magazine articles have stated that Indira's decision to live in her father's house was the cause of her splitup with Feroze. This is not true. He willingly, if with some doubts, agreed to the arrangement; and they lived together for many years after that. But it is true that it was not a good arrangement from a family point of view and they finally drifted apart.

In 1958, about two years before he died, Feroze moved into his own house and lived there alone. He continued to come to my brother's house for meals, and relations between him and Indira were cordial and friendly, but he made it quite clear to everybody that he was not staying at the Prime Minister's House.

Shortly after this, Feroze had the first of a series of heart attacks. Though he took good care of himself he had always been rather stout and this probably was one of the reasons for his illness. However, he continued to be active as a member of the *Lok Sabha*, and it was there that his final fatal illness began. One day he felt very ill and told an eighty-year-old cousin of ours who was sitting next to him that he was going to see his doctor. She begged him not to drive to the hospital, but he did anyway. As soon as he got there his third heart attack began.

Bhai, who was visiting the villages near New Delhi, was informed immediately, but Indira was traveling in the south and could not be reached quickly. Someone telephoned to me from my brother's house telling me what had happened, and saying that no one was there. I immediately booked on the evening flight to Delhi. Then another message came saying that Feroze's condition was not considered serious and that Indu would be coming through Bombay very early in the morning. I was to wait for her. They rang me up every two hours, each time saying he was better.

Indira arrived at the airport in the early hours of the morning. By then she had been told of her husband's condition, though even yet no one thought it was serious. She sent word for me to wait until she telephoned me some definite word.

Indira reached Feroze's bedside at about eight-thirty in the morning. Bhai was with him, and he was constantly asking for her. He recognized her and was perfectly conscious until he died a little over an hour later.

Though Bhai telephoned us immediately, Raja and I had to wait

243

for the evening plane and so missed dear Feroze's funeral, which, according to our custom, was held that same day. He was, as I have said, a Parsee and those of his faith are forbidden to burn or bury their dead. In India they are exposed on "the Towers of Silence" until the vultures pick the flesh from their bones which fall to a well beneath and are flushed into the sea.

Gentle Feroze could not bear the thought of this. Again and again during his last illness he said, "I want to be cremated." My brother ordered it done according to his wishes. His fifteen-year-old son, Rajiv, lit the funeral pyre.

Raja and I arrived in New Delhi late that evening. The lawn in front of my brother's house was filled with people who had come from all over to mourn Feroze. Old men, old women, youngsters, even some who had come on crutches, were still there in the darkness standing or lying on the grass or sleeping sitting up.

Raja and I rushed up to my brother's room and burst in without knocking. He greeted us sadly. I had always had the feeling that Bhai was irritated by his son-in-law, by his criticisms of the government and many other things he did in Parliament, but now he spoke regretfully. "I did not know that Feroze was so popular," he said. "I did not know that he had done so much good for the people of India. . . ."

As I have always said, no man or woman should marry a Nehru, for it is always difficult for them.

22
the captains and the kings

Even after Indira and Feroze had moved to the Prime Minister's House my brother would summon me back to New Delhi to be his hostess whenever Indira was away. Though the tasks of government were so onerous for him, I must admit I enjoyed these occasions. Meeting the leaders of all nations who came pouring through New Delhi was both intensely interesting and great fun. Men and women who have risen to such eminence invariably have, in addition to great ability, a special charm. Without this quality they would not have attracted loyal supporters, as necessary to achieving political power in totalitarian states as in democracies. The exception is, of course, hereditary monarchs and princes, but since they have been trained from childhood in the art of pleasing, they are usually equally affable, even if less high-powered.

By this time my brother had moved from 17 York Road, which is now the Italian Embassy, to the house that had been the British Commander in Chief's residence. Built in the days of imperial splendor, its style was what might be called British Monumental. It was a massive, red sandstone house with straight, simple lines and was on a direct line with the President's House, down a broad avenue called Teen Murti, which means Three Statues. In front of the house, where five roads converged, was a circle in the center of which was a lawn with gay flowerbeds and three statues of an Indian soldier, a sailor, and an airman in uniform.

At the entrance to the house were two high, wrought-iron gates and two small side gates for the staff. The big gates stood open all day long in my brother's time but there were security men in front of them and others in a little guardhouse. The long entrance drive curved around in front of the house through lawns and beds of brilliant flowers. One entered the house through a high-ceilinged hall and could walk on through another imposing hall to a large, quiet garden in back, with splendid trees, green turf and gay beds of English flowers—pansies, petunias, small herbaceous flowers, tall gladioli and vivid blue delphiniums in season. There were inlaid brick walks and two mirror pools with lotus flowers—Bhai's favorites—floating on their surfaces.

Just off the entrance hall was the receptionist's lobby with a round table and a statue of Mahatma Gandhi. To the right were the pantry, kitchens and all the serving places. On the left was a very large room where, every morning, people could come, though they had no previous appointments, to see my brother. Of course, only a certain number were allowed in. Sometimes students came and sometimes foreigners who just gave their names and wished to shake hands with him; and many people came who felt they had suffered injustice or needed help. Others waited in the front garden outside the house. When my brother came down from breakfast he would spend fifteen minutes to half an hour greeting these people and talking with them.

On the floor above there was an enormous ballroom. Though it was never used for balls in my brother's time, he gave receptions and buffet suppers there. A very large dining room was next to that and a big drawing room. There were several guest rooms to the left of the public rooms and my brother's suite and office. He had a long table-desk in his office with numerous fountain pens and writing paper scattered on it; and all around the room were overflowing bookcases. A few good paintings hung in what wall-space was left and photographs of his family, friends and colleagues stood on the bookcases.

Bhai's bedroom was very simple. It also had bookcases around the walls and pictures of Kamala, Indira and the family—including all his grandchildren. He slept in a plain wooden bed with no springs, just a plank with a mattress on it. All the furniture of his bedroom and office was old-fashioned, but his dressing room and bathroom were very modern, with all the latest gadgets.

246

The right wing of the house had a guest suite on the ground floor and above it the suite where Indira and Feroze lived. All the reception rooms were air-conditioned and in my brother's bedroom there was a machine so powerful that it could have turned an Indian summer day into a polar night; but my brother never used it. He hated air-conditioning and never seemed to feel either heat or cold. Nor was he affected or depressed by the monumental character of his residence; while he lived there it was a happy house.

Edwina Mountbatten remained my favorite visitor—and Bhai's too. She always came to stay with us for a few days on her annual trips to inspect the many charitable enterprises of St. John Ambulance throughout Asia. Those were the only times Bhai recovered his youthful gaiety. Nothing Edwina did was wrong. When I was still with my brother, in the old days, I loved wearing jewelry. One day Bhai flared up at me saying, "Do you have to wear so much jewelry and flashy diamonds around the house, especially in the morning?"

Luckily Edwina was staying with us and she changed for every meal; not only her clothes, but her jewels. If she had on something tan she wore a set of amber jewelry. If she wore blue it was sapphires, or rubies, or emeralds or diamonds, according to her costume. So I flared back at Bhai and said, "You don't get angry with Edwina, in fact you keep admiring her jewelry, all the different sets she wears. No matter what time of day or night she wears them you think it's wonderful. Why do you scold me?"

Bhai, looking puzzled, said, "Well, it's not quite the same thing—well, I don't know."

That was all, but he never mentioned my jewelry again.

Edwina was the only guest who came down to breakfast with us, with the exception of Prince Philip later on. She was easy to talk to and full of fun even the first thing in the morning. You had to be in the breakfast room at eight-fifteen when it was still dark in the winter in Delhi. I always thought my brother should change the time. He said he had—from eight to eight-fifteen.

Apart from liking Edwina so much, I enjoyed having her stay with us because she was such a wonderful companion for my brother, who in his lonely role lacked companionship. All his time was taken up with officials and even the womenfolk whom he met were aloof and scared, whether they were Indians or not. But Edwina always talked as a friend would, laughing and putting everyone at ease—not only my brother but everyone. Every so often she would tell Bhai he didn't know how to cut his soft-boiled egg. That was a standing joke. He would say, "Now don't tell me, Edwina. I know I do it wrong."

In the evenings if he was able to get some time off, we would all go rowing on a little canal that came off the Ganges. Drifting slowly through the blue-black, flower-scented Indian night was as close as either of them got to serenity in those days—a wonderful recess from care. I never saw my brother so gay and light-hearted and unlike the solemn statesman he had become.

His friendship with the Mountbattens, forged in the trying times of partition and communal troubles, was precious to him and endured until he died.

One of the most delightful official guests my brother ever had was Prince Philip, Duke of Edinburgh. When extremely important people came on official visits they stayed first at the President's House for two days and then moved on to the Prime Minister's residence for two more. On the occasion of Prince Philip's visit, security was especially tight to guard against the possibility of some fanatic, who did not know the revolution was over, taking a shot at him. Security men were at the gates and stationed outside his ground-floor room. My brother told me to see to his comfort, make sure he got a proper English breakfast, and anything else he wanted.

The first morning, from my bedroom window, I saw him walking across the lawn in front of the house in plain sight of the road. I dashed downstairs and practically ran across the grass until I reached him. "Prince Philip," I panted, "what are you doing out here? Have you had your breakfast?"

"No," he said. "I decided to have it in the breakfast room with your brother."

"That's fine," I answered. "But you shouldn't come out here leaving all those security men guarding your empty room. How did you get out?"

He grinned and said, "They were not guarding the window in the bathroom so I popped out that way."

I took him back to the house telling him I would not leave him for one minute until I saw him safely at the breakfast table. Punctually at eight-fifteen I took Prince Philip in. Bhai looked a bit surprised. I said, "I caught the Prince trying to escape from us."

That was a delightful breakfast. Usually in India we have lots of servants around at mealtimes but the Mountbattens had changed all that. They liked to have breakfast in peace so they had a table set up with hot plates, and everybody helped themselves to eggs, coffee, toast or whatever they wanted. My brother continued this custom. Indira, Feroze and their children were there, and we were very gay.

The next time, Philip came with the Queen and he was much more serious. Though it was a cold and foggy day, the largest crowd ever, up to that time, turned out to greet her and lined the streets from the airport, cheering wildly for the Queen who represented the monarchy they had fought against so long.

There was a notion in India that the Queen was a rather stern-looking person who seldom smiled, but I had been to her coronation and knew better. The Indians were surprised and delighted by her gaiety. When we met her at the airport she smiled at the President, joked with my brother and seemed very light-hearted. Naturally, I saw a good deal of her in New Delhi and even more in Bombay. Among other receptions and banquets arranged for her there, we staged an Indian fashion show, with twenty-four girls dressed in spectacular saris, and also Western-style dresses made of exquisite Indian materials. I was in charge of the girls and also the superb jewels lent by various jewelers. Keeping track of those young beauties and a maharaja's ransom in gems was a rather ticklish business but I managed to return them all intact.

The show was held at Government House, a magnificent palace built on a bluff above the sea by Lord Curzon in one of his more extravagant moments. It had superb gardens in which a platform was erected that made an excellent stage. There were numerous little rooms nearby that we could use for the girls to change their dresses.

The only hitch was that the Indians literally crashed the gates, bursting them open and pouring into the gardens. By the time the *Corps Diplomatique* arrived there were no seats left. I saw some of my diplomat friends standing on a jeep outside trying to get a glimpse of the Queen. It was a shambles.

However, the Queen seemed enchanted by the clothes; and everything she particularly liked was afterward presented to her. Prince Philip humorously complained to me, "Why are there only women's clothes? There are plenty of pretty girls—far too many pretty girls for my peace of mind—but you should have some men to show off the different costumes they wear."

After the fashion show I did something I was not supposed to—as usual. The girls and the designers, who had worked hard for three months on the show, naturally wanted to meet the Queen, but I was told it was not proper and would annoy her. I waited my chance. As the Queen stood up, she recognized me and said, "I believe you had a great hand in arranging this show."

"Yes, Ma'am," I said. "And would you do me a favor?"

"A favor?" She looked rather startled.

"Yes," I said. "The girls would like to meet you. They have worked hard and it would be a great thing for them. Would you mind coming up the steps?"

"Of course."

Before any of the people there, either the Governor or my sister, who was in the Queen's party, could object I took her quickly up the steps with Prince Philip and the others trailing behind, and introduced her first to the designers, two of whom were Englishwomen who had remained in India, and then to the girls. Some of them greeted her Indian fashion, bowing with folded hands, others curtsied, and some just stuck out their hands, which she took. Both she and Philip said something to every girl and their delight was unbounded.

As a result the girls all thought I was a wonderful person; but the reception committee did not.

Another monarch, who had come to pay his respects to the Queen in Delhi was the old King of Sikkim, the father of the present king who has married an American wife. A tiny man, no more than four and a half feet high, he came to a luncheon my brother gave for the Queen wearing a lama-like robe that fell to his ankles. It was made of gorgeous red-and-gold brocade, with golden flowers embroidered on it, and he had a cap to match. It all looked a little too much for noon, but it was magnificent.

I sat next to the King at luncheon. We had a traditional Indian meal served on large silver trays with the little silver cups for spiced meats, vegetables and yogurt. These same *thalis* were placed in front of Prince Philip and the Queen, but they were also served with fish and chicken cooked in Western fashion, in case they did not like Indian food. For desert we had *khir,* which is a little like rice pudding, only nicer, covered with sheets of gold beaten until it is as thin as tissue paper. One is supposed to eat the gold, though most foreigners push it aside thinking it is just decoration.*

No alcoholic drinks were served, as it was against the government's policy to do so; but there was a fruit punch which the King of Sikkim tasted, though it seemed to make him very unhappy. He drank only water and ate only meat and rice, leaving the vegetables, though he polished off the dessert, gold and all. Then he turned to me and asked, "What do we have to drink after this?"

"Tea or coffee," I answered.

"Isn't there anything else that you drink?"

I guessed he meant liquor and said, "No."

"Not even brandy?" he asked unhappily.

"No," I told him. "I don't think there is anything like that in the house. My brother does not drink, or serve liquor either."

The little King seemed quite upset. "In our country," he said nostalgically, "we drink a glass of good strong wine with every course and there are sometimes thirty or forty courses."

While I am describing visiting royalty I must mention the Shah and Queen of Iran who came shortly before the breakup of their marriage. I did not meet them until they came to Bombay, where the Governor asked me to look after Queen Soraya, and escort her to the various functions. She was very lovely and very sad. The people were delighted to have this woman, so full of beauty, in our city and besides there are many Iranians in Bombay, so they turned out in great numbers. I went to fetch her from Government House to a woman's luncheon. As we approached our destination the whole street was covered with superb Persian carpets over which the cars rolled. These Iranians had been away from their homeland so long that they were thrilled at seeing their Queen.

The crowds were cheering enthusiastically, but Queen Soraya just

* This kind of beaten gold and silver is used in many of our medicines, along with crushed pearls, if you can afford them, which is why Indian medicines are so expensive.

sat back in her corner of the car wearing her dark glasses, as she always did in the daytime. I had seen her at night at the receptions and knew how beautiful her eyes were so I said to her, "Your Majesty, will you please take those glasses off and smile at the crowds? They are all waving to you and have been waiting all morning, and will wait until you finish lunch and pass this way again. So why don't you smile at them, when you have such a beautiful smile?"

In a very soft girlish voice she asked, "Do you really think so?"

I said, "Yes, I do." And I almost took the glasses off her and pushed her forward so the crowds could see her.

The Iranian Consul General in Bombay had given me strict instructions that we must have only women for security police at the club where we gave the luncheon, as no men there must see her.

"That is ridiculous," I told him, "because she goes to receptions where there are men and women together, so why should it be different at the club?"

He said, "No. There will be all sorts of people at the club and we don't want any of them to look at her. The King does not want it. At a reception at the Governor's House or at the Prime Minister's House, that is different. You meet the right people there, but these are not the right people."

"Well, in any case they are just looking at her," I said. But I had to send for a platoon of policewomen. We have quite a large contingent of them in Bombay. They wear white trousers and a sort of white bush coat with brass buttons and a white Gandhi cap. I think they are quite attractive—if they are not too fat.

Queen Soraya, who had never seen women dressed like that, asked, "What are they?"

I said, "They are your guards. They are here to protect you in case someone might want to kidnap you."

To my surprise she did not think it funny or even smile a little.

When I took her back to Government House she thanked me and went to her room. Then I learned from her lady-in-waiting why the young Queen was so sad and distrait. She was worried even then about what her fate was to be, because if she did not have a son she would be divorced. Throughout the five days she was in Bombay I seldom saw her smile spontaneously, but only out of politeness when someone was presented to her. As a woman, I think the Shah should

252

have been more courageous and stood by her, even if it meant losing his kingdom for lack of an heir. Of course, there was not even a nephew to carry on the line, so perhaps he was right; never having belonged to a dynasty I would not know about that.

In the end it was Soraya who brought things to a head. Being a Muslim the Shah could have taken another wife, or two, and she would still have been the chief wife; but she would not stand for that and asked for a divorce.

This, though, I believe: that they were truly in love with each other. There was a tea at Government House and they were sitting together on a settee. I was sitting opposite to them with Raja standing beside me. Every now and then they would just slip their hands across and cling for a moment or two like a very young married couple. In the light of what we knew, it was infinitely touching.

Another Muslim, King Ibn Saud of Saudi Arabia, was a very different sort of guest. He brought no women, but a hundred and fifty men with him, of whom fifty were princes of the blood. He announced that each prince must have a separate car to ride in. This sent the Bombay government off rounding up all the big American cars in town. They asked for our Buick with a chauffeur. We told them we had no chauffeur and if they wanted our car, Raja or I would have to drive. They did not accept.

We were also informed that the wives of ministers of the government, and even women ministers themselves must not offer to shake hands with Ibn Saud as he was very orthodox; so we bowed to him with folded hands saying, "*Namaste.*"

The King insisted that his barber must be put up in Government House with him. The Governor, who was very strict about protocol, had had enough, and told the King it was "just not done." The barber could have the spare room in the Royal Bungalow, a small house on the grounds where my brother now stayed when in Bombay. This did not suit His dictatorial Majesty and within forty-eight hours he managed to rent a palace on the sea close to Government House from the Maharaja who owned it; and he and his whole entourage, barber and all, shifted over. No visiting dignitary had ever acted thus.

Furthermore, the princes were not so precious about their dignity. One night, when they wanted to go out on the town, all fifty of them piled into five cars and went roaring off looking for trouble. They paid their way with bars of pure gold stamped with the seal of Saudi Arabia. Nobody could cash them and they had to be returned.

When King Ibn Saud went to Hyderabad, which is a strongly Muslim state and is known for its beautiful women, those women said his alleged orthodoxy was nonsense. At the airport they all put out their hands and the King, taken unaware, shook them. For their courage they each got a beautiful gold watch which the King gave to everyone, men and women, who shook hands with him. We women of Bombay were furious at missing out on the fine presents because we had taken Ibn Saud's orthodoxy seriously.

Of the statesmen I met, Ho Chi Minh was one of the strangest. He was a tiny, wispy man with a straggly beard, but he had sparkling eyes and a sense of humor, which has not been apparent lately. For some reason he took a liking to me and invited me to visit him if I ever came to Southeast Asia. Each time we met he said, "I have always wanted a sister and I shall adopt you as my sister."

Finally I said, "I have one brother whom I adore and that's enough."

One day the municipality of Delhi was holding a reception for Ho Chi Minh in the Red Fort. I was tired and decided not to go. About half an hour after my brother left the house I heard sirens, and looking out of my bedroom window saw motorcycles and Bhai's official car. One of the secretaries came racing up the stairs and said, "Hurry up. A car has been sent for you, and you *have* to go to the Red Fort."

"Has my brother sent for me?" I asked.

"Of course the Prime Minister sent the car, but it was Ho Chi Minh who asked why you were not there."

"I can't go in these clothes," I said. "I'll have to change."

The secretary just stood there saying, "There's no time for that. You must go as you are."

So off I went in an old sari with the motorcycles screaming ahead. Normally Bhai did not use sirens and I had never ridden behind them. The Red Fort is in the old city—a forty-five-minute drive. We made it in twenty. It was all lit up with floodlights playing on the old red stones, and on its carved balconies and minarets. In the courtyard there was a dais with a canopy of flowers over it where the VIP's were sitting. As soon as he saw me Ho Chi Minh got up and said, "Oh I am glad you came. Come and sit next to me."

"I can't do that," I said. "It's not protocol."

He insisted; and I insisted on not sitting there because it was not done and I knew Bhai would be angry. Finally, we compromised by having me sit right behind him. When all the speeches were over and we were leaving Ho Chi Minh put his arm through mine and walked me to the car while a crowd of photographers walked backward in front of us popping flashbulbs in our faces. For once, mine was red with embarrassment.

Khrushchev and Bulganin also came to visit my brother. They landed first in Bombay, so I met them there, and again in New Delhi. Bulganin paid no attention to me; but Khrushchev was his familiar affable self. The only trouble was that he kept confusing me with my sister, who was then our High Commissioner in England, which was slightly annoying. That, and the fact that everything had to be translated by his interpreter, made conversation rather difficult. Khrushchev was wearing an exquisitely embroidered Ukrainian shirt hanging outside his trousers, which Ukrainians wear even on formal occasions. I admired it extravagantly in the hope that he would give me one for Raja, but he did not take the hint.

I cannot give a brilliant account of most of the world leaders whom I met because, as the sister of the Prime Minister, I dared not talk politics with them, for fear my words might be taken to have official significance; and what a kettle of fish that would have been, since my ideas were frequently not in accord with the government's policy! Raja, too, frequently disagreed with my brother's government and once ran for election as a Socialist against the Congress party candidate—he was defeated.

I missed some of the most famous men and women, like President Eisenhower, because Raja and I did a great deal of traveling in those years. Our boys were growing up—Harsha went to Kings College, Cambridge in 1953. We were no longer tied down, and Raja's family business was making more and more foreign contacts which made it necessary for him to go frequently to the United States and other countries. I love to travel and could always more than pay my way in America by lecturing—I had improved considerably since the first tour.

I think I mentioned that we were in London at the time of Queen Elizabeth's coronation. Harsha was obliged to have a slight operation* and we took a flat for a month or so. Bhai and Indira also came for the coronation, as did all the other Commonwealth prime ministers. Since we were there, we naturally received invitations to Westminster Abbey. I was a little reluctant to go because I did not want to leave Harsha alone in the apartment on crutches and in a plaster cast, but Bhai said that since our names were down it would be most discourteous not to appear. I got someone to stay with Harsha and invited some of his friends in to see the coronation on television.

That was an interesting but exhausting day! We had to get up at five-thirty in the morning to begin dressing. It seemed odd to be putting on a dress sari and all my jewels with the sun hardly up, but the instructions were that we must dress as though for a ball. I wore a silk brocade sari with multicolored flowers woven into it and a very beautiful silk shawl which had belonged to my grandmother. It was all wasted for we remained sitting the whole time and nobody saw us at all. Also I nearly froze in the Abbey which has been getting colder and colder for seven or eight hundred years.

We had to be at the Abbey promptly at seven o'clock. It was within easy walking distance from our apartment but again—it was not done, so a car from the Indian Embassy took us there. We were seated in the front row of our section with some of the Indian High Commission people behind us. Bhai was in another part of the Abbey with the Dominion Prime Ministers and Indu was seated next to Winston Churchill who said to her, "Don't you think it strange for us to be sitting here together when a few years ago we hated each other?"

"I never hated you,"

"Well, I did," Churchill growled. "But I don't now."

I was seated next to a lady from Australia or New Zealand who seemed to know everybody and their secrets. As the peers and peeresses began to arrive in their crimson-and-ermine robes and glittering

* Harsha had broken his leg in a motor accident. It was badly set in India, and we brought him to London to have it operated on by a famous British surgeon.

jewels, she kept up a running commentary on all those dukes and duchesses, marchionesses, countesses and such. Of one I said, "Isn't she wearing a magnificent diamond necklace?"

"They're paste," the lady answered. "She keeps the real ones in the bank." So it was with most of the peeresses, but of Lady Mount-batten, glittering in beauty, she said, "*She* wears the real ones."

We had a long, hungry wait. Many people had brought bags of sandwiches—it said on the card that you could bring food, provided it was not crunchy—but I had not done so as I did not think it proper to eat in the Abbey. There was a Greek Orthodox bishop at the end of the row who ate steadily all through the preliminaries. Finally I decided to go to the cloak room and pushed past him. To my horror I had to be escorted there by an usher who stood waiting until I came out. On my way past the bishop I knocked over his pile of sandwiches; and he gave me a dirty look. Then, my Australian neighbor wanted me to go to the cloak room with her and on my way out I did it again. I had an unhappy feeling that the bishop did not like me.

Finally, we heard the saluting cannon and the Queen came up the aisle in the slow, stately procession. Never have I seen anyone look as radiant as she. Not once during the long impressive ceremony did she falter or seem to tire, and when, at last, the triumphal music sounded and she walked solemnly out, wearing the heavy crown with its flashing diamond cross and carrying the orb and the scepter, she looked as fresh and happy and youthful as when she came in.

I felt far from fresh. We were in the Abbey from seven in the morning until two-thirty that afternoon with nothing to eat. There was supposed to be a buffet lunch afterward, but by the time we pushed through the crowd to the building where it was laid out the table had been swept clean. So we walked wearily home. At our apartment we found that Harsha's friends had consumed all the food I had stocked there. Nothing was left for us but a cup of tea and a few fragments of ham.

Raja and I had a most enjoyable trip to the United States in 1956. The highlight of it was a dinner that Sherman and Lorraine Cooper —he was then American Ambassador to India—gave for us at their house in Washington. It was a warm June night and we had dinner under the stars at little tables set up on their big flower-bordered lawn. Among the forty or fifty guests were many whose names I later became familiar with as they rose to prominence in American politics; or perhaps they already were important and I just did not know it at the time.

The couple who made the deepest impression on me were Senator and Mrs. John F. Kennedy. Jacqueline Kennedy was wearing a dress made from exquisite sari material; she looked so lovely that even a woman like myself could hardly take my eyes off her. Late in the evening, as the guests began drifting away, Raja became deeply involved in a conversation with Senator Kennedy who, with his alert mind and omnivorous interest in every phase of human experience, was probing Raja's knowledge of Indian economics and politics. The last guests left and the waiters were dismantling the tables but still they talked, while I made light conversation with Jackie. The Coopers, with whom we were staying, looked as though they wished they could go to bed. We wandered into the house and then out again. Raja and Jack Kennedy sat down on the steps and the rest of us, the Coopers, Jackie and I, drew up chairs and sat in a semicircle listening to their talk which I, at least, found so enthralling that I forgot to be tired. It was almost two o'clock before Senator Kennedy heeded his wife's frantic signals that it was time to go home.

After that we kept vaguely in touch with the Kennedys and when he was elected President in 1960 we were delighted because we felt that there was a man in the White House who would at least try to understand our problems and not be automatically hostile to my brother's policy of nonalignment.

When we heard that Jackie was coming to India I was naturally anxious to see her again, but I did not go to Delhi nor did my brother invite me. Then, on the night before she arrived, Raja and I were dining with some friends by the sea, twenty miles from Bombay. The telephone rang. It was the Prime Minister's House for me, and Bhai himself came on the line, a thing he rarely did because he did not like talking on the telephone. "I have two seats for you on tomorrow morning's plane," he said. "Pack up and come here. I would like you to be here when Mrs. Kennedy arrives because, though Indu and I have been their guests, you know them better and we feel that she will be more informal with you."

258

I was both thrilled and irritated, because it was just like Bhai to wait until the last minute. "You might have let me know before," I said. "I'll come but not on the morning plane. I can't even get home from here until one o'clock and I have to pack and arrange things."

Now Bhai was annoyed. "Why does it take so long to pack?" he asked. "Just throw some things in a suitcase and come."

"But it does!" I replied. "I also want to find out how many functions there are and what sort of clothes I should bring."

"Well, all right, if you want to be difficult you can," he snapped.

"I'll come on the evening plane," I promised.

Jackie was already in Delhi staying at the President's House when I arrived but she shifted over to my brother's the next morning. With her came an entourage of security men, secretaries and so forth. I did not know that her staff had been given my brother's secretary's office and had it all wired up so she could talk to her husband direct until I burst into it one morning and was confronted by a security officer. He did not actually pull a gun on me but I could see the bulge of it under his coat. He pushed me out. I said, "What's going on around here?"

"You can't come in," he said. "This is the office of Mrs. Kennedy's staff."

By that time I was surrounded by G-men so I meekly said I was sorry, I hadn't been told.

Jackie and her sister, Lee Radziwill, were the most charming guests we ever had. It was true that Jackie was quite formal with my brother but I used to pop into her room anytime to see if she needed anything. Of course, most of her time was taken up with functions booked ahead by our government or the American Embassy. She wanted very much to go out shopping, but she had so caught the fancy of the Indian people that there were always big crowds in front of my brother's house, just standing there, hoping to catch a glimpse of her. Also it is our custom for merchants to bring their goods to the house, so they came with beautiful fabrics, exquisitely wrought Indian jewelry and all the other handcrafted things that cannot be duplicated in the West, for Jackie to chose. But I did take Lee Radziwill out shopping.

Though Jackie's schedule was crowded, there were occasions when there was time for her to sit in the quiet garden behind the house and chat with my brother, who obviously enjoyed it—she is such a lovely person.

When my brother and Indu were in America the Kennedys took them to see *Camelot*; and Bhai often spoke of that happy evening. When that terrible day in Dallas came, we thought in agony of Jackie. Our hearts, like those of millions of people, were nearly broken, and sharply stabbed again when we read her interview with Theodore White in which she said so tragically, "There was a place called Camelot...."

23
juvenile
delinquents
in Bombay

All the splendor and the entertaining, the famous guests and the happiness of feeling secure and knowing that I and those I loved would never unjustly have to go to prison again, did not make me forget little Bachuli and the children like her whom I had known in Lucknow Central Prison. Right after Independence, in 1947, I began to do something about it.

Four other women and I started a little hospital to treat children crippled by polio and other diseases in an encampment that was vacated by the British military forces in Bombay. I knew many people in the British field hospitals and begged this installation from them. It was just a long hut made of bamboo in which we put up some partitions to separate the boys and girls while they were being treated.

The strange thing was that most Indians then believed that there was no polio in our country; it was a queer disease that the Americans and Scandinavians had. For example, when I went to the Chief Minister of Bombay, Mr. Morarji Desai, who long afterward ran for prime minister against Indira, to ask for money from the city, he refused, saying there was no polio and that the crippled children we saw had rickets or some other disease. This was true of many but not all. Mr. Desai was a strong man, but a bit of a fanatic, ardent for prohibition and the compulsory teaching of Hindi. His medical knowledge is indicated by the fact that he once advised a visiting Westerner to drink cow's urine for his health.

However, a friend of mine, Mrs. Ismail, had a daughter eighteen months old who became paralyzed. After taking the child all over India she found a doctor* in Madras who disgnosed the disease correctly and after that the little girl was treated successfully at the British Military Hospital in Poona for polio.

Mrs. Ismail wanted to help other children with polio and she recruited me and the three other women to help. We collected money from our rich friends to make a start. Three of us were completely untrained, but one was a woman doctor. We persuaded two men doctors to help us. We started with just six children, not all of whom had polio, and gave them massages on wooden tables and ultra-violet-ray treatment. I was in charge of the latter, and worked from nine-thirty in the morning until four-thirty, taking my lunch in a paper bag and virtually never leaving the room.

I knew the danger of looking into a violet-ray machine and always wore dark glasses. In spite of that I woke up one night feeling as though my eyes were full of pins. I walked to the bathroom and tried to wash them out with optrex and rose water, but I couldn't open my eyes, and dropped the bottle with a crash. That woke Raja who led me back to bed. There I lay in agony until six o'clock when Raja got our family eye specialist. He said I had burned all the tissue of my eyelids. I was in bed for three months. It was boring and also very frightening for I was not allowed to read and, in fact, could not even see big headlines in the paper.

Raja gave me little sympathy saying I must give up social work, but I recovered, except that I, who had never worn glasses, now need new ones every three or four years. But I went back to my social work.

When the poor people discovered we had this hospital for crippled children they came to us in increasing numbers. Since I could get no money from the city government, I wrote and asked my brother to visit the hospital when he came to Bombay. Despite his heavy schedule, he came and was shocked to see us working in such miserable conditions. When he returned to New Delhi he had the Central

* Doctor Kiri, who later became head of our Children's Orthopedic Hospital in Bombay.

Government send us 35,000 rupees and requested Bombay to match the gift. Knowing that my brother was interested in our work made our friends give much more generously. Between private and public donations we now have a fine modern building—The Children's Orthopedic Hospital of Bombay—with trained personnel: physiotherapists (some from abroad), registered nurses; and a modern operating room and facilities to treat two hundred children a day.

Not all our patients were grateful, however. I remember one small boy of fourteen who, wearing nothing but a loincloth, used to drag himself around the streets on his knees with the help of one crutch. He would open the door of my car and say, "*Salam!*" and then guard the car until I came out when I would give him a rupee. One day I said to him, "Would you like to find out if your leg could be operated on so you could walk properly?"

He said, "Yes, but I have no money."

I told him that it could be arranged. The operation was a success and the boy was able to walk with only a slight limp. He had no idea who his parents were, and when he left the hospital he was on his own again.

Many months later I saw him again at the very spot where I had first met him. He looked rather miserable and as he came up to me, walking very well, he said, "I don't think you have done a good job for me."

"Why not? Are you sick?"

"No, I feel well," he answered. "But as a beggar I could earn three or four rupees a day. Now I am lucky to make two."

I felt as responsible as when you save a man's life, so I got him a job with my Chinese shoemaker and when he learned the trade he got a good job in a shoe factory.

Though the hospital was a great success and I am still on the Executive Committee, my greatest interest, because of my prison experience, was in juvenile delinquents. In 1948, I accepted a post as an honorary magistrate of the Juvenile Court of Bombay; there were several honorary magistrates appointed by the government. We sat with the regular magistrate, a woman. At first we just listened to the cases and learned the procedure. Later, we were told that if the magistrate were ill or very busy we could make decisions of our own in minor cases, but could not judge serious charges such as rape or murder. However, it is very rare for Indian youngsters to come up for murder. In all the eighteen years I have been a magistrate, I have only seen three cases of boys fourteen or fifteen charged with murder, and even in those there was a good deal of provocation. They were sentenced, but not for long terms.

At first, most of the children were charged with minor offenses: petty theft or carrying rationed grain. Many of the young girls had been kidnapped and when the police picked them up they were sent home, if we could locate their parents. Nowadays the major problem is bootlegging; boys and girls do nothing else. I once told the Chief Minister who was largely responsible for starting prohibition in Bombay, "Thanks to you I have learned how to earn a living, if ever I must, in the wrong way."

The ingenuity of the children—or their bosses—is amazing. Boys innocently selling popcorn on a tray with a fire underneath to keep it warm have a false bottom under that, stocked with country liquor—moonshine, Americans would call it. Or they have tubes filled with liquor around their waists. In the beginning, the girls used to carry it quite openly in shopping bags, but when the authorities cracked down, the girls became quite clever designing all sorts of other means. We found out about that when a girl about fifteen years old was picked up because she looked pregnant, and brought into court. When the doctor and the nurse undressed her they found two bicycle tubes full of liquor wrapped around her waist.

When the teen-age girls were sentenced, they were usually sent for from six months to two years to various homes for delinquents and orphans run by religious groups—Hindu, Muslim, Christian— according to their religion. As a magistrate I could make surprise visits to these homes at any hour of the day or night and I discovered that the Hindu and Muslim homes were not well run. We had one difficult case of a Hindu girl who had run away from the home she was in three times. I decided to send her to the Catholic St. Catherine's Home, and the result was so successful that over the years I have sent many other Hindu girls there—the government pays a miserable eight to ten dollars a month for their upkeep.

St. Catherine's belongs to the Sisters of the Cross and was run by Sister Anna Huberta who was full of go and good will—she is now

Mother Provincial. All the other homes had high walls and little low gates you had to bend over to get through, but even so the girls escaped. In St. Catherine's there are no walls, just cottages dotted all over a big compound on the outskirts of Bombay. The nuns have made it very pretty with the help of the older girls. The inmates are of all castes and religions—Hindu, Muslim, Christian. Many of them come of their own accord asking the sisters to take them. They always do, giving the girls room, food and work to do. People of all religions leave illegitimate or unwanted children there. Very often I have seen a taxi drive up and just dump one child or two and dash off before it could be intercepted. There are now about 160 infants under two years, and over 700 children altogether in St. Catherine's. The older girls learn to sew and do most of the cooking and cleaning. They have a big vegetable garden and a beautifully appointed kitchen. There is also a small hospital and dispensary with a doctor in charge. Some of my delinquent girls went to the hospital to look after sick babies. They have now learned to be nurses and taken jobs outside; a few of them have even become nannies in Indian and English homes. So far we have heard of none misbehaving.

With the money from my committee for delinquents I arranged to take the children on bus rides to interesting places, which was never done before. They went in batches of twenty-five or thirty. They always wanted me or some other committee member to go with them and we would take food along. At first Mr. Desai was against it—how could we manage so many girls and what if they ran away? We had to take a matron or superintendent, but when we found that the children were not at ease, we decided against it. Not one of the girls or boys has ever tried to jump out of the bus or escape.

Of course, I was criticized for sending Hindu girls to a Catholic home, by those who feared the sisters might try to convert them. But there is no proselytizing; none of the girls is forced to go to chapel though all of them, even the little tots, are taught to sing hymns as they are taught nursery rhymes. Nor is there much mixed marrying. The Muslim girls marry Muslims and the Hindus, Hindus. I have seen a Hindu girl marry her Hindu probation officer and Sikh girls marry Sikh officers in the Home. The sisters ask who knows how to arrange a Hindu wedding; a Hindu priest comes and they walk around the fire. And that's that.

What troubled me most as a magistrate was the problem of the youngsters waiting to be tried. They used to sit in a house of detention for months, girls on one side of a wall, boys on the other, with nothing to do, just waiting and wondering....

In 1950, I formed the Committee for the Prevention of Juvenile Delinquency. It was composed of social workers who would work outside the court with preventive measures, and also take care of those poor children awaiting trial. I was, and still am, chairman of the Executive Committee on which we had two American women, one French woman, one Belgian and the rest Indians. After forming the Committee, I went to Mr. Desai to get permission to do something for the detainees because they were kept for such a long time, even when charged with very minor offenses. I thought this quite unnecessary. Of course he objected at first, but finally he gave in. Then, I went to all the rich people I knew like Mr. Tata of our great Tata Company and other magnates of Bombay. I asked them for just enough for one teacher's salary for a year. They were amazed because most people started by asking for five or ten thousand rupees. I only asked for four or five hundred. Some were very generous like the Tatas who gave a thousand rupees and asked me to remind them in a year to renew the gift. I also asked for saris for the girls and clothes for the boys.

Then I started classes inside the House of Detention. The girls and boys were taught tailoring, cutting and to sew properly on a machine. We taught basket-weaving and painting the pottery jars used at festivals. We had to throw quite a lot of the stuff they made away, but in the end they got better and better. Weaving was the most popular of all the things we taught.

After a bit, our committee decided we should pay these children for their work to give them an incentive to improve. Of course, we could not give them the money there. It was kept in the office, but we kept track of the hours they worked and how much was paid in, so the superintendent or matrons could not steal it. Our greatest financial success was beach sandals, which we sold in the shops.

We also gave the children lessons in reading and writing, geography, and history, and we told them stories from Indian mythology. Even after they left, the girls often kept on studying. The boys were more difficult. We don't have compulsory education and they either did not want to study or else had to earn money. I was quite at a loss as to how to help them after they were released, but I hit on an idea of giving them each a brush, a cloth and boot polish and I said to them, "Don't just go begging. Earn your living." Now you see quite a crowd of them polishing boots. But most of them stand outside the movie houses and ask if they can look after your car, wipe the windshield or polish it. If you say, "Yes," you are fine, but if you say "No," you are apt to find a hubcap missing. So it is better to say "Yes."

This part of the work of the committee gradually lapsed, because the courts have improved and cases are tried much more quickly, in three weeks at most. The children can't learn much in three weeks.

In addition to my own committees, being weak-minded enough to say yes, I got on all sorts of other things. At one time I was on the All India Women's Council, the International Women's Council, the State [of Maharashtra] Women's Council, the SPCA, the Children's Aid Society and the Executive Board of the Planned Parenthood Committee, besides my own two committees. In fact I was spread as thin as almshouse butter.

However, I refused to join any committes that were communal or sectarian like committees of Gujaratis or Hindus or Muslims. Now, having acquired slightly more wisdom with the passing years, I have resigned from all but a few of my favorites, which are Children's Aid, SPCA, Planned Parenthood and my own two. They keep me busy enough.

While I was trying to alleviate suffering in a small way, my brother was endeavoring to cope with it on a macrocosmic scale. In his bright dreams of an independent India he had envisioned a great industrial nation where the whizzing, shining machines he loved would raise our standard of living to parity with European countries. He literally adored modern inventions. When the first Indian-made jets took to the air, he stood on the airfield staring up at them with shining eyes murmuring to himself, "Gazelles of the sky!"

To effect the industrialization of India, he inaugurated a series of five-year plans copied partly from the successful Russian efforts, though with many American techniques. But the great Socialist state of his dreams was by no means Communistic. He had absolutely no use for the totalitarian Soviet system of government. Their dogmatic thinking, their ruthless methods, their secret police and their brutality toward their own people outraged his sense of justice and his belief in the democratic parliamentary system of government which had been firmly instilled in him by his English education.

Many things conspired to frustrate his plans, chief among them the enormity of Indian poverty, the low base from which he had to start, the lack of trained technicians and the slapdash temperament of the Indian engineers. Nevertheless, great strides forward were made. Indian production of steel, oil, electric power and manufactured products increased tenfold or more during his premiership. In part this was due to huge sums poured into the country in the form of aid and credits from the United States, the Aid-India Consortium, and Russia. But it was never enough to make more than a minor dent in the appalling problem of India's poverty-stricken masses.

The least successful of Bhai's efforts was in the most vital area of all—agriculture. As a result of his idealistic program of land reform, taking from rich landlords to give to the landless peasants, production of food grains did not increase as rapidly as industrial production; individual proprietors of small (thirty-acre) farms simply could not afford the necessary machinery and fertilizer. On top of that, in spite of the best efforts of the government to popularize birth control, the population of India increased by *over* 100,000,000 during the eighteen years my brother was prime minister. The great gifts of American food and large purchases made with scarce foreign exchange barely served to keep the people above the starvation level. Poor Bhai must have felt like Sisyphus rolling that stone up the mountain.*

* It is reliably stated that animals sacred to Hindus—cows and monkeys, etc.—actually consume more food than India receives from abroad.

24
China crosses the mountains

In the field of foreign affairs the heaviest blow to my brother's humanistic idealism came from China—the very nation in which he had placed his greatest trust and his highest hopes for co-operation in shaping the world nearer to his heart's desire for an honorable, peaceful, *generous* community of nations. He liked to point out that there had been three thousand years of peace between the two great Asian nations, whose mutual border ran for over 2,000 miles along the wild and lofty spine of the Himalayas.

The story of India's relations with Red China is an extraordinary tangle of misinformation, misplaced confidence, duplicity, and the willful blindness of men who would not see. When Mao Tse-tung drove the corrupt, inept and dictatorial regime of Chiang Kai-shek off the Chinese mainland in 1948, and set up a Communist state, my brother was frankly delighted. For the next three years he received glowing reports of the progress of the "agrarian-Communist reformers"—the excellent food situation, the way the people lived and dressed, and the surprising amount of freedom they had—from the Indian Ambassador to China, Sardar Pannikar, who had stayed on after first representing us during Chiang Kai-shek's regime, about which he had been equally enthusiastic. It was said of him, "He will be a Communist in Peking and a champion of freedom in Washington so long as it takes Mr. Pannikar somewhere." He was a short, heavy man with a goatee and mischievous little eyes that snapped and sparkled at his own wit, which one must admit was very quick and funny.

Though my brother realized that Pannikar was pro-Communist, Bhai was so prepossessed in favor of China that he believed much of what the Ambassador reported. Not even the Chinese takeover of Tibet in 1950 shook Bhai's faith, though he later gave the Dalai Lama sanctuary in India. I believe the first adverse news he got was from my husband.

In September 1951, Raja was invited by Mao's government to go to China with a cultural mission on behalf of the India-China Friendship Association. Ever since 1937, when he had been secretary of the China Aid Committee of the Indian National Congress, Raja had read everything he could lay his hands on about China—writers like Edgar Snow, Epstein, Gunther Stein. He looked forward to seeing it for himself with high anticipation.

What he actually saw was just what the Chinese government chose to show him, in carefully guided tours to the showplaces of the Revolution, "the Potemkin villages" which were all façade and no substance. But even this was enough to make him realize that all was not as rosy as Ambassador Pannikar had led the Indian government to believe. So he wrote a private memorandum to my brother giving a factual description of the situation in China.

Bhai did not entirely believe it, since he wrongly regarded Raja as being prejudiced against Mao's regime. Nevertheless he thought the memorandum sufficiently important to circulate it through the Indian Foreign Office, in the course of which it fell into the hands of Mr. Pannikar. This turned out to be very bad luck for Raja.

Less than six months later Raja returned to China with an official mission headed by my sister to attend the May Day celebration. This time he went as a journalist representing the Press Trust of India.* The delegation flew to Canton in an Air India plane and transferred there to a Chinese plane for the trip to Peking. At Canton Chinese officials took up all the passports and official papers. While Raja was there Chinese officials complained to the delegation's secretary that he had taken a photograph of a forbidden area. Raja explained to

* The Indian equivalent of Reuters or Associated Press.

the secretary that with other members of the delegation he had taken a picture of a charming Chinese child. He offered to take out the film and hand it over to the Chinese. That did no good. The secretary said that the Chinese were unwilling to take him to Peking, but said he would try to clear the matter up. Finally Raja was allowed to board the Chinese plane.

In Peking my sister and the delegation stayed at the Peking Hotel but Raja was asked to go with the Secretary of the Indian Embassy to the Chancery and wait there for Ambassador Pannikar. After greeting Nan and the delegation Pannikar came to the Chancery. Members of the delegation had questioned him about Raja's memorandum and he was furious. He told Raja that the things he had written had undone all his work in China. Therefore, Pannikar said, he had decided to prevent Raja from accompanying the delegation and filing any reports to the Press Trust of India. He added in an irritated tone that the Chinese also objected to his arrival in Peking until the whole business was cleared through the Chinese Foreign Office, and he ordered Raja to stay with the First Secretary in the latter's quarters.

Raja was a virtual prisoner there for several days. Since he had no money and no passport, to go out was to court immediate arrest. In addition he almost starved to death for there was no food in the apartment.

My sister and the other members of the delegation did not miss Raja at first because they thought he was busy with his Press Trust reports. Finally at an Embassy reception for the whole delegation Nan asked the Ambassador why Raja was not present. Pannikar sent for Raja. He arrived in a black fury and managed to get Nan aside and tell her what had happened to him. He also asked her to send a cable for him to the Press Trust which she sympathetically agreed to do. In it Raja informed his office that although the Chinese Foreign Office had agreed to welcome him he was being held incommunicado and asked the Press Trust to take the matter up with the Prime Minister.

This produced immediate results. Bhai cabled Pannikar for an explanation and the Ambassador replied that it was due to the Canton incident. Whereupon Bhai ordered the Ambassador to straighten things out and see to it that Raja was allowed to proceed with the delegation and cable his reports.

Pannikar promptly got Raja's passport back to him. But he told Raja that he had persuaded the Chinese to allow him to go with the delegation by promising that he would show all his dispatches to an attaché of the Embassy before cabling them to India. Raja saw through this. It meant that it was not *the Chinese* but Pannikar himself who had engineered the whole business to prevent the truth about China being known in India.

Despite these difficulties Raja managed to see quite a bit of the seamy side of Red China—the ill-dressed, sad-looking people wandering through the rotting magnificence of the Forbidden City; the noisome slums in the great cities; the wreck of commerce in once-rich Shanghai; the effects of inflation; the failure of the land reform program; the breakdowns of machinery in the great factories for lack of technicians; the ruin of small businessmen who were committing suicide in droves; and the black-market profiteers growing rich.

Raja saw some good things, too. But even these were tainted by the Big Brother brainwashing techniques of the government that even corrupted the fine old universities. As he wrote: "I saw a great people roused into life by a new hope, but only for a while. Now they are again caught in the gathering winds of darkness which seek to crush the passions of their nation; its humanity, gentleness, tolerance, and love of knowledge. The four hundred millions of China are being reduced to mere passionless bodies in the service of a dictatorship. They have bartered their humanity for their right to eat."

While Raja was held incommunicado, I was frantic. I could get no word from him; nor could the Press Trust, who were furious with him. They telephoned me; I telephoned them. Finally his dispatches began coming through. Then came the welcome news that he was coming home. I flew to New Delhi to meet him.

Raja stormed off the plane black as a thundercloud. I said, "Hello," very affectionately, but he just pushed me aside. "I'm fed up," he said. "I want to talk to your brother and no one else."

"You can't talk to Bhai," I protested. "It's past ten-thirty at night."

"I don't care what time it is," he said. "I'm going to talk to him right now."

We drove to the house and Raja burst into my brother's office where nobody was supposed to go without permission. Bhai was hard at work with his files piled up in front of him. He looked up in a rather dazed fashion and said, "Hello, Raja. Are you back?"

That was enough to get Raja started. He poured out the whole story torrentially like the Yangtze River in flood. Bhai could hardly believe these things of our Ambassador but the next day my sister confirmed Raja's story.

This put Bhai in an awkward position between two furious men, his Ambassador and his brother-in-law. He tried to smooth things over by saying to Raja, "I'll ask for an explanation."

Raja said, "No. I want an apology and nothing short of an apology will do. If I don't get it I shall write a book and tell the whole story of just what Red China is like."

"Don't do that," Bhai said. "You'll put our Ambassador in a very difficult position with the Chinese."

"The apology or the book," was Raja's ultimatum.

So my brother went to Mr. Pannikar and said, "You knew Raja at Oxford and all these years, and have liked him right up until now. Why don't you put your hand on his shoulder and say 'Sorry old chap,' and that will be that."

Mr. Pannikar flatly refused to do even that. He said that Raja's memorandum had made his position in China very awkward and he would not apologize.

So Raja wrote his book. Though he was still angry, he gave a dispassionate, accurate account of the situation in China. The book was published in the United States by Harper and Row who sarcastically titled it *The Great Peace,* and in England by Derek Verschoyle who called it *Window on China.* It was a tremendous success, translated into many languages including Japanese, Chinese, Siamese and the major languages of Southeast Asia. I thought I was the author in the family but I have never been published in so many countries. We still have stacks of Raja's books, many of which none of us can read.

Perhaps the most farsighted thing that Raja put in his book was that the Chinese did not believe that India was independent of Britain even yet. He quoted Chinese newspapers that belittled "Indian elections and Nehru," and referred to India as "the running dog of imperialism."

Then Raja wrote: "Along the 2,000-mile-long frontier between

273

China and India stands a powerful army, not perhaps to attack . . . but certainly to influence and promote the 'liberation' of India. *Mao needs India,* not only to strengthen his hand politically, but also as an economic asset . . . officially China is therefore friendly to India, but she will give all assistance to the Indian people's 'liberation.' "

This was, of course, something my brother did not believe. He simply could not conceive of Red China casting covetous eyes on India. As late as 1959, when it was suggested that an arrangement should be made with Pakistan for mutual defense, Bhai retorted, "Defense against whom?"

In 1954, Chou En-lai came to India as a State Guest. He is a very handsome man and as Raja said, "His suit was perfectly tailored and his conscious elegance [is] coupled with mandarin grace and charm." He was accorded a tremendous reception by the Indian people, and Bhai found him altogether charming. The result of their meeting was the famous declaration of *Pancha Shila,* the five principles of friendship between nations, which was in effect a pact of nonaggression and eternal friendship between the two great Asian nations.* It was the embodiment of Bhai's utopian concept of international relations. He firmly believed that China would stand by it and that both the East and the West would eventually come around to accepting that doctrine and abiding by it.

The people of India were wild with joy. Everywhere Chou went crowds greeted him shouting, *"Hindi Chini bhai bhai!* [Indians, Chinese: brothers! brothers!]"

In addition there was the agreement on Trade and Intercourse between the Tibet Region of China and India, also signed in 1954, in which India gave up any claim to the special position in Tibet that the British Raj had bequeathed her. Bhai thought that by this renunciation he had removed the last possible point of dispute between India and China. Later he returned Chou En-lai's visit by going to Peking.

The Bandung Conference of Afro-Asian nations the following year, which Bhai persuaded Chou En-lai to attend, was regarded as a great diplomatic triumph for my brother in his unceasing endeavor

* The five principles formulated by my brother were: 1) Mutual respect for each other's territory and sovereignty; 2) Mutual non-aggression; 3) Non-interference with each other's internal affairs; 4) Equality and mutual benefits; 5) Peaceful co-existence.

to unify the "have-not" peoples of two continents as a counterpoise to the great Euro-American power blocs. This, too, gave him confidence in China's friendship.

But there remained the border between China and India. In that wild, inaccessible Himalayan region of twenty-seven-thousand-foot peaks, mile-deep gorges and eternal ice and snow it was natural that the border had never been properly surveyed and defined. Nor had it needed to be until now. However, there were certain areas in which India's right had long been established. The first my brother knew of trouble in that far from paradisiacal region was when certain Chinese maps were placed before him, which showed the ancient Indian regions as part of China. The Chinese explanation was: "These are old maps dating from Chiang Kai-shek's time. Don't worry about them."

From 1955 on there were secret discussions and sometimes heated arguments with the Chinese about the border. Bhai regarded them as minor annoyances and no real threat to the friendship between our nations. He relied heavily on the *Pancha Shila* Declaration. China had given her word and that, to his idealistic thinking, was conclusive.

Another possible influence on my brother's attitude toward China was Krishna Menon. After succeeding my sister as head of the Indian delegation to the United Nations General Assembly, where he undid much of her good work by his acid tongue, Mr. Menon became Minister of Defense in my brother's Cabinet. His thinking was far to the Left of Bhai's. Though Menon always denied being a member of the Communist party, many of his closest friends were Communists and I know that whenever he came to Bombay he was always seen with the top Communists, some of whom I knew well because they had been to Oxford with my husband. In fact, most of them had been educated at the great English universities and had taken to communism later.

Though Krishna Menon always said he was neutral, and in the speeches he made to mass gatherings he would follow the nonalignment policy of my brother's government, immediately afterward he would entertain these Communists in his apartment; so whether he was a Communist or not I do not know. But since my brother's death, he has even more openly sought their company.

Though Krishna Menon was gaunt and grim some people found him very attractive and certainly immensely interesting to talk to. I cannot agree with them because I found conversation with him extremely difficult. He simply would not talk to me, but sat there looking glum and rather sinister. The only person I saw him smile at and talk with in an animated way was my brother, but the minute someone else entered the room he would fall silent, unless it was a member of our family. He just ignored us, except possibly Indira, of whom he seemed quite fond. He certainly disliked my sister because their whole political thinking was antithetical and he knew she detested him.

I did not count because I was not in politics, so he was quite polite to me, though superficial—"How are you? How are the children?" sort of thing. And he was hardly thoughtful. Once I was in the hospital with a bad case of shingles. That day the doctor had told me it might spread to my eyelids and affect my sight. I was almost hysterical when the door opened and in walked Krishna Menon, cane and all. He told me he was on his way to America and said, "I haven't come of my own free will. Your brother sent me to see how you are. He's very worried about you. Why do you keep on getting ill?"

That was perhaps better for me than sympathy; it made me angry. I said, "I don't particularly like having shingles, or any other disease. I can't help it!"

So he stood there and Raja gave him a cup of tea. He drank it and left.

That Krishna Menon had some influence on my brother's policies is true, but how great it was I cannot say. Perhaps it has been exaggerated, for their friendship was a personal thing, more than a political alliance. The fact that Menon had been educated in England, as very few of the Congress leaders had, formed a special bond between him and Bhai. Despite all their differences they spoke the same language, understood each other's jokes based on English slang or customs; and they delighted in reminiscences of English days. Not that Krishna Menon made many witticisms himself, but he could appreciate them. My brother could not talk to his Indian friends, not even to Lal Bahadur Shastri, who was close to him, as he could to Menon, for they would not have understood the jokes and references as Menon did. Nor could Bhai ever forget the devoted service that

Menon had given to India, working and almost starving for all those years on a pittance in London. This accounted for Bhai's fierce loyalty to him in the face of strong opposition within the Cabinet. However, Menon must certainly have convinced my brother of the sincerity of the Chinese, or else Bhai would not have delayed so long in recognizing the danger on our northern frontier.

The first harsh jolt to Bhai's belief in China's true friendship came in 1959, when it was discovered that the Chinese had secretly built a military road from Tibet to Sinkiang through Aksai Chin, a high plateau which juts out like the prow of a mountainous ship from Ladakh, north of Kashmir, between Sinkiang and Tibet. Aksai Chin had long been recognized as part of India. The road was of great strategic importance, not only because it cut hundreds of miles from the route between Tibet and Sinkiang, but also because a branch of it ran down to Pakistan.

Just how this road could have been built without the knowledge of the Indian Defense Department is still a mystery to me. Even though the area was an uninhabited wilderness in the most forbidding region of the world, with the exception of the South Pole, there were Indian outposts not too far away and the building of a road is not a very quiet undertaking. It is a major enterprise requiring thousands of workers, heavy lorries and other machinery and a great deal of blasting and loud noises. Why no Indian Army patrols or even civilian mountaineers had stumbled on it and reported it is simply inexplicable.

This *fait accompli* was a great shock to my brother, not only from the point of view of Indian defense, but because it rocked the innermost foundation of his belief in the essential goodness and honor of human beings. If India's trusted friends and fellow Asians could thus forswear their sacred obligations, his dream of a world made safe by *Pancha Shila* seemed shattered.

The discovery of the Tibet-Sinkiang Road was a great shock to the Indian people as well. They had thought that Pakistan was their only enemy; the greater part of the Indian Army was guarding its border. Now they found themselves with a far more powerful foe on a naked frontier thousands of miles long. Their bitterness was in proportion to their disillusionment. Anti-Chinese feeling was as violent as that against the British had ever been; and there was an upsurge of nationalism hitherto unparalleled in Indian history. This resulted in considerable criticism of my brother and his government, which, too, hurt him badly.

In April 1960, Chou En-lai again came to India to try to repair the broken friendship. He may have offered a deal to my brother of trading some of China's border claims in Himachal Pradesh (formerly the Northeast Frontier Agency) for part of Aksai Chin. Even had Bhai been willing he could not have accepted; because the feeling of the Indian people was so intense that not one inch of the sacred soil of India could be yielded up.

Nothing came of the meeting and relations with China continued to deteriorate. Then came the worst blow of all.

In the autumn of 1962, Raja and I were guests of the Raja of Bahdri, who was Governor of Himachal Pradesh, in the mountains north of Assam. The border between India and Tibet was only a few miles to the north. It had been established in 1914 by an agreement between Sir Arthur McMahon, representing the British Empire and India, and delegates from Tibet and the then-new Republic of China. Sir Arthur had simply taken a map and drawn a line along the Himalayas. Then he and the delegates from China and Tibet had initialed it. Though the McMahon Line had been determined so casually, it had been accepted for nearly fifty years by all three countries and India's right to the territory south of it had long been established.

Raja and I decided to go up to the border. Though there had been some border incidents there was no reason to suppose it would be unsafe. We dined the night before with General Daulat Singh, Commander of the Western Forces, who was a fine man and a great friend of ours. When we told him we wanted to go to the outposts and look over into Tibet he said, "Well, if you really want to, I'll arrange a military escort for you."

"That won't be necessary," I said, "the Governor is sending some security men with us and I personally don't think we even need them."

So it was arranged. The next morning at ten o'clock we were ready to leave with three or four days' luggage packed in the car—later we planned to change to a jeep, the only thing that could go up that rocky defile. Then a servant ran out to say that General Singh wanted to speak to me on the telephone. "You must call off your trip," the General said abruptly.

"That's impossible," I replied rather crossly. "We are all packed and ready to go. In fact, I had to get out of the car to answer the telephone."

"Packed or not doesn't matter," he said. "Last night, after you left, word came that the Chinese have crossed the border and are trying to break through into Assam. I can't permit you to leave."

We went immediately to the General's house where he greeted us grave-faced. "There is no use arguing," he said. "This is a very serious business. Even if I permitted you to start and you were foolish enough to go, it is a physical impossibility to get through. The only road is already choked with marching troops and convoys going to the front. I don't even know what the situation is myself. I'm going up now to find out."

"What do you think?" I asked.

"I'll tell you when I get back," he said. "Until then I won't know whether this is just a border raid or if the Chinese will try to penetrate further into India, and whether we can stop them."

We knew that road. Our reinforcements must climb up the jeep path from Tezpur through the forests of oak and banyan trees, then down to Bomdi-La and up again to the mist-hung Se-La Pass 13,500 feet high. There was nothing we could do except go back to Government House to wait for news. It was two days before we learned how serious things were. The Chinese had infiltrated into India at three points hundreds of miles apart though the main attack seemed to be against Himachal Pradesh. We decided to return immediately to New Delhi. Bhai had been very ill that spring and I wanted to be with him now.

Never had I seen my brother so shaken. He almost disbelieved the reports of his military commanders so sure had he been, despite the incident of the Tibet-Sinkiang Road, that China would never attack India.

November 19, 1962 was Indira's forty-fifth birthday. As usual many people, relatives and her close friends, came early in the morning for breakfast, bringing presents for her. A big birthday cake gave a festive air to the breakfast table. We would not eat it until night, but the cake was there. The room was full of gaiety as Raja came in with Indira's sons. Then came Indira. She looked like a stone sculpture of herself and when I put my arms around her and wished a happy birthday, she gave me the sickliest smile I have ever seen and thanked me coldly for the present I gave her. She seemed to be making a tremendous effort at self-control.

A few seconds later Bhai came into the room. He had aged twenty years since I had kissed him good night, his hair seemed whiter, his face more deeply carved with wrinkles; catastrophe was written plainly on it. It was the first time I ever thought of him as old.

Normally, he would have greeted everyone in the room with a kiss or a joke, but he went straight to his chair and sat down. Our cheerful chatter suddenly stopped. In the silence I went up and put my arms around him saying, "Good morning, darling, aren't you feeling well?"

Like a Himalayan bear he snarled, "Haven't you put your radio on this morning?"

"No, darling," I said. "What's happened?"

Very wearily he answered, "The Chinese have broken through the Se-La Pass."

Then I knew, then we all knew the peril of India. For the Se-La Pass through the mountains guarding Assam was supposedly impregnable. Later we learned that 20,000 Chinese troops had attacked the Pass. With the latest-model Russian rocket guns and mountain howitzers they had silenced the old-fashioned Indian artillery, knowing where each battery was located, picking them off one by one until only the infantry, armed with World War I Lee-Enfield rifles and a few machine guns, stood in their path. Then they had launched a "human wave" attack; massed thousands of them pouring through the Pass, hurling our Indian soldiers back as the Ganges in flood sweeps trees and houses, cattle and people before it. Our men fought well but all they had was courage and it was not enough against modern automatic weapons.

The days that followed were more dreadful for my brother than the worst days of the fight for independence. For he felt that he had betrayed the trust of the Indian people as he was himself betrayed by China. Bhai had once said, "From time immemorial the Himalayas have provided us a magnificent frontier. We cannot allow that barrier to be penetrated because it is also the principal barrier to India." Now it had been penetrated.

When my brother spoke in the *Lok Sabha* a little later the agony in his face was the measure of his disillusionment. The Chinese Army stood on the Brahmaputra River, the threshold of the rich, flat, defenseless plains of Assam. It seemed certain they could go on and on. Bhai told the Parliament the truth, sparing himself nothing; that the Indian Army had been decisively defeated at Se-La Pass and Walong. His enemies and even his friends shouted furious questions in Hindi and English. "We shall do everything possible to strengthen our defenses to turn back the aggressors," he told them. "We are trying to get help from friendly countries." And he characterized the Chinese attack as "imperialism of the worst kind."

Bhai had lost pride but not his courage. He did take all possible measures to defend the country and, contrary to his principle of non-alignment, he sent Army Chief of Staff General K. S. Thimaya to plead with American Ambassador John Kenneth Galbraith for help. On his own authority Ambassador Galbraith promised full United States support. As a first step America sent sixty planes, among them twelve huge C-130 Hercules transports, which flew Indian troops to the battle zone. In the streets people were shouting, "Yankees *bhai bhai! Chini hai hai!* [Yankees brothers! Death to the Chinese!]"

The Commonwealth countries rallied to India's support. England airlifted 150 tons of arms to us. Canada sent six transport planes, and Australia opened a credit for India of $1,800,000. A United States mission, headed by Averell Harriman, flew to India. From England came Winston Churchill's son-in-law Duncan Sandys who was Commonwealth Minister.

Then, quite suddenly, even before the planes or the guns or statesmen had arrived, it was all over. With Assam at their mercy the Chinese unilaterally announced a ceasefire. Furthermore, they announced that by December 7 they would withdraw all their troops to the line they had held in 1959, further back than where they had started. Neither my brother nor anyone else knew whether or not to believe them. We suspected a trap. Astounded, we watched the Chinese do exactly what they had said they would.

To this day no one knows why they retreated, or why they attacked us in the first place. Was it to teach India that she was at their mercy?

Or was it to show their power to the world? Or was it some internal Chinese politics? Did the Russians, who then still had some influence with Mao, call them off fearing a general war? We do not know. They have become as inscrutable to us as they are to the Western world. But this we do know: we shall never trust them again.

One fortunate result of the Chinese aggression was that the Indian Army was thoroughly overhauled and strengthened. The Battle of Se-La Pass showed up some of its weaknesses and the ensuing inquiry brought others to light—for example the Army was terribly short of ammunition for those old Lee-Enfield rifles. As a result of these revelations Minister of Defense Krishna Menon had to go. Loyal to the end, my brother tried to save him by taking on the Defense Ministry himself and making Menon Minister for Defense Production. But Bhai's colleagues would not have it; and the *Lok Sabha* was howling for Menon's head. The Army Staff had never liked him, but Bhai would not listen to them. When Bhai pleaded with the Executive Committee of the Parliament that he needed Menon's experience and brilliance, and must keep him, ten clenched fists banged the council table, as ten voices shouted, "No!"

So Menon left the Cabinet to be replaced as minister of defense by Y. B. Chavan, a tough, strong-willed gentleman who did an excellent job of revitalizing the Army.*

* After Krishna Menon's resignation Bhai again appointed my sister to lead the Indian delegation to the United Nations General Assembly in September 1963, and repair the damage Menon had done to India's relations with the West.

25

"a handful of ashes"

Nineteen sixty-two had been a bad year for my brother and the beginning of worse ones to come. In that winter, six months before the Chinese aggression, he had his first serious illness in nearly forty years. Indira and my sister were both lecturing in the United States, so I was in New Delhi acting as Bhai's hostess. It began with him feeling unwell but still continuing all his regular duties and his backbreaking schedule seven days a week; rising before dawn to read the newspapers and late dispatches and do Yoga exercises; then breakfast and afterward walking through the front garden greeting all the people who gathered there every day to ask for help or protest some injustice, or merely to shake his hand. Anyone could come to his garden. Then he went to his office in the Secretariat Building where he worked until six or seven o'clock. He received and answered an average of five hundred letters and one hundred telegrams a day. Bhai came home to a late dinner with a big dispatch case full of papers on which he worked until midnight or later.

By the time he gave up, Bhai was desperately ill with a high fever that continued for more than two weeks. Being alone and responsible for him, I was terribly anxious. None of the doctors seemed to know what was wrong with him. Sometimes they seemed to think it was a kidney infection and, at other times they were honest enough to say they just did not know. So they filled him full of antibiotics and hoped for the best, while he seemed to be getting weaker and weaker as the fever continued to burn him up.

My greatest difficulty was trying to keep him quiet and to keep unnecessary visitors away from him. It seemed that everyone in the government had an urgent need to see him; but I turned most of them away, and became totally unpopular with many people. President Sarveppali Radhakrishnan of India and Vice President Zakin Hussain came every day. I could not keep them out of Bhai's room. Lal Bahadur Shastri, who was then minister for railways, came twice and sometimes three times a day. I welcomed his visits for he was so gentle and kind that he did my brother good and he was a great comfort to me.

I had known Mr. Shastri since I was thirteen years old when he joined Gandhiji's Civil Disobedience Movement at the age of sixteen in 1920. At that time he looked about twelve years old with his small frame and round innocent face, but he was full of spirit. Once, when the municipal authorities of Allahabad refused to let us fly our national flag from the pole atop the courthouse, Shastri dressed himself up in the tentlike robes and hood of a Muslim woman and got through the guards. Then, throwing off his disguise, he bounded up the stairs like a chamois and hoisted the flag before anyone knew what he was doing. During our fight for independence he spent a total of nine years in prison.

Shastri often came to Anand Bhawan in those days. As a child, I was very fond of him because he was always sweet to me. Both my father and Bhai liked him very much. After I moved to Bombay, I did not seem to see him as often. Our friendship began in 1962.

Mr. Shastri was a tiny man hardly five feet tall, slightly built with a round, merry face and large brown eyes full of warmth and affection. When he came into a room he seemed almost timid because of his diffident manner, but this only concealed an inner strength. A leader of the Congress party aptly described him as "a man like Gandhiji with the softness of silk and the hardness of steel."

I remember one day, early in Bhai's illness, when I was particularly upset about his condition. I asked Mr. Shastri to come over. He came and said very gently to me, "Aren't you ashamed of being so nervous?"

"I'm not ashamed," I said. "Here I am all alone with none of the family to help me. I'm responsible for Bhai, and I'm so afraid something will happen to him."

"But your brother has to live to do all the things that still have to be done, which no one but he can do," Mr. Shastri said. "He will live. He's not going to die!"

Then this little man reached up and put his hands on my shoulders and said, "I know how you feel but you must not behave like this. I will come every day, but I don't want you to call me up just because you are feeling hysterical. You must be strong."

As my brother got no better, I wanted to send for Indu and Nan, but the doctors did not think it necessary. They counted on Bhai's strong constitution and enormous vitality to pull him through. He was, in fact, in wonderful physical condition for a man his age, but, after all, he was seventy-two years old. Finally I felt that something drastic must be done before Bhai became too weak to respond. I decided to get Doctor Roy, in whom I had complete confidence, because he had been our family doctor and friend all the years in Anand Bhawan. He was now Chief Minister of the State of West Bengal with headquarters in Calcutta. I rang him up there and told him about Bhai's condition. He was worried, but he said, "Look, Krishna, I am not just a doctor. I am Chief Minister and also I am a doctor, but this makes complications; for it is against medical ethics for me to come unless I come just as a friend, which I am willing to do. But I cannot take the Prime Minister's case out of the hands of his official doctors."

So then I called Mr. Shastri, in spite of what he had said to me, and asked him to come over. I told him that I wanted to get Doctor Roy because he knew my brother's case from long ago and I trusted him. "Look," I said to Mr. Shastri. "Doctor Roy will come if I ask him, but only as a friend; and it will do no good if he doesn't take over from the doctors and find out what is wrong with Bhai, and scrap all those useless medicines they are giving him. Will you do me a great favor and ring him up, and officially ask him to come?"

Mr. Shastri must have been getting rather worried about Bhai by that time for he said immediately, "Yes, I will ring him up. I will go home and do it."

"No," I said. "Ring him up now from my room here in my brother's house."

Mr. Shastri did as I asked and the next day Doctor Roy came. When I went to meet him at the airport the first thing he said to me was, "I suppose you are being nervous, emotional and hysterical."

"Well, you come and see why," I replied.

The very sight of Doctor Roy gave you confidence. He was eighty-four years old, but he stood six-foot-something high and was stalwart and broad, an enormous Indian. He came into my brother's room and in his great booming voice said, "Hello, old man, how are you?"

So faintly that you could hardly hear him, Bhai said, "Who are you calling an old man? You are twelve years older than I am."

The very tone of Bhai's voice and the sight of him so worn and thin brought tears to Doctor Roy's eyes and he turned his head away. Then he recovered himself. He sat down beside the bed and started chatting, telling jokes and laughing heartily at his own humor. My brother was not easily fooled. "Did Betty send for you?" he asked suspiciously.

"Oh no," Doctor Roy said. "I had some business in Delhi and thought I'd look you up. I heard you weren't well."

"I don't believe it," Bhai said. "Betty is worse than any security officer the way she guards me."

When Doctor Roy left the room he was very upset. He had a session with the doctors. I was not there so I don't know what was said, though I presume that it was carried out with a façade of medical etiquette. But I do know that Doctor Roy threw out all the medicines and wrote some new prescriptions. Everything was changed, including the diet. Doctor Roy stayed only three days, but he left very strict instructions as to how everything should be done, and everything he ordered was done. My brother gradually recuperated and got back, not quite to normal, but very close to his old self again.

The Chinese aggression that autumn was a tremendous strain on my brother, and in 1963 the trouble about Kashmir began again. The government of Pakistan had never followed the democratic methods which Bhai had done so much to foster in India. M. A. Jinnah's death from cancer only a little over a year after the birth of the nation he had almost single-handedly brought into being was followed by years of confusion in the counsels of the State and a succession of weak governments. Finally, in 1958, Field Marshal Ayub Khan seized power and established a virtual dictatorship. A strong government in Pakistan meant greater pressure against India on the question of Kashmir. After the Indian defeat at Se-La Pass the pressure increased further. With India involved on her Chinese border and her army apparently demoralized, Ayub Khan began moving toward a military confrontation.

Meanwhile, the Government of the State of Jammu and Kashmir had also had its troubles. For example, Sheikh Abdullah, who had been its first prime minister, had been clapped into jail by his successor and held there for eleven years. During this time my brother had personally paid for his son's education in England. Now that Pakistan was pushing again, Bhai put tremendous pressure on the Kashmiri State Government to release Sheikh Abdullah, who regained his freedom in April 1964.

In addition to all these troubles there were internal difficulties in India itself: the revolt of the primitive Naga tribesmen who were fighting for a separate country with bows and arrows; renewed communal rioting; and, above all, the never-ending struggle to give India a viable economy that would alleviate, if it did not cure, the curse of abject poverty.

The doctors told my brother that he must take things easier and he obeyed them for a while, but by mid-1963 he was going flat out again. The stress and tensions were unbearable, and added to them was grief for old comrades in the Movement who were dying in the inevitable progression of age—Maulana Abul Azad, Vallabhbhai Patel; dear Edwina died in 1960. Several close friends died in 1963. One old friend he kept ever more closely by his side, Lal Bahadur Shastri. Bhai made him Minister Without Portfolio and, in effect, his deputy. No one was closer to him except Indu, who gave up every outside interest to take care of her father and ease his burdens.

None of Bhai's immediate family were far away. After serving an unprecedented two terms as India's High Commissioner in London, Nan had been appointed Governor of the Maharashtra, the huge state in which Bombay is located. She came to live in the superb Government House, or Raj Bhawan as it is now called, on the southern point of Malabar Hill which juts out into the Arabian Sea. It was a series of white, one-story buildings with red-tile roofs. From the balustraded terrace which encircled it one could look eastward to the sea or west across Back Bay to the fine sweep of Bombay's Marine Drive. Fine lawns interspersed with beds of brilliant flowers and small fir trees sloped down to end abruptly at the edge of the rocky cliffs.

At first I think my sister thoroughly enjoyed the magnificence of her surroundings and kept busy redecorating Raj Bhawan. Originally, it had been furnished with Indian pieces made of our rare, beautiful woods, but the wife of one of the last British governors had them all painted white! By the time Nan moved in it had become somewhat dreary and she had a fine time restoring it.

When that was done she became rather bored. The governor of an Indian state occupies a purely ceremonial position and wields no real power. Greeting distinguished visitors and opening charity bazaars was not my energetic sister's idea of a fitting employment for her talents.

I was also in Bombay most of the time, though I made frequent trips to New Delhi to see Bhai and occasional lecture tours in the United States. I was very anxious about him, for he never seemed to me to have recovered completely from his 1962 illness. My friends and all my family told me I was overanxious; but as it turned out I was not.

Early in January 1964, my brother went to Bhuvaneshwar in Orissa for the annual meeting of the Congress party. He was extremely keen on this meeting because of the criticisms of his policies; and he had prepared a long and eloquent speech urging the Congress to reaffirm the Socialist platform which was the key to his economic planning for India. Just as he ended the speech, he was stricken on the platform before hundreds of delegates. Indu caught him as he pitched forward.

In Bombay we heard on the radio that my brother had had a stroke. I immediately telephoned to Indu in Bhuvaneshwar offering to come there at once. She told me that as far as anyone knew Bhai's life was not in danger. "Don't come here," she said. "It is so far from Bombay. As soon as possible we are taking him to Delhi where the medical facilities are better."

It was a week before they could move him while I waited anxiously in Bombay. By the time he reached New Delhi, I was there in his house. I watched him carried in through the front door with my heart bursting, for he could not walk. Never before, even in the worst stages of his earlier illness, had he been unable to walk.

I stayed with Bhai and Indu for another three weeks while Bhai got better. New arrangements were made in the Prime Minister's House. The entire upper floor was converted into a hospital with a room for physiotherapy, another for the doctors' consultations and one for the nurses. My elder son, Harsha, who was working in Delhi as a journalist for the *Hindustan Times,* had been staying in my brother's house. Bhai was very fond of Harsha. Up to that time they often rode together in the early mornings and Bhai would not hear of him living in his own apartment, as he wanted to do. Now Harsha shifted over to the apartment.

By the end of January my brother's amazing constitution and will-power had triumphed again. He was able to walk, though he dragged one leg and would never run swiftly up the stairs, two at a time, again. His power of clear speech came back. It was officially announced that he had completely recovered, which was not so; but he began to act almost as though he had. He began taking charge of all important official business and in February, he was present at the opening of Parliament—though he still had to speak sitting down. From that time on, he made various public appearances, still looking dapper with the red rose pinned on his sherwani and his Gandhi cap at a rakish angle. Mr. Shastri took much of the routine work off his shoulders, but my brother, whose mind was as acute as ever, made all the important policy decisions. I went back to Bombay, but I shuttled over to Delhi almost weekly. Everyone said he would soon be quite well, but I was uneasy.

Everyone seemed to be right. By April, Bhai was able to make his speeches standing up. He also conferred with President Ayub Khan of Pakistan and journeyed to the high border of Nepal to talk with the King on Chinese border problems. Then, on April 13th, he made a speech in the *Lok Sabha* condemning the rising tide of Hindu feeling against Muslims in general and Pakistan in particular. "The Pakistanis are decent folk," he said, "but when you excite people with religious slogans, nobody remains decent; they become brutal, be it Hindu or Muslim." He spoke of the killing of Muslims in Orissa and Bihar and said, "It was scandalous in the extreme that our people should do what was done there. We Indians should not become self-righteous . . . we Indians think that every evil is being done by Pakistan and China and that we are completely free from wrong-doing. . . ."

Walter Crocker, in *Nehru: A Contemporary's Estimate,* writes: "This brave and moving speech provoked interjections, but Nehru, maimed in body though he was, insisted on his point, 'that the only way for Pakistan and India to live together was in peace.' "*

In mid-May, Bhai came to Bombay to address a Congress party meeting. He stayed at the Raj Bhawan with my sister. It was good to have him back among us; good to see the glint of his old humor; and the flash of anger when he spoke to Congress party delegates sitting on their mattresses and bolsters on the floor of the big hall. Again he told them what they did not want to hear—that the rise of anti-Muslim feeling must be checked and that it was urgent to take a new and softer approach to the problems of China, Pakistan and Kashmir.

Sheikh Abdullah had been speaking in Kashmir to the effect that its accession to India was not irrevocable and he had gone back to his old ambition, saying that the best solution might be an independent Kashmir jointly guaranteed by India and Pakistan. This raised the temper of Indians to boiling point. Krishna Menon's newspaper shouted that Sheikh Abdullah should be jailed again. In these circumstances it took a brave man to face the overwrought Congress delegates with proposals for peaceful discussions, but even his worst enemies never accused my brother of lack of courage.

On the morning of May 18, 1964, after the Congress meeting, we gathered at the Raj Bhawan to ride with Bhai to the airport. The entire thirteen miles of the route was lined by great crowds of men, women and children as it always was when my brother passed that way. They cheered him wildly—whatever his colleagues might think, the people of India felt he could do no wrong—and he responded to them gaily, smiling and waving in the hot sunshine.

At the airport all the cabinet ministers of Maharashtra State, officials of the government of India, and many friends, were gathered to see my brother off. It was a long and formal business until the end. At the foot of the stairs to the plane Nan and I kissed Bhai good-by.

When he was halfway up the gangway an irresistible impulse made me rush up it and fling my arms around him.

"What's the matter, darling?" he asked.

I could not answer, but clung to him for a moment before running back down the stairs. It was the last time I ever saw him.

* Walter Crocker, *Nehru: A Contemporary's Estimate,* Foreword by Arnold Toynbee (New York: Oxford University Press, 1966).

On the way home Nan said coldly, "I do wish you wouldn't be so hysterical."

Back in Delhi, Bhai received the President of the Sudan on a state visit and conferred with the Dalai Lama. He invited Sheikh Abdullah to visit him and had long friendly talks with the man whom many people felt was stirring up trouble for India in Kashmir. Though Sheikh Abdullah might well have felt bitter after spending eleven years in jail he was still devoted to my brother.

Then on May 23, Bhai flew in a helicopter to Dehra Dun where Father had met his young son and heir so gaily over half a century ago and where Bhai had spent so many years in jail.

On the evening of May 26, 1964, we read in the evening newspaper that Bhai had returned to New Delhi. All the stories spoke of how rested and well he looked. Later we learned that he had spent that evening with Lal Bahadur Shastri, and working on his papers. He went to bed about eleven o'clock.

Early the next morning the telephone shrilly awakened Raja and me with a message that Bhai had been taken ill; just that, no details. The morning flight to Delhi had already left so I booked on the evening plane. Then I rang my sister at Raj Bhawan and told her I was going. "You are silly to be so nervous," she said. But she added that she would follow in a day or two.

Within the hour we got another telephone message that a government plane was being sent for us. Then we knew it was terribly serious. Nan and Raja and I left on the plane with two doctors.

My brother had called his servant at six o'clock that morning and said he was in terrible pain. Later the doctors said he must have been suffering for some time but he would not disturb the household, not even his valet. The servant sent a security man to call Indira and another for Doctor Bedi, who had slept in the house ever since my brother's stroke. That night, of all nights, he had gone home. However, he reached my brother within fifteen minutes.

This was not another stroke. Somewhere deep inside him, Bhai's aorta had burst. An immediate transfusion was essential. Bhai had a rare blood type so Indu gave her blood for the first transfusion. Some of the doctors wanted to hurry Bhai to the hospital for an immediate operation. Indu gave her consent but other doctors and the Cabinet, who had assembled in an adjoining room, were afraid. At eight-thirty Bhai lapsed into a coma.

On the special plane we were all fearful and silent. Shortly before three o'clock I saw my husband go into the pilot's cockpit. I asked the air hostess why. She told me the captain had sent for him. I guessed immediately that something was very wrong. When Raja came out of the cockpit one look at his face told me that the worst had happened. He stopped to speak to the two heart specialists who were with us. Rushing up to him I heard him say, "He has gone."

The suddenness of it, hearing of it on the plane, cut off and high above the world, gave the moment a nightmarish unreality. We knew but did not realize; we moved and spoke in a trance, having no feeling, mercifully having no feeling . . .

We landed in Delhi about four o'clock. Harsha was there to meet us. He put his arms around me and said, as his grandfather might have, "Be brave, Mummie!"

It was a twenty-minute drive from the airport to my brother's house. Huge crowds were around it with hundreds of police trying to hold them back. They got the car up to the high wrought-iron gates, but each time the guards started to open them to let it through, the crowd surged forward and they were slammed shut again. Finally we had to get out and walk through the jostling and din of the mourning masses of people and slip into the comparatively peaceful compound through a side gate. Groups of people, mostly from the household, were standing aimlessly in the driveway.

Nan, Raja, Harsha and I rushed across the lawn and into the house. The great halls and rooms were filled with Cabinet ministers, members of Parliament and others whom I did not see or remember. We went straight to the door of Bhai's room. Nan entered first, then I went in, with Raja and Harsha following. Indira was sitting on the floor beside her father's bed with an agonized expression on her face. Bhai, lying there so quietly, looked young again, younger by twenty years than he had two weeks ago. Nan and I kissed our brother. The sharp pain of returning reality stabbed us and we burst into tears. Weeping, we sat with Indu on the floor beside Bhai's bed.

The room behind us was full of members of the family, standing or quietly moving in and out. As it became more and more crowded, Nan and I realized that we must do something to establish order. Indu never moved from beside her father's bed but we got up and began to do what was necessary. All the corridors and rooms of the big house were filled with people and more were coming every moment.

Vice President Hussain was there—President Radhakrishnan had already come to pay homage and had gone—so were most of the Cabinet, the high Army officers and many, many friends of my brother's. We had to keep them out of his room, or let the ones closest to him in and then move them on. Indu sat like an image beside the bed, never moving.

Outside, the enormous crowd burst through the gates and poured into the compound flooding the house with the sound of their lamenting. I tried to go down and say a few words that would calm them but now they were trying to get into the house. One of the Ministers jumped on a railing and spoke to them saying that my brother's body would be brought out to lie in state on the front portico at six o'clock. In all the noise and confusion unreality gripped me again and the rest was one long nightmare.

Meanwhile, the doctors were preparing my brother's body but it was eight o'clock before they were ready and all the time the crowd was swelling to gigantic proportions. It was a terribly hot night, and though the house was air-conditioned the portico was, of course, open. Huge blocks of ice were set on trestles with electric fans to blow over them, and Bhai was placed on a catafalque in front of them. He was draped in our national flag and entirely covered with lilies, roses and golden marigolds, except for his serene face with a *tika* on his forehead. Above his head we put two lotus flowers with their stalks crossed. The family stood beside his body while the foreign ambassadors and other dignitaries came and paid their respects and their homage.

Through the whole night we stood there and the crowds passed slowly by—men and women and small children shouting their grief, and sobbing, especially the children. Some of them had been there for twelve hours, since eight or nine o'clock in the morning, when the news of Bhai's illness was first known.

Early the next morning the leaders of the nations began to arrive by plane from all over the world. It seemed to me, although it cannot be true, that Indira never moved but stood beside her father like a rock throughout that night and morning. At about seven-thirty I had gone to my room to wash my face and freshen up—the heat of the day was closing in on us. When I came out I saw Dickie Mountbatten and his daughter Pamela. He put his arms around me—it was the first time he had ever done that—and kissed me. Then he took out his handkerchief and wiped the tears from his eyes. I led him to my brother.

After that, many representatives of other nations came, bringing flowers and wreaths—the Prime Minister of Great Britain, Sir Alec Douglas-Home; Secretary of State Dean Rusk from the United States; heads of state from all over the world. Many of them could not get into the house because of the crowds that grew and grew and filled the earth and sky with the noise of their grief.

We Nehrus do not believe in rituals or religious ceremonies and my brother had written in his will: "I wish to declare in all earnestness that I do not want any religious ceremonies performed for me after my death. I do not believe in any such ceremonies and to submit to them, even as a matter of form, would be hypocrisy and an attempt to delude ourselves and others."

In spite of this we could not help it. The force of religious feeling was too strong. Muslims, Hindus, Christians, Jews and others who came asking for permission to say a prayer for him could not be turned away without inhumanity to them. I remember the first who came that blazing hot morning while Bhai's body lay in state. A receptionist came running to me saying, "What do I do? The priests, they want to come in."

I said, "Well, let them come in."

He answered, "They not only want to come in, they want to sing. We cannot let them come in."

I went to greet them. This group of people was led by a Catholic bishop who was a friend of my brother's and of mine. I asked him what he wanted and he told me, "Your brother loved 'Ave Maria' and I have brought people who will sing it—just in the background, not on the portico near the body but from inside this room. It will go through." And he added, "Your brother always asked us to do this."

I could not refuse him but I went to Indu who said, "I don't know...."

"What harm can it do?" I asked. "Others of all faiths are praying out there without asking permission, the Buddhists chanting in that corner, Hindus in another place."

She nodded and I told the bishop he might go ahead. So they sang "Ave Maria" in the room. It came through the open doors somehow against the noise of the crowd, and it destroyed my self-control, for it was a song that both Bhai and Gandhiji loved.

In the intense heat of afternoon the funeral cortege started for the place by the Jumna River where long years before Gandhi had been cremated. The pallbearers lifted Bhai's body, draped in the flag he loved so much, to a gun carriage drawn by ninety men of the Armed Services. Ahead went a jeep with the Commanding General and the Honor Guard with reversed arms, then the gun carriage. Following it in an open car sat Indira and her youngest son, Sanjay. Rajiv, who was at Cambridge, could not arrive in time. My sister and I came next, followed by many other cars with the President and Vice President, Members of the Cabinet, Chiefs of the Armed Services and foreign dignitaries.

Slowly, very slowly, with muffled drums we moved through that vast weeping, lamenting crowd who were throwing flowers at my brother lying on the gun carriage. Some said there were three million people and some said two million but no one said there were less than a million people along the line of march. The lines of soldiers and police held while the funeral procession went past the huge circular Parliament House and the Secretariat Building, where Bhai had worked so long, and up the Raj Path. Then, as we turned down Tilak Marg, the enormous pressure of the people burst the lines and only the first few cars got through. Some of the officials and other dignitaries in the rear got out and struggled along on foot. So we came to the cremation grounds on a round hillock by the Jumna River.

Bhai's body was lifted onto the pyre of sandalwood and those who were close to him gathered around. Looking down from the little hill, the crowd looked like a vast white ocean stretching to infinity. The President and a few close friends of different races and creeds, including Krishna Menon and Sheikh Abdullah, sobbing loudly, filed past the pyre, laying their tributes of flowers on the slight body under the flag. We of the family were the last to pass by. Then the flag was replaced by a white silk scarf on which we scattered more flowers. The Honor Guard fired the traditional English three volleys and bugles sounded The Last Post. More logs of sandalwood were piled on Bhai's body. Finally, Sanjay, looking pale and grim and younger than his seventeen years, took the flaming torch and plunged it into the pyre.

As the flames shot upward, the vast, frightening mass of people stampeded forward. The straining guards shouted at us, "Get away! Get away!"

Our family tried to stay together but we were knocked apart and overwhelmed by the rushing people. I found myself on a road with thousands of strange people all around me in an hysteria of emotion. In the distance I could see the flames that were devouring Bhai's body towering up in a whirling, twisting column of crimson fire and black smoke. I was lost and frightened and hysterical with grief. Then I saw the Papal Nuncio's car moving very slowly, creeping, through the crowd. He recognized me and stopped to take me in. I sat in his car and he drove me home.

I did not know where Indu or Raja or my sons were for they were all scattered. But each one finally came separately, in cars of people who had picked them up. So we were together again, except for Bhai, in his house.

We were quiet that night and Rajiv arrived from England. But the next morning people began to come to pay condolences, according to custom. They came all day long. On the third day we went to the priests and brought my brother's ashes home. Yes, despite my brother's wish, there were priests at the cremation. The government had made all the arrangements for a traditional ceremony. We had nothing to do with that. And besides, the only people who knew how it should be done—building the pyre and all the other details—were the priests.

They brought my brother's ashes mixed with rose petals—we call them "the flowers"—in a very beautiful big bronze urn and several smaller urns. These ashes are always kept outside, never under a

296

roof, for it is supposed to be inauspicious to have the ashes in your house. We put my brother's chair—in which he used to sit after his stroke—under his favorite tree in the garden and placed the large urn on it with the smaller ones on little tables around it. The place was roped off and guards stationed there day and night while many people came to look sorrowfully at the urns. Some of these people were frantic with grief and fear, too, from feeling that they had lost their great protector. One day I heard a scream and looking down saw a crowd standing and groaning instead of walking past the urns. So I dashed out and found the guards grappling with a youngish woman who seemed hysterical. "What are you doing?" I asked.

"Look what she has done," they said. "She has thrown her baby into the enclosure."

"I have lost four children, all girls," the woman sobbed. "This is my fifth, a boy, but I don't want him to live in an India without Panditji."

I took her by the shoulders and I said, "Stop it! Stop this screaming and pick up your child! This is ridiculous."

"No," she said. "I just can't imagine how the child will grow up without him."

The guards picked up the baby and gave it to her, but its mother would not take it back. We had quite an argument. Finally I took her to a quiet place and washed her face with the garden hose, and calmed her and made her lie down, and gave her some water to drink. After about two hours she was able to take the child and go home.

During all those days of official mourning, the crowds kept coming. Also we ran into the religious problem again. Some people, especially the foreign press, criticized us for having services in spite of my brother's expressed wish that there be none. But they had it all wrong. We could not help it if people—Muslims, Hindus, Christians —all came and wanted to hold services. At first Indira said "No" to them, but later she thought, and rightly, I believe, that she was hurting them because they were doing it of their own free will. So then we decided to let whoever so desired hold services from six-thirty to seven-thirty in the morning. There was a big verandah at the back of my brother's house where we arranged for the priests to sit and everyone else sat on the floors or out on the grass. Indira insisted that they should not be of one faith or sect, so Hindu priests, Muslims, Christians and others all prayed and sang and worshipped together. After the first two days the crowds became so great that we had to have loudspeakers set up because if people in the distance, far down the lawn, could not hear the prayers and singing they made a disturbing noise. All India Radio picked up the services every morning.

Thus, in the way it was done, it was at least in accordance with Bhai's desire to avoid the divisive influences of different religions, and it came about through none of our wishes. The people wanted it and we could not say no.

On the thirteenth day after the cremation we took the big urn to Allahabad to immerse Bahi's ashes in the Ganges according to his wishes. Our special train, so unlike the Nehru Wedding Train over the same route, moved very slowly through the familiar countryside, stopping at every town and village, large and small. There were great crowds everywhere, even along the railway line in the open country far from any village. They stood on the tracks and some tried to throw themselves in front of the train. This journey, which normally takes ten hours, took twenty-five hours.

We arrived at about seven-thirty in the morning and went straight to Anand Bhawan. The streets were lined by great crowds of people but, unlike the crowds in Delhi, they were quietly sorrowful, and very orderly, which would have pleased Bhai because he believed in order and discipline and always lost his temper when crowds behaved riotously. This was his home town; the people had learned over the years what he liked and in tribute to him they behaved magnificently. So we came to the gates of Anand Bhawan and saw our national flag flying at half-staff as it had for our father.

There were many of our relations at Anand Bhawan and all our old servants who had retired. We went into the house and the urn was put on a platform, which had been specially built in the garden, where those who had loved Bhai could come and put flowers on it. Beside it, on the platform and beside it on the train as well, a little square basket stood by the large copper urn. Now I asked Indira, "What is that little basket doing on the platform?"

She said, "Papu always kept this with him. It is part of my mother's ashes, and, as he said in his will, I want no part of my ashes left behind, I thought it best to submerge them with my father's ashes."

Then I remembered this little basket. Nobody had known it existed or that Bhai was that sentimental. I had seen it myself but never thought it was anything but just a basket. It had stood on a corner of his dressing table, in whatever room or cell he had occupied, for almost thirty years.

After two or three hours at Anand Bhawan, we started in a small procession for the Ganges. My brother's ashes in the urn were placed on a platform built on a mechanized gun carriage so the people could see them. We of the family, Indira, Nan, Raja, Indira's two sons and myself, with Vice President Hussain and Lal Bahadur Shastri, sat beside it on the gun carriage. My sons and Nan's daughters followed in an automobile. We moved very slowly in order to give the crowds on either side of the road a chance to throw flowers and garlands on the gun carriage. They continued to show the discipline they had observed from the beginning; no one made a dash at us or even stepped out of line. Even so, there were places where the road narrowed and it was difficult to get through. Although it is not very far from our house to the Ganges, the journey took three hours. Throughout the trip a friend of my brother's who had been governor of one of our states, piloted a little plane over the procession, flying back and forth, dropping rose petals on the urn.

When we reached the banks of the river, boats were waiting for us. Only Indira and her sons, Nan, Raja and I went in the boat with Bhai's ashes. We sailed well out onto the bosom of our sacred river. Then Rajiv and Sanjay tilted the urn, pouring the ashes of their grandfather into the Ganges. As they did so Indu quietly immersed the little basket of Kamala's ashes.

Soon the surface of the river was covered with rose petals, which had been mixed with the ashes, and hundreds of people in hired boats each tried to pick up one petal to keep for posterity.

Then we came swiftly back to our desolate house.

That night, at eleven o'clock, we started back to Delhi on the special train. The journey was much quicker and we arrived early in the morning. There was one more task to carry out in accordance with the instructions in my brother's will. Indira flew to Kashmir and back in one day, with one of the small urns, to scatter his ashes on the high mountains and clear cold streams he loved. I took a helicopter and flew over the villages outside of Delhi scattering his ashes over the people working in the fields. I was horrified to see that there were recognizable bones. Nan did the same in Bombay, and all the Cabinet Ministers took his ashes to their states and scattered them over the land in all parts of India.

For my brother had written in his will, which Raja read aloud to the family sitting around him on the floor (he could hardly read for weeping):

I have received so much love and affection from the Indian people that nothing I can do can repay even a small fraction of it and, indeed, there can be no repayment of so precious a thing as affection. . . .

When I die, I should like my body to be cremated. If I die in a foreign country, my body should be cremated and sent to Allahabad. A small handful of these ashes should be thrown into the Ganga and the major portion of them disposed of in the manner indicated below. No part of these ashes should be retained or preserved.

My desire to have a handful of my ashes thrown into the Ganga at Allahabad has no religious significance; so far as I am concerned I have no religious sentiment in the matter. I have been attached to the Ganga and the Jumna Rivers in Allahabad ever since my childhood and, as I have grown older, this attachment has grown. I have watched their varying moods as the seasons changed, and have often thought of the history and myth and tradition and song and story that have become attached to them through the long ages and become part of their flowing waters.

The Ganga, especially, is the River of India, beloved of her people, round which are entwined her racial memories, her hopes and fears, her songs of triumph, her victories and defeats. She has been a symbol of India's age-long culture and civilization, ever changing, ever flowing, and yet ever the same Ganga. She reminds me of the snow-covered peaks and deep valleys of the Himalayas, which I have loved so much, and of the rich and vast plains below, where my life and work have been cast. Smiling and dancing in the morning sunlight, and dark and gloomy and full of mystery as the evening shadows fall; a narrow, slow and graceful stream in winter, and a vast roaring thing during the monsoon, broad-bosomed almost as the sea, and with something of the sea's power to destroy, the Ganga has been to me a symbol of the past of India, running into the present, and flowing on to the great ocean of the future. And though I have discarded much of past tradition and custom, and am anxious that India rid herself of all shackles that bind and constrain her, and divide her people, and suppress vast numbers of them, and prevent the free development of the body and the spirit; though I seek all this, yet I do not wish to cut myself off from the past completely. I am proud of that great inheritance that has been, and is, ours, and I am conscious that I, too, like all of us, am a link in an unbroken chain which goes back to the dawn of history in the immemorial past of India. That chain I would not break, for I treasure it and seek inspiration from it. And as witness of this desire of mine and as my last homage to India's cultural inheritance, I am making this request that a handful of my ashes be thrown into the Ganga at Allahabad to be carried to the great ocean that washes India's shore.

The major portion of my ashes should, however, be disposed of otherwise. I want these to be carried high up into the air in an aeroplane and scattered from that height over the fields where the peasants of India toil, so that they might become an indistinguishable part of India.

JAWAHARLAL NEHRU.

So everything was done, as far as we were able, according to my dear brother's wish.

26

Indira,
Shastri
and Tashkent

So great a vacuum had been left by the death of the man who had been the first and only Prime Minister of India for eighteen years and her political leader throughout most of our struggle for independence that people wondered if an orderly transition could be made or if parliamentary democracy would collapse. But Bhai had built better than that. Immediately upon his death Home Minister Gulzarilal Nanda became Acting Prime Minister at the suggestion of the President, and many thought that he would be the choice of the Congress party to become Prime Minister in fact.

In the first days of grief there was great confusion in the party councils. This was resolved mainly by the efforts of Congress party President Kumarswami Kamaraj with the help of S. K. Patil and Atulya Ghosh. Mr. Kamaraj was not one of the intellectual types who had predominated among Congress leaders. He was a powerful, broad-bodied man whose fringe of white hair around a bald dome and luxuriant white mustache stood out in sharp contrast to his dark skin. He came from Virudhupatti in the south of India and spoke no language but his native Tamil—a true peasant leader, and an adroit, intelligent politician who could bring men of different opinions and ambitions to a compromise agreement.

Mr. Kamaraj believed that Lal Bahadur Shastri should be prime minister, not only because he had clearly been my brother's choice as his successor and had worked so closely with him the last few years that he knew all the intricacies of internal and external affairs better than any other man, but also because, though he was firm in his quiet way, no one disliked him. Mr. Kamaraj felt he would be a unifying influence that would keep the party from flying apart. It had all happened so suddenly and everyone was so stunned that the strong men of the Congress party, like Chavan and S. K. Patil, who might have aspired to first place, had no time to play politics. Only Moraji Desai, with whom I had numerous quarrels in Bombay, proposed to run against Shastri in the Congress party meeting. In a long private interview Kamaraj talked him out of it and Lal Bahadur Shastri was unanimously elected Prime Minister.

It was settled on the ninth day after my brother's death, and while the urns were still standing under the tree in the garden, Mr. Shastri came to ask Indira to become Foreign Minister in his Cabinet. No one in India was better fitted for the post because she had met the foreign ministers and leaders of all the important nations in her travels with her father or as his hostess in New Delhi, and was familiar with his negotiations and conversations with them. She knew how they thought and what Bhai thought of them.*

That was the first time in all those days that Indira broke down. Weeping she told Mr. Shastri that she did not want any place in the government; she only wanted to work for the memorial to her father. "I would like to have six months of quietness," she said, "before I take any job in the government."

But day after day, sometimes twice a day, Mr. Shastri came back; not only he, but the Vice President and the other ministers as well. I think they felt they needed her, not only because of her knowledge and ability, but because they wanted the Nehru name to give a sense of continuity that would bolster the new government and win the confidence of the Indian people.

They all arrived and tried to persuade her, and in the end she gave in and took a smaller job in the Cabinet, which they told her was Minister of Information and Broadcasting. She accepted but said she would not take up her post for a month because in front of her there were still the immersion ceremonies at Allahabad and the scattering of the ashes. After that she told them she needed a little time to recover from her grief.

* Mr. Shastri had been outside of India only once, to Nepal.

As it happened we came back from Allahabad at seven-thirty in the morning and on the eight o'clock news broadcast it was announced that Indira was the new Minister of Information and Broadcasting and would take the oath of office at the President's House at nine o'clock. It was too much! For the second time she collapsed. Her magnificent endurance had been used up. It had carried her through the interminable days of heartbreaking ceremonies, the climax of going to our beloved home and the ceremony of pouring the ashes into the Ganges. Now her body and her soul were emptied of all strength.

I rang up the President and assailed him with a torrent of words which were some relief to my own pent-up emotions. "How do you expect Indira to come to you and take the oath of office after this nightmare experience?" I asked. "We have traveled from Delhi to Allahabad—twenty-five hours it took to get there—and the crowds; and going back to the home that was no longer the bright home we loved. So much has happened in that home. Our father died and our mother, and Indira's mother, Kamala. And just now we have been in a big procession to bring her father's ashes there. How do you expect Indira to come with the other ministers to take the oath? She is in a state of collapse. She can't come!"

The President was very understanding, perhaps taken aback by my vehemence. He said soothingly that he would not expect Indira to come; that she could take the oath later on, alone, after a few days. "Of course she does not have to come now," he said.

Indira did not go for a week. But after a week she took the oath. Because, as in England, Members of the Cabinet must also be Members of Parliament, Indira was nominated to the *Rajya Sabha*—the Upper House.

In October 1964 my sister Nan resigned as governor of Bombay and stood for election to the *Lok Sabha* in Bhai's old constituency of Phulpur, near Allahabad. She, too, won easily in a strongly contested election.

Contrary to the expectations of many who did not know of the steel beneath the silk, Lal Bahadur Shastri made a fine Prime Minister. He had his own ideas which differed somewhat from Bhai's; for example, he was more conservative in economics. He said, "Our objective is socialism but we must not be dogmatic." Also he put somewhat more emphasis on agriculture than industrial growth, but this was necessary at the time. To see him among his Cabinet, every one of whom towered over him, one might think he would be overwhelmed. No such thing happened. If he governed with so light a rein, the fact remained that he *governed*. As he himself once said, "I am not as simple as I look."

Mr. Shastri did not move into my brother's house, which was kept as a memorial to Bhai, but remained for a while in his small bungalow-type house. Later he moved next door to Number 10 Janpath, a house formerly occupied by the Canadian High Commissioner. There he lived with his wife, three unmarried sons and his eighty-one-year-old mother. One of the boys slept in the same room with him. He had such a large family of sons, daughters, sons-in-law and grandchildren that the security people had a difficult time keeping track of them all. One of the charming sights of Delhi was Shastri happily playing badminton on the lawn with his sons, dressed in a *dhoti* and *kurta*. He hardly ever wore the more formal sherwani until he became prime minister and then only on state occasions. Even the cares of high office could not alter his sweet simplicity or dim his elfin gaiety.

Shastri rose even earlier than Bhai—at five o'clock in the morning. He carried on my brother's custom of keeping closely in touch with the people. There were no guards in front of his house and the small lawn was filled every morning with people patiently sitting cross-legged, waiting for him to appear. His first trip after becoming Prime Minister was to a tiny primitive village near Nagpur. Even his jeep got bogged down in the mud, and he waded barefoot through the slime to call on the noted sage, Vinoba Bhave. He touched the old man's feet and humbly asked his advice as to how to improve the condition of the people of that primitive place.

When she became Minister of Information and Broadcasting, Indira moved from the great house on *Teen Murti* to a smaller government-owned residence at 1 Safar Jung Road. It was one of the most charming the British built. It had pleasant, high-ceilinged rooms, a large library crowded with books and a classic columned portico and arbor covered with pink bougainvillaea, where she liked to work. There was a lovely garden with lawns where her three golden retrievers could romp. They are the last of the many dogs Bhai owned and loved.

Though her new residence was quite a large house, Indira had to make two of the guest rooms into offices and a third into a reception room for the people who came every day to ask for help or just to see her, as they had come to her father's house before he died. She kept his custom of seeing anyone in the early morning and she still does.

After recuperating for about three weeks, during which I stayed to take care of her, Indira plunged into the work of her ministry with amazing energy. In the short eighteen months of her tenure she raised it to much greater importance by sheer drive. She was particularly interested in getting news—that is, enlightenment—to the villages. Since the literacy rate was still so low (it had been raised from 12 per cent to 40 per cent since Independence) the best way to do this was to encourage the manufacture of inexpensive transistor radios with short-wave reception that would pick up more than one station. Only the most expensive Indian-made radios had a range of more than a few hundred miles, though I had one that would even get French and Russian broadcasts on short wave. The latter were usually beamed to India in Hindi, which the Russians seemed to prefer because it was more intellectual than Hindustani—which would have won them more listeners. But any radios the villagers could afford, even by joining together and buying one for a whole village, were limited to a very short range.

In her study of the situation Indira visited villages all over India. She was criticized for being away from New Delhi so much, but that was inevitable. Had she remained in her office she would have been criticized for losing touch with the people.

She also made an effort to improve the quality of the programs, which certainly left much room for it. Many of our stations only operated at certain hours and the quality of the broadcasts was as wanting as their quantity.

Though she did not succeed in realizing her full ambition for improvement—who ever does?—Indira doubled average radio broadcasting time from nine to eighteen hours a day. More important still, she opened the air waves, which up to then had been a government monopoly and the mouthpiece of the ruling party, to members of the opposition parties and to independent commentators. Indian intellectuals, and peasants as well, listened in amazement to voices attacking the government over its own facilities.

In so short a time she could do little about television. It operated only in the New Delhi area and was definitely dismal. But after Indira became prime minister, she began laying the coaxial cables which carry the telecasts from New Delhi southwest to Bombay and eastward across India to Calcutta and points in between.

Nor did she confine herself to the field of her ministry. Wherever trouble broke out—food riots, communal difficulties—she was invariably the first minister to arrive on the scene, mingling unguarded with the people, learning at first hand the cause of their trouble and calming their passions by her gentle assurance that they were not forgotten by their far-off government.

Typical was her action in southern India. Our Constitution provided that after twenty years the official language of the Central Government should be Hindi. As the twentieth year (1967) approached the government began to move toward this end. This touched off violent antigovernment riots in the Tamil-speaking south where the people felt that it would put them at a disadvantage. With Shastri's blessing, Indira flew to Madras, the hot-point of trouble, and calmed the angry mobs by telling them that the matter would be reconsidered and they would receive fair play. Partly on her advice and to keep her faith with the people the Prime Minister pushed through the *Lok Sabha* a constitutional revision temporarily retaining English as the "associate official language."

Lal Bahadur Shastri was a true disciple of Gandhiji, more unquestioning in his devotion to non-violence than Bhai had ever been. Thus it was particularly ironic that he finally established his reputation and won wide popularity in war. He had inherited the unsolved problems of Kashmir and the Chinese border troubles from my brother's government who, through no fault of theirs, had not achieved satisfactory solutions. In addition, the quick defeat of the Indian Army at Se-La Pass had led Chinese and Pakistanis alike to regard our men as cardboard soldiers.

Toward the close of 1964, with an untried, peace-loving Prime Minister at India's helm and her army presumably still in disarray, President Ayub Khan of Pakistan felt it was a good time to apply pressure. His first move was in the Rann of Kutch, a virtually uninhabited, desolate area of swampland where the western Indian states bordered on Pakistan. Because it was utterly useless for industry, agriculture or even human habitation the border there was loosely defined. However, Pakistan suddenly advanced claims to what was clearly Indian territory and troops began to maneuver.

Probably to President Ayub's surprise, the Indian government reacted promptly, sending troops into the desolate waste. There was a flurry of gunfire and a lot of hard words after which the situation simmered down to another festering sore spot in Indo-Pak relations.

Mr. Shastri attended the Commonwealth Prime Ministers' Conference in London early in 1965, as my brother had always done. He had to buy several new sherwanis as he literally had nothing to wear. At the Conference, British Prime Minister Harold Wilson brought him together with President Ayub in a series of private meetings. In that atmosphere of sweet reason they agreed that there was no point in going to war over a piece of ground that nobody really wanted. Mr. Shastri agreed to a new delineation of the border and, at the price of a few square miles of nothing, removed one irritant from the delicately balanced relations between our two countries, and secured the good will of President Ayub—or so he thought.

However, in aggressive action nothing is truer than the old French saying, *"L'appétit vient en mangeant."* Having probed and found what he misread as weakness beneath the apparently firm policy of the Indian government, President Ayub decided to make a move toward his real objective, Kashmir; but more subtly. He began a campaign to influence the *mujahids,* the local warriors of Azad Kashmir on the Pakistan side of the ceasfire line, which had been static ever since the brief fighting in 1947. They were armed and given a brisk refresher course in guerrilla warfare at which they were naturally adept. In August 1965, thousands of them were sent across the lightly guarded ceasefire line to cause trouble in Indian Kashmir. They could have hoped to accomplish nothing more, for there were 100,000 Indian troops in Jammu and Kashmir, unless they expected the inhabitants to rise and join them in revolt. But the sensible Kashmiris had no interest in dying for Pakistan. They had not changed since I talked with them in 1948: all they wanted was to be left in peace, to profit from tourism.

Once more, our peace-loving Prime Minister reacted more sharply than Ayub expected. Over three thousand of the infiltrators—the Pakistanis called them "freedom fighters"—were killed or captured, and the Indian Army was ordered across the ceasefire line to cut off the sources of infiltration. They advanced twenty-five miles, against little or no resistance, and halted temporarily.

However, this did not altogether stop the leakage of those well-armed bandits, and two weeks later the army was ordered to "correct" the line where it bulged out toward Shrinagar. They threw it back sixty-four miles, seizing and sealing the Haj Pir Pass through the mountains. When the government radio announced the taking of the pass and the "liberation of 5,000 Kashmiris," the Indian people went wild with martial enthusiasm. In a roundabout way Se-La Pass seemed to have been avenged.

The real war began early in September when, at dawn, a vicious barrage fell upon the defenseless villages of Chhamb and Dewa, in the Punjab far south of Kashmir. Following this treacherous blow, a mechanized brigade of infantry and seventy Patton tanks, which the United States had sent to Pakistan on the strict understanding that they were to be used *only* for defense against Russia or China, roared across the border of India and clanked over green fields laced by small canals until they halted on the Munawar Tawi River. They were poised to strike across the flat horizon-to-horizon Punjab plains at New Delhi itself.

This was a vastly different matter from disputed Kashmir. As Minister of Defense Chavan announced, India itself had been invaded. The Indian Air Force in twenty-eight British-made Vampire jets counterattacked the Pakistani column, knocking out many tanks. They, in turn, were attacked by more modern American-made F-86 Sabre jets which had been supplied to Pakistan on the same understanding as the tanks. Four of our planes were shot down. India and Pakistan were at war in all but name.

The myth that Hindus won't fight was shattered by the warlike reaction of the Indian people to this senseless act of aggression. The whole country rose in martial ardor to support the government. As I have written, I immediately volunteered to go to the front in any capacity but was turned down. All I could do was to join a Red Cross canteen. Every morning at five-thirty I went to the station to distribute coffee and food to the men bound for the front in long crowded troop trains. Later, as the wounded began coming back, we tended and comforted the men who had been fighting so valorously in the terrible heat and dust clouds of September in the Punjab where the glaring sun almost boiled the blood in their veins and turned the interior of the tanks into kilns.

But if I could not go to the front, Indira could and did. She was the first Cabinet minister to visit the battle zone, before even Minister of Defense Chavan. Though her Ministry had nothing to do with military affairs and consequently she did not interfere with such matters, her presence gave an immense lift to morale. Throughout the weeks of most intense fighting she visited front-line hospitals and troops in the field in every combat area, ignoring the terrible heat and the physical strain imposed by battlefield conditions. Her reports on the splendid *élan* of our troops made us all even prouder of them.

It was a very different Indian Army from the one that had given way before the Chinese in 1962. In less than three years it had been largely re-equipped and its morale had soared. The high command also knew its business. Instead of wasting time sending a defensive force against the Pakistan column down on the Munawar Tawi River, our Chief of Staff, General Joyanto N. Chaudhuri, ordered the Army to take the offensive. They struck across the Pakistan border in five places. Three columns attacked at Dhankeal and Kasur, converging on the great city of Lahore and threatening the Pakistani capital city of Rawalpindi, where President Ayub Khan, in his role of Field Marshal, sat in his map room directing his armies. This forced the original Pakistani attackers to abandon the advance and send their tanks north to the defense of Lahore. In the fierce fighting around Lahore and further north at Sealkot the Pakistan First Armored Division lost half of its 220 tanks and two Pak generals were killed.

Supporting the Army, the Indian Air Force attacked Lahore with French Mystère jets, sending rockets slamming into trains in the station and the marshaling yards. Other Indian planes bombed Rawalpindi, Peshawar near the Kyber Pass, and ships in the harbor of East Pakistan's greatest city, Karachi. In return the Paks bombed the holy Sikh city of Amritsar.

The boys who flew our planes had a mixed lot of equipment. Besides the British Vampires and French Mystères, there were Russian MIG–21's, Indian-made jet fighter Gnats and British Canberra bombers. Such a mélange does not make for efficiency, but it was all we had, and our pilots handled them magnificently.

The Paks had much newer and more homogeneous equipment supplied by the United States, because Pakistan had joined the CENTO Alliance while India pursued my brother's policy of non-alignment. This turned out to be a liability because Pakistan's source of supply for military matériel was cut off when the United States abruptly stopped arms shipments to both countries, while we could still get them from the French and Russians.

The news of the actual invasion of Pakistan, and Indian victories, brought even wilder rejoicings in India. Our people were as passionate in joy as in sorrow, and displayed it as riotously. The cliché about dancing in the streets became an actuality in our great cities. Only part of this exuberance was due to their delight in seeing Pakistan humbled; the rest was because of pride that our Army had proved itself a fighting force to be reckoned with. As many said, "We have been kicked around long enough!"

Then, at the height of the rejoicing a terrible new threat was posed. Red China had made its sympathy for Pakistan evident in slanted news reports and propaganda broadcasts denouncing "Indian aggression." Now, she suddenly demanded that India dismantle all her defensive works on the Sikkim border of China or "face grave consequences." We had fortified the 14,000-foot-high passes of Natu and Jelep. If China took them, it would close our direct route to part of the Northeast Frontier Province and give China an easy access to East Pakistan.

My cousin B. K. Nehru, our Ambassador in Washington, immediately requested the United States to resume arms shipments to India. which they refused to do even in this emergency. However, Mr. Shastri staved off the threat by a combination of firmness and diplomacy. He agreed to allow a Sino-Indian inspection team to go through the fortifications and report whether any of them was on Chinese territory.

Meanwhile, all the great powers were in a frenzy of alarm that the war would spread. Their ambassadors beseiged both governments with pleas for peace and proposals of mediation. United Nations Secretary General U Thant rushed to Pakistan and then to New Delhi in a frantic effort to end the fighting by some compromise arrangement. He returned to New York to report the failure of his mission.

Yet, perhaps he had not really failed. It was a strange situation. India and Pakistan were at war, yet not at war; for though Pakistani troops were fighting on Indian soil and Indians were in Pakistan, neither side made a formal declaration of war and the attacks across the borders were called "defensive advances." To the credit of both governments, religious passions were damped down in their respective countries. With both Muslims and Hindus in a tremendously emotional condition, it was almost a miracle that there were no mass killings.

The truth is that almost no one in the world wanted an all-out war. Mr. Shastri was a true Gandhian, but he never forgot that Gandhiji had once said to him, "Where there is only a choice between cowardice and violence, I would advise violence." Shastri was firm in maintaining India's rights, but he held a tight rein on the military and refrained from escalating the fighting. After the Indian victories near Lahore, no attempt was made to take the city. Also, because there was only one Pak division in East Pakistan, separated from its main army by a thousand miles of Indian territory, it would have been easy for the Indian Army to take that whole great province including Calcutta. Yet they did not.

So after those first weeks of fierce fighting there was a sort of unofficial truce. The armies remained more or less in the positions to which they had advanced. But with thousands of men glaring at each other across narrow strips of easily negotiable country, the danger was obvious. The slightest spark might start a general conflagration.

In this situation Russian diplomacy scored its greatest triumph for peace yet recorded. Premier Aleksei Kosygin invited President Ayub and Prime Minister Shastri to explore with him the possibility of a peaceful settlement at Tashkent in Uzbekistan, on the Russian side of the Himalayas, a city until then bypassed by history. After considerable diplomatic fencing, the meeting was agreed upon. Early in January 1966, Mr. Shastri went to Tashkent accompanied by Defense

Minister Chavan and Foreign Minister Swaran Singh, a tall Sikh made even taller by his large white turban.

President Ayub brought his best advisors and, to help things along, Kosygin brought his ablest diplomat, Andrei Gromyko, the wily veteran of a thousand diplomatic chess games.

Seated at the big round council table, which looked like an enormous doughnut with a formica top, surrounded by the burly soldiers and diplomats of India, Pakistan and Russia, Lal Bahadur Shastri, as always, looked pathetically ineffectual. However, as he ever did, he proved his mettle in tough negotiations that lasted for seven days. The meeting ended with India gaining all she had hoped for; an agreement that both armies would withdraw behind their respective borders and the establishment of a ceasefire line, which India and Pakistan agreed to respect. More important was the agreement of both nations to renounce war as an instrument of policy between them. This virtually amounted to a nonaggression pact. Other points included noninterference with each other's internal affairs; halting hostile propaganda; resumption of economic, communication and cultural ties; and implementation of already existing agreements.

This agreement produced such a joyous mood of good will between the rival negotiators as had not been seen since Pakistan became a separate nation. To increase the general euphoria and celebrate a vital contribution to the peace of the world, the Russians promptly staged one of their magnificent parties, with tons of caviar, gallons of champagne, toasts in vodka, and long tables spread with mountains of rich meats and pastries to which only a Russian in good gastronomic training could possibly do justice. The event was further enlivened by the chunking of frenetically played *gijaks,* wailing songs in twelve-tone-scale minors and Uzbek girls dancing in their glittering native costumes.

Naturally, our abstemious Prime Minister ate little and drank nothing alcoholic, though he is said to have enjoyed watching the expert gyrations of the lovely girls. After about two hours, Shastri warmly shook hands with Kosygin and President Ayub and went happily home to his villa to sleep, while the Russians and their guests continued to revel until dawn lighted the white Himalayan peaks.

In New Delhi and in Bombay the news from Tashkent in the

evening broadcasts set off even greater rejoicing. We Indians had proved ourselves in war but we truly loved peace; and now our great little Prime Minister had brought to us an honorable peace.

But even while the crowds churned joyously through the streets of our great cities and the revels at Tashkent were barely ending, Lal Bahadur Shastri woke in his bed with a terrible pain in his chest. He cried out in Hindi, "*Mere Bap! Hey Ram!* [My father! Oh God!]." And died.

To those of us who had gone to bed joyful in the news of peace and the hope of a new era of friendly relations between India and Pakistan, the news in the morning papers that Shastri had died of a heart attack at the very moment of his great diplomatic triumph seemed utterly incredible. All our love for him as a friend and our admiration for him as an Indian patriot combined to make our hearts reject the words our minds realized were true.* As the news spread rapidly through Bombay, Delhi, Calcutta and all the others, sorrowful people spontaneously closed shops and offices and went silently to their homes. For in his brief nineteen months as prime minister, Lal Bahadur Shastri had won the respect, the trust, and the love of all India.

* Mr. Shastri previously had a minor heart attack in 1959.

27
prime
minister

At this critical time in our relations with Pakistan and our internal difficulties it was urgent to find a replacement for Mr. Shastri as quickly as possible. Gulzarilal Nanda again became Acting Prime Minister, this time with high hopes of being elected to that office. Other strong men were equally ambitious, with good reason. Moraji Desai, whose square spectacles resting on a long nose gave him a pedantic appearance that belied his puritanical zeal and burning ambition, was a perennial contender. He was supported by extremist Congress members on both the far Right and far Left. Minister of Defense Chavan was very popular with the Armed Services, and with the people, too, because of the splendid job he had done in rejuvenating the Army. He was a very quiet man who did not go around speechifying, but a strong one who had grown tremendously in stature during the past year. S. K. Patil, a brilliant politician, who had the great city of Bombay and Maharashtra State with its fifty million people in his pocket, was also a powerful contender.

My sister cancelled her lecture tour and came tearing home from America. Having been Indian Ambassador to Russia and the United States, High Commissioner in London and a world figure because of her presidency of the United Nations, I believe she thought she had a chance. But I learned in Delhi that Mr. Kamaraj had not even thought of her as Prime Minister because, though she was so well known and popular abroad, she had been away from India too much and had been so little in the villages that she would not be a strong candidate.

Congress Party President Kamaraj was unquestionably the most powerful politician in India, the kingmaker. He could have had the post but he disqualified himself because he felt that a prime minister who spoke only Tamil would be disadvantageous to India. His choice fell on Indira.

There were many reasons for his decision. I think the main one was that he felt she was the one who would be the most acceptable to the Indian people and therefore would be a unifying influence. Desai was a Gujarati; Chavan and Patil were both from Maharashtra; and Nanda was identified with the Punjab. But Indira was not thought of as belonging to any particular locality, neither to our home town of Allahabad nor to Kashmir from which we sprang. Just as my brother had belonged to all of India, she, too, was considered as belonging to the nation. She had traveled to every part of it, both with Bhai and alone, and was known and liked throughout the land. Undoubtedly Mr. Kamaraj also took into consideration her knowledge of and her contacts in foreign countries. Finally there was the name—that always helps.

However, the Congress President had no such easy time arranging things as he had in the case of Mr. Shastri. First of all, he had to convince Indira herself, who was very reluctant to take on the enormous responsibility of the leadership of five hundred million people. During those hectic days in Delhi he held many meetings with her in which he urged his point of view strenuously and she as firmly declined. I have never talked with her about it, but knowing her so well, I am convinced that it was not the hard work she feared, nor even the infighting with which any head of a democratic government must contend. Nor was she afraid of responsibility for herself. Rather it was the fear that she might not be up to it and that if she failed it might tarnish her father's memory. That she accepted was because Kamaraj had made her see her duty plainly.

Meanwhile, the delay had given the other candidates time for building followings among the Congress members. It was difficult to persuade them to relinquish their high hopes. For a little while it looked like a battle royal in the Congress election, with four or five contenders hitting every head that showed above the crowd. But Mr. Kamaraj's powers of persuasion in private conversations are remarkable, and, in the end, all the other candidates agreed to withdraw in the interest of party unity—all except Moraji Desai. This time he was determined to stand, come what might.

During all this political maneuvering I was in bed in Bombay with an injured back. The doctor had refused to let me get up to go to Mr. Shastri's funeral. But from the time I heard that Indira had accepted Mr. Kamaraj's offer to stand for election, I rang up every day. Each time her secretary told me that the house was so filled with people from morning until night that he could not get her out of the crowd. Then one day she spoke to me. Her voice sounded faint and she told me she was utterly exhausted. I said I would like to come to Delhi for the election, but she was so concerned about my back that I did not press the matter. Instead, I said, "I don't have to wish you luck because I know you'll win."

She answered, "Well, I don't know. . . ."

The election was to be held in the Parliament House on the nineteenth of January. All the members of Parliament were not involved; only members of the Congress party, which had a large majority, were to vote for whom they wished to be their Prime Minister. So it was like a party caucus.

Until the eighteenth, I did not know whether I should go to Delhi or not. My doctor was adamant that I must remain flat on my back. That night I decided that I had to be there to see my Indu, whom I loved so much, elected prime minister, if it killed me. I caught the early morning plane and reached New Delhi about twelve-thirty. From the airport I drove straight to Parliament House. The streets converging on it were lined four deep with people waiting to hear the result. There was a great crowd around the building itself, held back by police and the high wrought-iron gates. The guards recognized me and let me through, but security was very tight and no one who was not a member of Parliament or an employee was allowed into the great Central Hall.

Inside, the voting was already going on. It took a long time, for it was by secret ballot and there were over five hundred and fifty members of the Congress party, each of whom in turn had to have his credentials verified, write the name of a candidate, either Indira or Mr. Desai, on his ballot and put it through a slit in a ballot box.

I stood outside the Central Hall between two fountains resting my back against a pillar. It was a bright, cold winter day with a bitter wind blowing. I felt very cold and my back ached. Someone brought me a chair. Just as I sat down the doors of the Central Hall opened and the crowd of reporters and photographers stampeded forward nearly knocking me over. As members of Parliament were constantly going in and out, the wave of newsmen rushed forward and back like breakers on a beach, so I thought it was safer to stand.

After about an hour and a half, Indira came out through the tall doors. She looked very beautiful with her black hair streaked with gray and her soft brown eyes in her pale classic face. She wore a brown shawl over her white sari with a rosebud pinned to it in memory of her father. While guards kept the newsmen in check she greeted me without surprise—she knew I would come. She said, "I was up so early. I'd love a cup of tea." I got it for her at one of the tables set up in the court beside the fountains and she drank it standing. People kept coming up to greet her and ask, "How is it going?"

To all of them she smiled and said, "I don't know. They are still voting. The count has not even begun."

After about a half an hour, Indu said, "I must go back in. Won't you come with me?"

"No," I answered. "You refused other people so I won't go in. I don't want them to think I claim special privileges because you may become Prime Minister."

But after a little while a man came out and said to me, "Mrs. Gandhi would like you to come inside. Just sit in a corner if you like, but come inside."

As I stood up, another messenger from Indira came to say that the press would be allowed in shortly so it was quite all right for me to go in.

I went and sat on a chair in the back. The vast, completely round, high-domed Central Hall was paneled in dark wood against which white sherwanis, *dhotis* and saris of the men and women members, sitting in the concentric circles of seats, were strongly contrasted. On a dais facing me there was a large table at which were President of the Congress Kamaraj, looking unusually solemn; Acting Prime Minister Nanda, a lawyer; two people representing Indira; and two from Mr. Desai's camp.

Indira was seated very inconspicuously in the twelfth row but Mr. Desai was right up in front. Some members of Parliment were still queued up before the ballot boxes, but the voting was soon over and, as the counting of the ballots began, the press were allowed to come in and stand behind the members' seats.

The counting seemed to take an interminable time. Mr. Desai's people challenged vote after vote, and tension built up until it was almost unbearable. I asked the world at large, "How long can it take to count five hundred votes?" Even Mr. Kamaraj, usually so big and fat and jolly, looked strained, every hair of his drooping mustache quivering with anxiety.

It was about three-thirty when the Presiding Officer advanced to Mr. Kamaraj and handed him the totals. One look at the beaming smile, that burst like a Burmese sunrise on his face, told me all was well. He stood up holding the paper and made the announcement in Tamil, which a majority present did not understand. A burst of applause was silenced as the announcement was repeated in English: "The result of the balloting is: Mrs. Indira Gandhi, 355 votes. Mr. Moraji Desai, 169 votes. Mrs. Gandhi is elected Prime Minister."

A roar of cheers, a storm of clapping swept the hall, quickly repressed by Mr. Kamaraj. Indira, her white sari shimmering in the television lights, moved toward the dais with that quiet, noble dignity she has, even though there were tears on her cheeks. As she came to Mr. Desai, she bowed, joining her hands and said, "*Namaste*. Will you bless my success?"

Gravely he answered, "I give you my blessing."

Then Indira was on the dais and people were cheering and clapping again. Though I had know she would win, a sudden realization of the fact swept over me and with it wonder at the marvelous turnabouts of all our lives. That the little girl I had cared for and comforted while her father and mother and grandfather were in prison should become the Prime Minister and leader of the great free nation of India seemed fantastic, beyond imagining, a tale so bizarre that if it were not true no man would believe it. I was so proud of her!

Mr. Kamaraj made a brief speech in Tamil, which had to be translated into English. Then Indira spoke in Hindi. She thanked the people who had voted for her. Then with deep emotion in her voice she said, "As I stand before you my thoughts go back to our great leaders: Mahatma Gandhi, at whose feet I grew up; Panditji, my father; and Lal Bahadur Shastri. These leaders have shown the way and I want to go along the same path."

After that Mr. Nanda spoke and finally Mr. Desai, who said he did not think he had done wrong to stand for election against Indira, who otherwise would have been elected unanimously. But, he said, she had his good wishes and he would co-operate with her. They shook hands while the people clapped and cheered again. Then the members crowded around Indira to congratulate her.

By the time I got outside, the world knew Indira had won. The people had shouted at the first person who came out, "Is it a boy or a girl?" And when he said, "It's a girl!" the crowd went mad. They were shouting, "Indira *Ki Jai!*" in a high-pitched chant over and over again. When she came out on the portico she was engulfed by television men, photographers and reporters and friends. I was jostled and almost thrown down. At the sight of her, the shouts of "Indira *Ki Jai!*" rose to a frenzied scream. As usual the police lines broke and the crowd came pouring through the gates. Then it was bedlam.

A cousin of mine, who was a member of the *Rajya Sabha,* grabbed my arm and dragged me through the maelstrom to a place where my sister was sitting in her car. She had left the hall immediately after the announcement, which did not seem to please her greatly. We got in with her. I'll never know how Nan's chauffeur managed to get us out through that hysterical mob, nor how Indira finally escaped. While I was having tea with Nan, Indira drove up the Raj Path in an open yellow convertible, with people strewing flowers in her path and throwing garlands at her, to the President's House where she mounted that cascade of steps up which the viceroys used to walk. Inside, President Radhakrishnan formally asked her to form a government, and she formally accepted.

I reached Indira's house about fifteen minutes before she did. She was greeting hordes of people. Then she went up to a riotous press conference which was going on, with television lights glaring, flash-bulbs winking and reporters shouting questions that she answered soberly and sensibly. Specifically she said that she would abide by and implement the Tashkent Agreement. Even after the press left, the place was crowded with people anxious to congratulate Indira, new ones constantly replacing those who left. I saw to it that Indu got some food, but she hardly had a mouthful because every time she went into the dining room to sip a cup of soup someone called her out again.

I stayed until midnight and they were still coming. Because Indu had had to convert her last guest room into a conference room where she could talk quietly with her ministers and advisers, I stayed with my cousin, Mrs. Marmohiji Sahgal. I was back at 1 Safar Jung Road at eight o'clock in the morning. The crowds were there again. They were not saying much, each just wanting to call on Indira and congratulate her. There were lots of ministers from the different states in other parts of the country, besides many friends and relations.

I stayed there helping out for five days, only going to my cousin's to sleep, and all that time it went on, until finally, Indu had to make a rule that she would only see people from seven-thirty to nine in the morning. Then she would go to her office to work. I hardly had a chance to see her alone. It is not like America and England where lawyers, businessmen and government officials take Saturday and Sunday off. In India they work all week long and all days are the same.

My Western friends often ask me how the Indian people felt about having a woman prime minister. My answer is that our reaction was nothing like as violent as it would be in their countries. One can picture the consternation in London if a woman moved into 10 Downing Street, and the stupefaction in America if a woman became President. But, after all, those countries have a rather old-fashioned attitude toward women in politics.

Of course, it was somewhat surprising even in India. On the other hand, we have had many women leaders—queens who ruled great states, and warrior women who led their armies in battle. Then, during the struggle for independence, when women fought beside the men and went to jail with them, they won themselves a kind of equality, for there is nothing more equal than people in jail. So, after independence was won, many women entered politics and government service—my sister and Padmaja Naidu, who was governor of West Bengal—and dozens of others are in Parliament, far more than in the House of Commons or the American Congress.

Naturally there were old fogeys who viewed Indira with alarm, and others not so hidebound, who yet wondered if she would be able to handle such a difficult task—as, indeed, she wondered herself. For the problems she faced were appalling—famine and drought; tension between India and Pakistan, and between India and China; trouble with the Communists down in Kerala; Sikhs demanding a separate state in the Punjab. Some people, who were pessimistic in any case, thought she would not be able to cope with these numerous crises.

The yellow press and the leftist papers did not help any. They ran headlines saying, "The Nehru Dynasty is going to be restored—who is coming next?" Many of them prophesied that my sister would be taken into the Cabinet, which she was not. One paper, wiser than the rest, said, "Indira Gandhi has not put on a crown of roses but of thorns."

But all these barbs were only the pinpricks that any prime minister must expect. The people of India, the great masses in the cities and the villages, who after all do the voting, were delighted to have Indira.

Soon after Indira was elected I left for the United States, so I was there when, in March 1966, she came for the official visit Mr. Shastri had planned to make. On the day before her arrival, I flew to Washington where I stayed with my son Ajit, who was working in the World Bank. The next morning I was invited to go to the White House to watch Indira arrive by helicopter from Williamsburg, where she had stayed the night to see the restored colonial capital of Virginia.

It was a bright and windy morning, bitterly cold for that time of the year. The whole crowd of us huddled in our coats for forty-five minutes before we saw the helicopters landing far down the lawn. Automobiles were waiting and they came in a little motorcade. The President and Mrs. Johnson came forward to greet Indira who was wearing a plain orange sari with a black coat over it. Mrs. Johnson gave her a great bunch of American Beauty roses—she was smothered in roses everywhere she went, red, yellow and pink roses, a golden rose from Tiffany's and a rose etched on a stone plaque. Then we all stood at attention while the band played the Indian National Anthem, which not so long ago would have got them jailed in India, and the "Star Spangled Banner."

Escorted by President Johnson and an American general, both of whom looked like giants beside her, Indira inspected the Guard of Honor. She almost had to run to keep up with their long strides. Then the President made a speech warmly welcoming Indira to the United States and she replied with grace and dignity.

That was that. While Indira went to Blair House, where honored guests of America stay, I rushed to the Embassy residence of my cousin, Ambassador B. K. Nehru (Bijju we called him at Anand Bhawan) to change for Dean Rusk's luncheon at the State Department. Contrary to my expectations, I thoroughly enjoyed the luncheon, for with remarkable tact, the American Chief of Protocol had put me between two old American friends, former Ambassadors John Kenneth Galbraith and Sherman Cooper. Again Indira spoke and spoke well, while I beamed from a distance.

There is no point in recounting the formal events of those hurried, harassed days, except to mention that everywhere Indira handled herself with such a remarkable combination of poise, intelligence and warmth that she was quite evidently winning the hearts of the American people, the American press and the American President. Most of the time she threw away her prepared speeches and spoke extemporaneously, which is much more effective—if you can do it. One event however is worth recording.

On the last night of Indu's stay in Washington, our Ambassador gave a dinner for forty at which Vice President and Mrs. Hubert Humphrey were to be the guests of honor since President Johnson made a great point of not accepting return invitations from visiting statesman. Dinner was for eight-thirty, but Bijju and his charming Hungarian wife had asked me to come early so I could have a chat with Indira before the guests arrived.

Ajit drove me there at a quarter of eight to find the driveway blocked with enormous black Presidential limousines, and the American Secret Service in full security regalia complete with guns and fierce police dogs on chains. The President was paying his farewell call on Indira. They did not want to let me through but I showed them my invitation and they grudgingly agreed I could go in. However, I had a big suitcase, for I was going on to New York with Indira in the

President's plane the next morning. That was frightfully suspicious and they got difficult all over again. I practically had to prove I was the Prime Minister's aunt before they would let Ajit carry my bag into the Embassy.

From the hallway I could see the President talking to Indira in the drawing room. I thought she looked especially lovely, in a coral pink sari with little golden flowers embroidered on it. The President evidently thought so too. Luci Johnson was sitting in another part of the room chatting with Indu's two sons. I asked a secretary of the Embassy when the President was due to leave. "Any time," he replied. "He should have left twenty minutes ago."

I sat in the hall for ten or fifteen minutes. When the President did not leave I just walked into the drawing room. Bijju and Fori, his wife, jumped up and presented me to President Johnson who said, "We've come to the end of our talks." But he continued to sit! It was nearly eight-fifteen and Bijju and Fori were getting very nervous. She whispered to me, "Don't take a drink while the President is here." I suppose he thought it would spoil the purity of India's image—of course, Indira, like her father, never drinks. Bijju was also worried about how his guests could get in with the Presidential cars blocking the whole driveway. "What had I better do?" he asked me.

"Ask him to dinner," I suggested. "Then he's sure to go home."

Was I wrong! Bijju's wife asked the President, who said, "No. It wouldn't be right. Everybody but me in black tie. But may I stay a little longer?" Of course nobody was going to say no.

However, the President ordered the driveway cleared and told Luci to go along home and take Indu's sons with her. They were quite annoyed when she just left them off at Blair House instead of taking them to the White House or out on the town.

The guests began to arrive. They had been dressed by Dior, St. Laurent and all the other top couturiers and were blazing with jewels. Their bewilderment was quite comical when they saw the President sitting there in the rather rumpled business suit he had worn all day. At about eight-forty, the President finally accepted my cousin's invitation to stay to dinner. She said, "Shall I telephone Mrs. Johnson and ask her to come?"

"Don't you bother," the President replied. "Lady Bird's not feeling well and she has already gone to bed."

Then there was general chaos behind the scenes as to where to seat the President and how to change all the place cards. I went out to help, and then I suddenly saw our Deputy High Commissioner to London getting his coat. "Where are you going?" I asked.

"The dining room only seats forty," he said. "Somebody has to go and I am it."

He is a very quiet man who doesn't like large parties so he was very happy about it.

The dinner was a smashing success. Mrs. Humphrey sat on my cousin's right and the President sat next to Indira. In fact, he hardly let anyone else talk to her all evening, and was quite evidently having a fine time at his genial best. Any image of Indians not drinking went down the drain, as three kinds of wine were served and toasts were drunk to everything you could think of. President Johnson made a funny charming speech in which he said, "I'm the man who came to talk and stayed for dinner," and toasted Indira. She got up and thanked him very gracefully and drank to his health—in water!

The President not only stayed to dinner, he stayed on for liqueurs and coffee. It was almost midnight when he left. After bidding Indira good-by with the warmth of genuine affection, he said to the world at large, "I won't have anybody hurt this little lady!"

The next morning, we flew to New York in luxurious Air Force One, the President's plane. Mayor Lindsay met Indira at Kennedy Airport. They had a lot in common because both of them like meeting challenges. From the airport, Indira was swept into a typical New York hurly-burly of lunches, receptions, dinners, press conferences, interviews, and hordes of children lined up and shouting, "Hi, Indira Gandhi!"

In a sense it was anticlimax after Washington and in another it was not. For Indu spoke better and better all the time. She seemed to get into the groove, as Americans would say. She would have a piece of paper in her hand with notes on it but most of the time she never looked at it, and I believe she was able to make the American people understand India's position and problems better than they ever had before. At the dinner for eight hundred people given by the Economics Club she made a speech that can only be described as magnificent.

Then, as Air India was still on strike, she flew to London in President Johnson's plane.

Time magazine wrote:

The result of Mrs. Gandhi's visit was primarily a new mood of increased warmth and understanding between the U.S. and India. She and the President decided during the week that they were going roughly in the same direction, and that they could accomplish things without making demands on each other. Mrs. Gandhi proved to be not only "a very proud, very gracious and a very able lady," as the President called her, but a fiercely independent ruler with a determination, equal to his own.

Indira also proved that a woman Prime Minister has certain advantages. No Indian man could have established the same rapport with President Johnson in so short a time, a sincere friendship between leaders that promised to be advantageous to both our countries. Another advantage Indira had was that when she made one of her highly intelligent, closely reasoned, far-seeing speeches it had all the greater impact because she was a woman. The Americans were astonished and delighted to hear this delicate, lovely creature talking with such good sense.

Indeed, Indira succeeded almost too well in America. For we Indians are very jealous of our freedom of action, and Bhai's policy of nonalignment has become almost an article of faith in our country. Indians were concerned by the thought that we were getting too closely involved with the United States.

To counteract this reaction, which she foresaw, Indira flew from London directly to Moscow to confer with Kosygin and Brezhnev before coming home. But even this tactful detour did not altogether allay the uneasiness of the Indian Left. President Johnson had promised Indira an additional $500,000,000 worth of American food for India in 1966. He had also proposed to set up an Indo-American Foundation for educational purposes to be financed by $300,000,000 in rupees which India owed the United States, but which were by agreement blocked in India because of our shortage of dollar exchange. The first gift was accepted gratefully; the second Indira had regretfully to decline because of the noisy resistance of hard-core

326

Indian neutralists who feared that the new Foundation might become an instrument of U.S. propaganda.

Indira returned to find more troubles piling up. As one Hindu leader put it, "All the Punjab is afire." Ever since Independence, the Sikhs had been agitating for a Punjab state of their own within the Indian Union. My brother had refused because he would not permit a state to be carved out on a religious basis. The Sikhs argued that the proposed state would not be based on religion but on language, as several other Indian states were. About two weeks before Indira went to Washington, Sikh Sant Fateh Singh threatened to go on a fifteen-day fast and to end up by burning himself to death. The Congress Working Committee, of which Indira is, of course, still a member, agreed to the formation of a Sikh state. I am sure Indira was overruled, for though she is very gentle, she is firm and will not be bullied by threats of this sort. If it were up to me I'd tell them to save the trouble of fasting and get on with it, or send a firing squad to hasten them to sainthood.

The folly of yielding was shown by the fact that Indira came home to find that the Hindus, who would be a minority in the new state, had risen in wrath. Protesting the new partition of the Punjab, the Hindu religious leader Yagga Dutt Sharma, went on a counterfast in the marketplace of Amritsar and thousands of Hindus marched through the streets shouting, "*Punjabi Suba Murdabad* [Death to the Punjab State]," and "Indira Gandhi *Murdabad!*"

In Delhi, for the first time in our history, Hindus attacked the main Sikh temple. The Sikh guards in their turbans stood fiercely impassive at their posts, ignoring insults and ducking rocks thrown at them. When the crowd grew to 2,000, with more coming every minute, the Sikh guards drew their long curved swords and yelling their ferocious war cries charged the mob, scattering it and wounding several people.

The riots in Delhi and the Punjab were a great blow to Indira who, like her father, hated communal rioting above all else. It was almost nine months later, in December 1966, that the whole trouble seemed to be settled by a series of sensible compromises and safeguards for the Hindu minority in the Punjab state.

This was only one of the problems Indira had to face in her first year in office. Others included bad crops in Bihar and Gujarat due to the failure of the monsoon; our always thorny relations with

Pakistan; and the herculean task of getting India's economy going on a self-sufficient basis.

In all things Indira followed her father's general policies and practices, not slavishly, but with the flexibility to fit changing conditions. Like him, she worked a sixteen-hour day every day. She also continued to keep close to the people, following his custom of talking with anyone who came to her house in the early morning, with no appointments required. In addition, she continued to fly to trouble spots, and from the Punjab to Kerala, walked fearlessly among the angry mobs and calmed them with gentle dignity and common sense.

Indira met frequently with her Cabinet and the Congress Working Committee to profit by their advice and their feeling for the ground swell of public opinion. The Cabinet meetings were held around a big oval mahogany table with the ministers sitting in Chippendale chairs. For less formal Working Committee meetings, the floor of Indira's book-lined study was covered with mattresses and strewn with fat bolsters. Indira and the other members, many of whom were also in the Cabinet sat cross-legged on the floor or reclined against the bolsters just as they had in her father's and grandfather's time.

In foreign affairs Indira's government continued to follow the policy of strict nonalignment. India remained friendly with both sides of the riven world and committed to neither. In our relations with Pakistan, as she had promised, she tried hard to implement the spirit of Tashkent, though this became increasingly difficult as the Pakistani attitude toward India gradually hardened and violations of the ceasefire line became increasingly frequent.

With the Chinese, Indira's government appeared to be more successful. During the first year she was prime minister there were no serious clashes between the two great Asian nations.

In internal affairs Indira shifted the emphasis back to increasing industrial production, with more stress upon her father's Socialist principles. However, she recognized that India simply did not have the capital to build the great industrial plant she needed to put the economy on a viable basis. So she made much greater efforts than Bhai did to attract private capital from the Western nations by offering their great companies and industrial entrepreneurs tax incentives and guarantees that they could get their money back with a reasonable profit. As a result, the Indian economy spurted forward against the trend in most other nations where 1966 was a year of somewhat reduced industrial activity.

Raising enough food for the hundreds of millions of Indians who live on the razor's edge of starvation continued to be the Prime Minister's greatest worry. The failure of the monsoon for the second year in a row again forced India to appeal to the generosity of other nations for grain and rice. That her minimum needs were met and that there was no actual famine was a sort of triumph, albeit a meager one.

And still looming over us and devouring any increases of goods or foods we might produce, was the continuing increase in population—India smothered under the enormously growing weight of her own people. Contraceptive techniques and education in their application appear to be the only answer—as indeed it is for every country in the world, though with less dire urgency than in India. No one is more aware of this than Indira, and her government strains every financial sinew to assist and encourage this. Admittedly, it is very difficult in a country so poor with so many people wedded to their ancient customs. However, tremendous advances are being made.

On the constructive side the government is building dams to control floods and irrigate the lands, digging wells where dams are impractical, encouraging the manufacture of fertilizer and the production of better seed, and beginning the long, slow process of educating the peasant farmers in modern agricultural methods and providing them with the necessary tools—at least steel plows to replace sticks of wood.

It is a race—a race against famine and overpopulation—a race whose prize is abundant life for our people and whose penalty, if we lose, is death. Indira believes we shall win.

A book about living people never ends; it merely stops. So this one must stop with most of its answers pending and many of its characters still striving toward their goals.

We Nehrus who are left are still trying hard to serve our country in our different ways. We are still a close-knit family. We still have Anand Bhawan, which is the place we all call home. In the private part of his will my brother left it to Indira for as long as she could maintain it. If she could not, it was to go to the Nation. But he also stated that my sister and I must ever be welcome there, as we always were in his time.

Indira's story is the most unfinished since she is so much younger than my sister and I, and is just reaching the peak of her truly remarkable powers. Of one thing, though, I am certain: whatever the vicissitudes of politics and in whatever capacity, she will continue to serve India with all her strength and heart and soul.

For she is a worthy daughter of a great and beloved man.

epilogue by
Alden Hatch

Krishna and I had finished the book before the elections in February, 1967. They were the hardest ever fought in India. Public opinion polls showed that the once supreme Congress party was in trouble. The causes of popular dissatisfaction were numerous. Foremost was the partial failure of the harvest for two successive years in Bihar and Gujurat.

Though no power on earth can make the rains come, the government was blamed. In addition, there were local disappointments: India's foreign exchange was in precarious condition—partly due to the necessity of purchasing wheat to supplement what was generously given by the United States and other nations with surplus productivity. Also, the reactionary, extremist Hindu party raised a great dust storm to force the government to forbid all slaughter of cattle in India. It had no power to do this as the matter is left to the states by the Constitution. Finally, because the Congress party had been in power for all of the twenty years of India's independence, some people may have voted against it like the ancient Greek who voted against the great Alcibiades because he was tired of hearing him called "the just."

During the pre-election campaign there were dire predictions of defeat for the Congress party, and many said that even if it won Indira would be defeated for prime minister by the party caucus. The truth is that several strong men of the party, among them S. K. Patil, Atulya Ghosh, Y. B. Chavan and Moraji Desai aspired to the Prime Ministership.

Anyone who thought Indira was not a good politician had his eyes opened during the campaign. Though she was running for the *Lok Sabha* for the first time in the constituency of Rae Bareily* she flashed from one end of India to the other in a white jet speaking for

* She had been an appointed member of the Upper House, the *Rajya Sabha*.

331

Congress candidates who were in trouble. In the excited mood of the Indian people it was not only arduous but perilous. Confronting one howling mob, Indira was hit in the nose by a stone. With blood streaming from her face she continued to speak quietly for a few moments before she was led away to have her wound treated.

The results of the election followed the polls. The great majority which the Congress party had previously held was reduced to a mere twenty votes as they suffered a net loss of 214 seats in the *Lok Sabha*. Their losses in the assemblies of the various states were even greater and in several of them, opposition parties formed new governments, including the Nehrus' home state of Uttar Pradesh. The Communists won a smashing victory in Kerala State. Many of the famous leaders were defeated. S. K. Patil went down in Maharashtra; Ghosh was defeated. Even the powerful Kumaraswami Kamaraj lost his seat though, of course, he remained president of the Congress party. Of all Indira's principal rivals, only Moraji Desai survived.*

By contrast, Indira, though neglecting her own interests to campaign for others, carried Rae Bareily by a margin of almost three to one. That was the justification of her leadership, the vote of confidence which every politician wants, the "Well done!" of her own constituents. It was also the powerful lever for being again chosen by the Congress party as their leader. With all her rivals except Mr. Desai knocked out by the voters, the whole situation was drastically changed.

Kumaraswami Kamaraj wanted above all things to unify the Congress party. The electoral losses had been a great shock to him and he saw that without complete concord in their ranks no Congress government would last long. A unanimous choice of their leader was essential and Indira was the only hope of unanimity. However, Moraji Desai again wished to run against her in the party caucus.

Once more Kamaraj employed his great powers of persuasion, first on Desai and then on Indira. He got Desai to agree to withdraw, provided Indira would accept him both as Deputy Prime Minister and Home Minister. Indira refused; she felt this was too much power to give any single member of her cabinet. The whole thing was off and it looked as though the contest Kamaraj dreaded would take place.

* Krishna Menon on the Socialist ticket was defeated in Bombay.

Indira was confident of winning and Desai had some hopes, but both of them realized that a unanimous choice was best for the party and for India.

Kamaraj finally brought about a compromise. Indira accepted Desai as Deputy Prime Minister and Minister of *Finance,* and he withdrew from the contest. Indeed, he went further. At the meeting of the Congress party members of the *Lok Sabha* on March 12, 1967, Desai handsomely proposed, "Sister Indira as our leader," and he added, "I hope you will accept my proposal with the same enthusiasm."

When her name has been seconded, the Presiding Officer, K. Sen, asked, "Are there any other nominations?"

A tremendous shout of "No!" shook the high-domed roof of the chamber. Then Mr. San declared Indira unanimously elected.

So once again, wearing garlands of red roses and marigolds, Indira drove up the Raj Path to the President's House to be officially asked to form a government and become Prime Minister of India. But this time, because of her great personal victory at the polls, she came confidently and with the assurance of her people's approval.

ALDEN HATCH

bibliography

BOURKE-WHITE, MARGARET, *Half Way to Freedom*. New York, Simon & Schuster, 1949.

BRITTAIN, VERA, *Envoy Extraordinary*. London, George Allen & Unwin, Ltd., 1965.

CROCKER, WALTER, *Nehru: A Contemporary's Estimate*. New York, Oxford University Press, 1966.

EVANS, HUMPHREY, *Thimaya of India*. New York, Harcourt, Brace & Co., 1960.

FISCHER, LOUIS, *The Life of Mahatma Gandhi*. New York, Harper & Row, 1950.

HALIFAX, LORD, *The Earl of Birkenhead*. Boston, Houghton Mifflin Co., 1966.

HUTHEESING, KRISHNA, *With No Regrets*. London, Oxford University Press, 1944.

————, *Nehru's Letters to His Sister*. London, Faber & Faber, 1963.

HUTHEESING, RAJA, *Window on China*. London, Derek Verschoyle, 1953.

NANDA, B. R., *The Nehrus*. New York, The John Day Company, 1963.

NEHRU, JAWAHARLAL, *A Bunch of Old Letters*. Bombay, Asia Publishing House, 1958.

————, *Glimpses of World History*. New York, The John Day Company, 1942.

————, *Letters From A Father to His Daughter*. Allahabad, Kitabistan, 1930.

————, *The Discovery of India*. New York, The John Day Company, 1946.

————, *Toward Freedom: The Autobiography of Jawaharlal Nehru*. New York, The John Day Company, 1941.

NORMAN, DOROTHY, *Nehru: The First Sixty Years*. London, The Bodley Head, Ltd., 1965.

index

about
the authors

Krishna Nehru Hutheesing is Jawaharlal Nehru's youngest sister, the aunt of Prime Minister Indira Gandhi. She has been an important Indian revolutionary in her own right, active in Indian political and civic affairs since her girlhood. She lives with her husband in Bombay.

Alden Hatch, with whom Mme. Nehru Hutheesing wrote this book, is a well-known author whose books include last year's most successful and well-received *The Mountbattens*, as well as *A Man Named John, Pope Paul VI, The Wadsworths of Gennessee*, and others. He and his wife live in Sarasota, Florida.